The World of
RICHARD WRIGHT

Special Collections, John Davis Williams Library, University of Mississippi

# The World of
# RICHARD WRIGHT

*Michel Fabre*

UNIVERSITY PRESS OF MISSISSIPPI
*Jackson*

Copyright © 1985 by the
University Press of Mississippi
All rights reserved
Manufactured in the United States of America          Second Printing 1987

## Center for the Study of Southern Culture Series

The University Press of Mississippi thanks all publishers for granting permission to reprint these essays. The press also thanks the Collection of American Literature and the Beinecke Rare Book and Manuscript Library at Yale University for permission to reproduce unpublished material from the Richard Wright Archive. The copyright for all Wright's work is held by Ellen Wright and is used with her permission.

The essays in this volume were originally published, occasionally with slightly different titles, as follows: "Richard Wright's First Hundred Books," *CLA Journal*, 16 (June, 1973), pp. 438–74; "Black Cat and White Cat: Wright's Gothic and the Influence of Poe," *Poe Studies*, 4, No. 1 (1971), pp. 17–19; "From Revolutionary Poetry to Haiku," *Studies in Black Literature*, 1, No. 3 (Autumn, 1970), pp. 10–22; "Beyond Naturalism," in *American Literary Naturalism*, ed. Yoshinobu Hakutani and Lewis Fried (Heidelberg: C. Winter, 1975), pp. 136–53; "From Tabloid to Myth: 'The Man Who Lived Underground'," *Studies in the Novel*, 3 (Fall, 1971), pp. 165–79; "'The Man Who Killed a Shadow': A Study in Compulsion," in *French Approaches to Black American Literature*, ed. Michel Fabre. (Paris: Université de la Sorbonne Nouvelle, 1980), pp. 45–64; "Fantasies and Style in Richard Wright's Fiction," *New Letters*, 46, No. 3 (March, 1980), pp. 55–81; "Richard Wright's Image of France," *Prospects: An Annual of American Cultural Studies*, 3 (1977), pp. 315–29; "Wright and the French Existentialists," in *Critical Essays on Richard Wright*, ed. Yoshinobu Hakutani. (Boston: G. K. Hall, 1982), pp. 182–98; "Richard Wright's Exile," *New Letters*, 1 (December, 1971), pp. 136–54. Two items found in the appendix were reprinted from the following: "An Interview with Simone de Beauvoir," *Studies in Black Literature*, 1 (Autumn, 1970), pp. 3–5 and "A Letter from Dorothy Padmore," *ibid.*, pp. 5–9.

Works by Richard Wright found in the appendix were reprinted from the following: "Superstition," *Abbott's Monthly* (April, 1931), pp. 43, 46–47, 64–66, 72–73; "I Have Seen Black Hands," *New Masses*, 11 (June 26, 1934), p. 16; "Rise and Live," *Midland Left*, No. 2 (February, 1935), pp. 13–14; "Obsession," *ibid.*, p. 14; "I Am a Red Slogan," *International Literature*, 4 (April, 1935), p. 35; "Ah Feels It in Mah Bones," *ibid.*, p. 80; "Transcontinental," *International Literature*, 2 (1936), pp. 52–57; "Red Leaves of Red Books," *New Masses*, 15 (April 30, 1935), p. 6; "Spread Your Sunrise," *New Masses*, 16 (July 2, 1935), p. 26; "Between the World and Me," *Partisan Review*, 2 (July–August 1935), pp. 18–19; "Hearst Headline Blues," *New Masses*, No. 19 (May 12, 1936), p. 14; "Old Habit and New Love," *New Masses*, 21 (December 15, 1936), p. 29; "We of the Streets," *New Masses*, 23 (April 13, 1937), p. 14; "Red Clay Blues," *New Masses*, 32 (August 1, 1939), p. 14; "Rest for the Weary" and "A Red Love Note," *Left Front*, No. 3 (January–February, 1934), p. 3; "Everywhere Burning Waters Rise," *Left Front*, No. 4 (May–June, 1934), p. 9; "Child of the Dead and Forgotten Gods," *The Anvil*, No. 5 (March–April, 1934), p. 30; "Strength," *ibid.*, p. 20; "King Joe (Joe Louis Blues)," and Additional Lyrics, *New Letters*, 38 (December, 1971), pp. 42–45; "The FB Eye Blues," *Richard Wright Reader*, ed. Ellen Wright and Michel Fabre. (New York: Harper & Row, 1978), pp. 249–50. Wright's haiku are reprinted from *New Letters*, 38 (December, 1971), pp. 100–01 and from *Studies in Black Literature*, 1 (Autumn, 1970), p. 1.

**Library of Congress Cataloging in Publication Data**

Fabre, Michel.
  The world of Richard Wright.

  (Center for the Study of Southern Culture series)
  Includes index.
  1. Wright, Richard, 1908–1960—Criticism and interpretation—Addresses, essays, lectures.
  I. Title.  II. Series.
  PS3545.R815Z65133   1985        813'.52   85-6230
  ISBN 0-87805-258-5

# Contents

The World of
RICHARD WRIGHT

# Introduction

> If I could fasten the mind of the reader upon words so firmly that he
> would forget words and be conscious only of his response, I felt that
> I would be in sight of knowing how to write narrative; I strove to
> master words, to make them disappear, to make them important by
> making them new, to make them melt into a rising spiral of emo-
> tional climax that would drench the reader with a sense of a new
> world. This was the single end of my living.
>
> Writing depends upon the associational magic of passion.
>
> RICHARD WRIGHT, *American Hunger* (1977)

WRITTEN over the last two decades, the following essays on the
work and career of Richard Wright were not originally intended
as a collection, but their organization as such does underscore Wright's
literary and intellectual development in several interesting ways. In
*Black Boy,* he movingly documented the destitution and emotional insecurity to which he was heir from his childhood in Mississippi while his
mother's unending illness filled him with an abiding sense of existential
anguish. His mother was the one who taught him "to revere the fanciful
and the imaginative," and his autobiography also makes clear the part his
own vivid imagination played in a youngster who withdrew into himself to
compensate and keep painful experiences at a distance. Not only the
pleasures of learning at school, of reading and story-telling, but also the
exercise of his own creative gifts help explain the early awakening of
Wright's literary interests.

While working in Memphis after graduating from the ninth grade, he
began stuffing himself on a steady diet of books and magazines. The
irreverent criticism of H. L. Mencken may have been an introduction to
the muckraking tradition of American naturalism and Wright mentioned,
among other discoveries, the naturalistic explanation of culture and
character by Theodore Dreiser, and the debunking of middle-class pretence by Sinclair Lewis. But cheap pulp tales, detective stories, and
Sunday supplements attracted him as much as the classics he borrowed
from the public library by forging notes to circumvent the Jim Crow
regulations. And from the evening young Ella told him the tale of

3

Bluebeard in spite of his grandmother's prohibition, Richard's bent toward "the fanciful and the imaginative" was strong indeed. The bibliographical essay, "Richard Wright's First One Hundred Books," in which I document the contents of the novelist's scanty library up until the writing of *Native Son* may shed light on his literary sources but it does in no way explain his creative genius.

The social criticism that emerges from *Black Boy* invites us to consider Wright mostly as a victim of racial discrimination in its violent or subtle manifestations or as an embattled young man, determined to surmount the barriers of prejudice and poverty. Yet in spite of his often crude efforts at capturing the social changes in which he was caught up in the Middle West in the late 1920s, in spite of his experiments with words, scenes, and moods prompted by the reading of Gertrude Stein, Henry James, and Joseph Conrad, in spite of his turning to the social sciences at the University of Chicago, Wright's first recorded ventures in the field of fiction prove both traditional and romantic. As "Black Cat and White Cat" shows, his early short story "Superstition" was based on uncanny black folk beliefs but couched in the style of Edgar Allan Poe. It remains a good starting point to gauge not only a beginner's clumsy attempts at mastering the craft and his real potential for creating a gripping atmosphere but also the gap which separates that piece from Wright's first achievements in capturing the revolutionary spirit in verse a couple of years later.

Wright's early poetry only occasionally reflects an attempt on his part to achieve ideological perspective. When, after a series of ill-paid, temporary jobs, he was forced into unemployment and onto relief rolls by the depression, he was able to see his plight not only in the racial, nationalistic terms of the lingering Garvey movement but illuminated by the theories of Marx and Lenin on the wider world scene. Communism was an answer to his frustrations as one of the urban poor; in addition, joining the John Reed Club was to him the only avenue toward equal acceptance into a group of left wing white artists and writers. The poems he contributed to *Left Front, Anvil, International Literature,* and *New Masses* reflect his vision of his literary role as he expressed it in "Blueprint for Negro Writing" a few years later. Strong suggestions of his critical independence of thought appear in that essay. He took his mission as a proletarian writer seriously enough to consider that the Communists themselves "had oversimplified the experience of those they sought to lead. . . . They had missed the meaning of the lives of the masses." Wright believed that his responsibility as a black writer lay in correcting this vision, in voicing the specific, racial dimensions of the black working class. He wrote: "The Negro writer who seeks to function within his race as a purposeful agent has a serious responsibility . . . a deep, informed, and complex consciousness is necessary; a consciousness which draws for its strength upon the fluid lore of a great people and molds this lore with the concepts that move and direct the forces of history today."[1] In other words, Wright made his own the task assigned by Joyce to Stephen Dedalus in *Portrait of the Artist As a Young Man;* i.e., to create the specific features of his race. But with a difference—Wright spoke of the necessity to "create values by which his race was to struggle, live and die." He assumed that the black writer and intellectual had the responsibility of creating the ideological and symbolical means through which a black mass movement could emerge.

The fact remains, however, that in his early poems as well as in his first achievements in "naturalistic" fiction, Wright's imagination and emotions tended to carry him away from ideology towards personal, idiosyncratic modes of self-expression. His poetry ceased to be militant even before he left the American Communist Party in the early 1940s. He devoted time to composing blues. "Red Clay Blues," written in collaboration with Langston Hughes in 1937 and "King Joe," which was recorded in 1941 by Count Basie and sung by Paul Robeson, are fine examples of these and there exist unpublished scores of them, written largely in the 1950s. "F.B. Eye Blues," satirizing the evils of McCarthyism, is a more vivid example than "The Dreaming Kind," composed to be sung by a nightclub crooner in the film version of *Native Son.* For many years Wright toyed with the idea of a flexible form of poetic prose, rather Whitmanesque in its celebration of human and cosmic life, but never as successful as his later haiku poems. Into this strict Japanese mold, he was able to inject a deeply personal flavor. His haiku poems represent his disciplined best and, sometimes, his most agonizing expressions of grief and despair, as my essay "From Revolutionary Poetry to Haiku" attempts to establish.

However, it is an illusion to believe that Wright's fantasy found its best outlet in poetry. It certainly created more varied and more striking effects in prose. Admittedly, *Native Son* deserves to be hailed, as it was in certain quarters, as "a black *American Tragedy,*" along the lines of Dreiser's deterministic novel. Yet in the perspective of Wright's own development it deserves the closer look that I have tried to provide in "Beyond Naturalism." Boris Max's plea unquestionably rests upon environmentalist premises, making society rather than Bigger Thomas responsible. As a result, Bigger's crime appears inevitable. But it is also a compulsive attempt at breaking free from the conditioning imposed by a racist social system. From this angle the exploration of the unconscious determinants in so-called criminal behavior (a question that literally obsessed Wright all through his life) looms large and it will reappear in other stories like "The Man Who Lived Underground" and, especially, in "The Man Who Killed a Shadow." But an even more interesting consideration at the time, Bigger's elusive freedom is assuredly existential. Not Jean-Paul Sartre but Feodor Dostoevsky comes to mind when we consider Wright's conception of self-creation through violence and murder. In this respect Bigger is radically different from Dreiser's weak and blundering protagonist in *An American Tragedy;* he accepts full responsibility for what he did and such acceptance makes him what he is. The creative act cannot be anything but free. That was the way in which, a decade later, Frantz Fanon read *Native Son* and found in it not only a clear depiction of racial oppression in the United States but also a springboard toward the concept of "revolutionary violence."

*Native Son* contains strands and elements that differentiate it from the purely reportorial, and even from the deterministic outlook of social realism. It explodes at times into visionary epiphanies. In my article "From Tabloid to Myth: The Man Who Lived Underground" I try to show that this is even more the case for that novella. In what remains his most sophisticated piece of fiction Wright not only explores the fantastic reaches of the human mind but also completes a truly existential fable in often surrealistic terms. His major themes are not only solitude and invisibility as supreme punishment—a sort of Sartrean *No Exit* in reverse— themes which Ralph Ellison, following Wright's lead, explored brilliantly in *Invisible Man.* The novella also deals with "the obscenity of existence," i.e., the guilt not only of admitting to a crime one had not committed or of committing a crime which will never be disclosed, but of merely being of this world. And it also deals with self-creation through the gratuitous, aesthetic gesture of Fred Daniels writing his name with a stolen typewriter and strewing the soil of his underground refuge with innumerable diamonds after having pasted the walls with hundred-dollar bills and hung them with watches and jewels.

In "The Man Who Killed a Shadow," Wright again denounced the absurdity of white civilization, but he did not have recourse to another existential fable. In "The Man Who Killed a Shadow: A Study in Compulsion," I therefore concentrate on his use of the psychoanalytical approach.

Just like "The Man Who Lived Underground," this short story is a fine "case study" based upon a real occurrence. In the second case, a comparison between court records and imaginative rendering discloses less exciting aesthetic effects but it betrays a significant interest on Wright's part in the psychological links between sex and racism and in the conditioning imposed by the latter. When he explores how, to Saul Sander's ears, a white woman's outraged cry sounds like the shrill sirens of police cars chasing an alleged black rapist, Wright also makes a subtle and very deliberate use of the reader's responses to his text.

This led me to pursue a wider inquiry into Wright's writing and style, focussing upon the somewhat obsessive repetition of certain words and metaphors along the psycho-critical perspectives evoked by French critic Charles Mauron in *Des metaphores obsédantes au mythe personnel* (From Obsessive Metaphor to Personal Myth, 1964) and applied by him to Victor Hugo and Stéphane Mallarmé among others. This critical approach relies principally upon psychoanalyzing the text instead of the author. "Fantasies and Style in Richard Wright's Fiction" reflects my endeavor to link recurrent situations and images throughout Wright's whole opus with his compulsion to return to traumatic events or "primal" scenes. Focussing on the recurrent surfacing of half-buried memories in his prose would thus enable to define a writer's "style," i.e., his idiosyncratic rather than broadly scriptural writing strategies.

"Richard Wright's South" is a reflection on *Black Boy* and "How Jim Crow Feels," considering the dual relationship of Wright to his father as well as to his birthplace, both of which he turned into negative metaphors: the South mingles with Nathan Wright, and geography with genealogy. Admittedly, when he declared that he wanted to lend his voice to his silent dark brothers by writing a generic autobiography, Richard Wright sought to create meaning from his youth by imposing upon it a pattern that would make his past the coherent story of a writer's growth against many odds. He established certain stages in his childhood and adolescence, linked them, and defined a consistent relationship between himself as a misunderstood and rebellious youngster and the outer world represented by the home of his Seventh Day Adventist grandmother, the black community, and the racist South. When he renewed his life by interpreting it in 1942–44, the point of view he took was not only based on his position as a famous American writer but on his ideological views at the time. He saw his past as a unified pattern and made it into an ideological construction asserting, in the best Afro-American literary tradition, the development of a Promethean will toward education and literacy against the opposing forces of white southern oppression and also, in his case, of black "lack of culture" and illiteracy. He was able to project his father as a victim, while during his childhood he had experienced the latter's desertion of their home and inability to provide as hostile and reprehensible behavior. By laying the blame on the social structure, Wright was making the South the villain, but this was also a psychologically satisfactory way (because morally irreproachable) for the son to "kill the father" by relegating him to the role of a helpless sharecropper.

Spatially, then, *Black Boy* is structured between the opposing poles of North and South, two mythical places merging with metaphors of motion and stasis. In the southern context, Richard's repeated migration from one city to the next only duplicates his father's drifting. Aimless motion is just another form of imprisonment, the result of being snarled hopelessly in the coils of modern slavery. Conversely, Richard's real action followed two parallel lines: inwardly toward self-awareness and self-reliance; outwardly toward freedom in the North. Admittedly, the North was an ambiguous place and Chicago loomed ahead as the scene of "death on the city pavements," as *Twelve Million Black Voices* made clear. Still it was symbolically a place where the hero could remain alive, although it would later be displaced by New York City, then Paris, then a Third World of the mind.

Wright perceived his own plight as representative of black America; he believed that the Negro was not only "America's metaphor" (as an embodiment of the transition from southern feudalism to urban mass society) or the metaphor of modern men tossed about in a meaningless world but, above all, a harbinger of changes to occur in the world. The black man's historical situation was exceptional because of the coming liberation of the colored masses. And he wanted to be one of them. Late in his life, he bravely, although somewhat erroneously, projected himself as a man without roots. In *White Man, Listen,* he claimed: "I am a rootless man but neither psychologically distraught nor in any way particularly perturbed because of it. . . . I like and even cherish the state of abandonment, of aloneness; it does not bother me, indeed it seems to be the natural, inevitable condition of man, and I welcome it."[2]

He saw himself as "an outsider between two cultures," a man searching. Ever since he had given up his membership in the Communist Party, if not his belief in the Marxist vision, in the early 1940s, he had kept looking for a system of thought capable of accounting for the complexity of the human situation. For a time, he held great hopes for the philosophy of existentialism. When in 1953 he published *The Outsider*, an avowedly existentialist novel, some American critics reproached him for adopting an alien ideology after six years of self-exile in Paris instead of writing in his old "true, racial vein." But matters were far more complex. On the one hand, Wright had always been imbued with an existential sense of life and, if one points to influences, Dostoevsky probably was his first "existentialist" mentor. On the other hand, as I try to show in "Wright and the French Existentialists," French existentialist thinkers did not significantly inform Wright's perspectives and writing. He himself described *The Outsider* as "the first literary effort of mine projected out of a heart preoccupied with no ideological burden save that of rendering an account of reality as it strikes my sensibilities and imagination. . . . My hero could have been of any race. . . . I have tried to depict my sense of our contemporary living as I see it and feel it."[3] My essay attempts to establish, precisely, how little Wright's fiction was influenced by J. P. Sartre, Albert Camus, or Simone de Beauvoir, the French existentialists he knew best and with whom he consorted in the late 1940s. Existentialism as an ideology remained for him a sort of transition from Communism to growing preoccupation with Third World liberation and African nationalism. At this time Wright became more interested in nonfiction and he wrote from a new, no longer exclusively American (though not un-American) perspective. "Richard Wright's Exile" emphasizes his awareness of the increasing political and cultural role played by the United States after World War II and the growth within him of the uneasy consciousness of being, psychologically as well as physically, both *of* and not *in* America. The companion essay "Richard Wright's Image of France," shows his typically American expectations and reactions to daily life in Paris. He was a man preoccupied with industrial output, modern conveniences, and the kind of activity that "does not leave a nation one of beggars and thieves"; but he also reacted as a black man, eager to escape the slights of racism and the pressures of a prejudiced environment upon his literary sensibilities.

Wright's ventures into an assessment of the African personality and of the potential developments in the Gold Coast, then on the eve of becoming independent, were admittedly limited and biased by what he called "apropos prepossessions" in his introduction to *Black Power*. Besides, he sometimes felt ill at ease when dealing with French-speaking African intellectuals because he, like Senghor, found them more French than

African. Yet he was not only instrumental in introducing African readers to the complexities of the racial situation and the aims of the Civil Rights Movement in the United States; he also brought closer together two essentially different perspectives: that of integrationism among Negro Americans and that of nationalism, cultural and political, among Africans. This is what my essay "Richard Wright, Negritude, and African Writing" tries to establish while concentrating on Wright's role in the *Présence Africaine* group and on his helping African novelists, notably Peter Abrahams, to reach a wider audience.

In Europe, Wright also paid more attention to his lifelong concern— the exploration of the relationship between the individual and society, between tradition and industrialization. This was already his preoccupation in *Twelve Million Black Voices* when he depicted the tremendous journey of black Americans from the plantations of the Lords of the Land to the steel and concrete jungle of the Bosses of the Buildings. "Tradition and Industrialization" was also the title of one of his lectures, gathered in *White Man, Listen* and, in his three volumes on the Third World, he broached the political and social issues involved. He died a man searching for answers in a changing world, a writer still experimenting in poetry, and planning new travels to Africa to report on its coming independence.

With the exception of "Richard Wright's South" and "Richard Wright, Negritude, and African Writing," these essays do not aim at reevaluating Wright's place and individualistic stance within the context of the Afro-American tradition. This has been done with competence and perceptiveness by several critics, notably George Kent, Houston Baker, and Robert Stepto. I tend to examine Wright's works within the American and European ideological and literary context, whether they deal with naturalism, existentialism, Marxism, or nationalism. This may be due to my initial discovery of his novels in the late 1950s and my perception of him as a "modern" (but not specifically Afro-American) writer. Only in the late sixties did I fully comprehend his significance and importance for the Afro-American literary tradition. To this day he largely remains, first of all, one of the most representative authors of our times, someone who was born black in America and who, because of what Ralph Ellison has called "the tyranny of time and the tyranny of place," had a very special message for whoever cared to listen. This may also explain why I have not concentrated upon the "black" components or aspects of Wright's style when exploring the challenging, individual expression of a writer whose tension and protest were the wellsprings of his creativity.

Over the years my own critical approach somewhat shifted from genetic (the analysis of the creative authorial process) to textual and intertextual concerns, while I simultaneously favored a more definitely ethnological and folkloristic type of investigation. Yet looking back I realize that I have always retained a preference for factual detail, precise sources, documented deductions over impressionistic interpretations, and theoretical construct. In each of the following essays I have tried to provide new, often unpublished, information and texts in order to substantiate and refine my insights into the literary process.

I am gratified that this collection, devoted to a Mississippi-born writer, should be published by the University Press of Mississippi in the series begun by William Ferris, director of the Center for the Study of Southern Culture at the University of Mississippi, who has done so much to promote unrecognized trends in the literary and cultural production of the Deep South. I consider it a sign of the profound changes that have taken place in a state where, when I first went to do research on Richard Wright in Jackson and Natchez in 1962–63, I was regarded with suspicion outside the black community.

I am deeply grateful to Keneth Kinnamon for his thoughtful remarks and many suggestions which have greatly improved the present text, and to Sue Hart and Seetha Srinivasan for their considerate and efficient editing.

*Michel Fabre*

1. "Blueprint for Negro Writing," in *Richard Wright Reader*, ed. Ellen Wright and Michel Fabre. (New York: Harper and Row, 1978, p. 43.
2. Richard Wright, *White Man, Listen.* (New York: Doubleday, 1957), p. 17.
3. Book-jacket for *The Outsider*.

# Wright's First Hundred Books

I take an author, study his works carefully, go into his life with the same thoroughness, follow the ways the facts of his life are related to the fiction he created. I have done this with Dostoievsky, Chekhov, Conrad, Turgeniev.

—RICHARD WRIGHT, *Daily Worker* interview (December 13, 1938)

Eliot, Stein, Joyce, Proust, Hemingway, and Anderson; Gorky, Barbusse, Nexo and Jack London no less than the folklore of the Negro himself should form the heritage of the Negro writer. Every iota of gain in human thought and sensibility should be ready grist for his mill, no matter how far-fetched they may seem in their immediate implications.

—RICHARD WRIGHT,"Blueprint for Negro Writing" (1937)

## I

RALPH ELLISON'S insistence on the dual tradition of the Afro-American writer is well-known; he has even been attacked by black nationalists for insisting too much on his indebtedness to the European/White American body of literature, to the detriment of the black folk cultural heritage. Richard Wright, on the other hand, has until recently often been considered as a passionate, spontaneous, and demonic novelist, writing from his inner self to the detriment of any close study of his literary parentage. Yet a closer look reveals not only that he was a much more sophisticated literary artisan than one commonly thinks but that he was, like Ellison, perfectly aware of this dual heritage of the black writer in America.

In order to gain an understanding of the development of Richard Wright as a major novelist of the twentieth century and also of the literary tradition of the Afro-American novel in general, precise knowledge of just what books Wright was reading during his formative years is very beneficial. Of course, he himself gave several clues in *Black Boy*[1] and in a number of articles and interviews. More recently, Margaret Walker has beautifully written of her formative literary relationship with Wright in

Chicago,[2] and I have dealt in detail with Wright's readings and attempts at writing in my biography of him.[3] Yet, having had the opportunity to make a list of the roughly one hundred books that Wright owned before the publication of *Native Son* in 1940 and having come across a number of hard-to-locate references to his readings, I believe that the following outline of Wright's library and readings through 1940 could constitute a basic and fairly complete guide for the future study of his fiction and thinking, in the perspective of literary filiation and comparative literature.[4]

Wright used to read the Memphis *Commercial Appeal* regularly during the years 1926–1927, and a close scrutiny here should yield interesting information on possible early influences. A quick perusal of the microfile at the Memphis Public Library enabled me to locate not one Mencken article, as mentioned in *Black Boy*, but half a dozen of them; for example, "Notes on Government" (January 10, 1926, Sect. 1, p. 9); "A Chance for a Millionaire" (January 24, 1926, p. 26); "Essays in Constructive Criticism" (March 1926, Sect. III, p. 8), in which Proust and Joyce are mentioned, as well as an editorial on Mencken ("The Joke Is on Mencken," June 9, 1926, p. 6), which does not fit Wright's allusion to an anti-Mencken piece in his autobiography.[5]

Several gothic detective stories are also to be found. "Even This Can Happen" by Lee Hutty (April 18, 1926, Sect. III, p. 11) may have left some impression on Wright's imagination with its secret passages, Poe-like heroine, and retired professor reading Camille Flammarion's *Haunted Houses*. (See Wright's 1931 story entitled "Superstition.") The weekly billings of the Strand, the Majestic, or Loew's Palace could be checked with profit to map Wright's early movie culture. And it is quite tempting to see a visual source impression for the central scene of *Native Son* on page 2 of the *Commercial Appeal* for January 25, 1926: a two-column photograph shows a plain-clothes policeman and two uniformed officers standing near the open door of a blazing furnace, into which they are throwing packages—"$250,000 Narcotics Burned," the caption reads. However, juxtaposed to the photograph, a larger sized caption, "Police Near Solution of Headless Murder," introduces an even more interesting article: the body of a murdered young woman was found in the remains of a fire, with the head lying at some distance; "in the ashes, the policeman scooped up a handful of glass beads"; also, the killer shot the woman's little dog that barked. Does it take too much imagination to see anticipated here the furnace scene, the severing of Mary's head, the burning of her body, the discovery of her earring in the ashes of the furnace by detectives, and even the potentially tell-tale pet?

A scrutiny of *Flynn's Detective Weekly,* or *Argosy's All Story Magazine* (in which Wright found Zane Grey's *Riders of the Purple Sage* and a few scientific horror tales) for the years 1923–1925 might be as rewarding as that of *The American Mercury* from mid-1926 on, or that of the numerous works by Horatio Alger that Wright avidly devoured.

Wright's vivid account of his discovery of the joys and importance of fiction through the initiation of Mencken's *Prejudices* and *Book of Prefaces* in Memphis is accurate; *A Book of Prefaces* certainly served as his literary Bible for years, introducing him to Dreiser and Conrad, to the French and British realists, to J. G. Huneker, Hauptmann, and Suderman, among others. Yet Wright only owned *A Book of Prefaces* (in the 1927 edition), and he borrowed *Prejudices* from the New York Public Library when he wanted to refresh his memories of it for the writing of *Black Boy.*

Mencken did not think much of the American classics of the preceding century, and Wright only praises a few of them. In a 1937 speech he alludes to Melville along with Anderson, Dreiser, Crane, and John Milton Hay (the author of *The Breadwinners* in 1884), and in "Personalism" (circa 1937), he reflects:

> Hawthorne posed the problem of evil, of those whom society had branded. Emerson speculated and sang of the possibilities of the spiritual and moral perfection of the individual under what he hoped would be a truly democratic civilization. Thoreau took refuge in self-sufficiency. Whitman chanted of a mystical future, of a mystical reconciliation of the individual and society, of a confused comradeship on an emotional plane. . . . Poe hid in the shadows of a dream world, a region almost akin to the Heaven of the surrealists. Melville dramatized his conflict with society in emotional terms, basically pessimistic. Twain hid his conflict in satire and wept in private over the brutalities and the injustices of his civilization. Dreiser tried to rationalize and justify the defeat of the individual in biological terms. . . . Anderson pictured the lonely soul of the crushed petty bourgeois. Sinclair Lewis, at heart a reformer, laughed and sneered. Abruptly there ends the major attempts of literary artists to deal with their times and age.

Emerson's *Essays* (First Series) in a second-hand copy of a 1930 edition was in Wright's library, but he never alludes to the writings of Emerson in his published works. After 1932, he acquired Melville's *Omoo, Typee, Mardi, Redburn, Israel Potter, White Jacket,* and *Moby Dick* in a collected edition, as well as Lewis Mumford's biography of Melville. Poe was certainly an early major influence. Wright owned both his *Poems and Tales* and Volume 4 of his *Collected Works*, which contains his criticism. Traces of this influence, so akin to Wright's own love for the horror tale, the gothic, the fantastic and the detective story, are to be found as early as 1931 in "Superstition," and also in *Native Son*, as I have tried to show elsewhere.[6]

Wright alluded several times to Mark Twain as a great novelist but he mentioned *Innocents Abroad* rather than *Huckleberry Finn* which he certainly read in Chicago. Walt Whitman was a more important part of his early baggage; he had not one but two editions of *Leaves of Grass* (1917 and 1922),[7] from which he was fond of quoting all-embracing verse, especially "Not until the sun excludes you do I exclude you," or the lines which adorn the end of *Black Power*.

Yet Henry James was rather unexpectedly a much more decisive influence. In unpublished notes for a 1941 Wright lecture, we find: "Experiments in words, Stein; experiments in dialogues, James; experiments in scenes, James; experiments in moods, Conrad." These experiments took place in the mid-thirties, and Wright was fond of discussing *The Portrait of a Lady, Daisy Miller* and *Roderick Hudson* with his friend Joyce Gourfain at the time he was writing his first important short stories. However, *Portrait of a Lady* (acquired after 1936) and a 1929 collected edition of *The Two Images, The Turn of the Screw* and *Covering End* (bought after 1932) were Wright's only holdings at the time.

Among American novelists of the twentieth century, Theodore Dreiser should be listed first, since he was incontestably the greatest American master in Wright's eyes. He read *Sister Carrie* and *Jennie Gerhardt* in Memphis, and several other novels in Chicago including The *Titan*, The *Financier*, and *An American Tragedy*, to which *Native Son* was clearly intended to be the black counterpart. As late as 1960, Wright significantly declared: "Among the great novelists I reread with the greatest pleasure are Sherwood Anderson, Mark Twain, James T. Farrell, Nelson Algren, Proust, Dostoievsky. But I'd give them all for a book by Dreiser: he encompasses them all."[8]

Possibly along with Frank Norris's *McTeague*, Stephen Crane and Sherwood Anderson were Wright's first incursions into American realism and naturalism, not to exclude Sinclair Lewis, whose *Babbitt* is mentioned in *Black Boy* and whose *Main Street* Wright used to praise to his fellow workers in Chicago. By Sherwood Anderson, Wright owned *Many Marriages* (bought in 1933), and he had read *Winesburg, Ohio* as well as *Dark*

*Laughter* and *Tar.* By Crane, he owned only *Men, Women and Boats* (1930?), but had read *Maggie, A Girl of the Streets* (which later became his favorite) around 1928, *The Red Badge of Courage,* and probably most of the short stories of a writer whom he considered a master of realism and whose "Blue Hotel" was mentioned very flatteringly in *A Book of Prefaces.*

Through the techniques of *Studs Lonigan* and *U.S.A.,* James T. Farrell and Dos Passos definitely influenced the writing of *Lawd Today* in 1935–1937. Wright only owned *Three Soldiers* by Dos Passos, but he later discussed *The Big Money* with Margaret Walker, though he confessed having difficulties in finishing *U.S.A.* He mentioned Dos Passos with the American realists on several occasions, and was careful to learn how to handle the "Camera Eye" and "Newsreel" techniques. Farrell was a close friend of Wright's from the mid-thirties on and gave him personal advice concerning *Lawd Today* after Wright had been awed and delighted by Farrell's stand on the politics versus literature controversy at the 1935 League of American Writers Congress. Apparently Wright owned only *Tommy Gallagher's Crusade* (1939), but he had read, meditated upon, and used several devices of *Judgement Day.* (See among others, the material representation of the bridge game in *Lawd Today.*)

In the same realist / proletarian group should be placed Robert Cantwell's *Land of Plenty,* William Rollins's *The Wall of Men,* and especially Nelson Algren, Jack Conroy, Erskine Caldwell and John Steinbeck. Wright was Algren's friend, and he read *Somebody in Boots* when it appeared and later took for his own novel the discarded title *Native Son.* He admired Algren greatly, wrote a glowing preface to his *Never Come Morning* in 1942, and listed him among his favorites as late as 1960. Jack Conroy was a friend too, and when it was published in 1934, Wright was impressed by *The Disinherited.* In a 1935 term paper that he wrote for his friend Esse Lee Ward, Wright alluded to "the new degree of persuasion that can be seen in such work as *The Modern Temper* by Joseph Wood Krutch, and Jack Conroy's *The Disinherited.*"[9] He felt closer to its author's authentic proletarian voice than either to propaganda writing or to the novels of the preceding generation, which lacked class consciousness, as he stated at the second American Writers' Congress.

Caldwell's *God's Little Acre* he bought in 1934, and he saw the stage adaptation of *Tobacco Road,* by John Kirkland, in May of 1935 in New York. He was quite enthusiastic about *Kneel to the Rising Sun,* and later

mentioned Caldwell's effective realism several times. He bought Steinbeck's *The Grapes of Wrath* for Ellen when their first daughter was born,
and he discussed it at length in an essay, but he did not know much of his
work by the time he spent a few days with Steinbeck, who was shooting
*The Forgotten Village* in Mexico in the spring of 1940.

Novels by Faulkner and Hemingway are conspicuously absent from
Wright's early library. However, Wright had read several novels by
Faulkner, including *Sanctuary*, before 1940, although he spoke of him
with admiration only in the late forties. Concerning Faulkner's attitude
towards the Negro, however, Wright was wary; he liked to say that Faulkner had never been so right as when he had declared that it was impossible for him to get into the skin of a Negro when creating black
characters. (See interview in *Oslo Dagbladet*, November 29, 1956.) The
case was different with Hemingway, whom he greatly admired. He
studied his short stories certainly more than his novels, and tried to apply
their techniques to his own. A close study of *Uncle Tom's Children* in that
light might be rewarding especially of "Long Black Song," of which
Wright says:

> All us young writers were influenced by Ernest Hemingway . . . We liked the
> simple, direct way in which he wrote, but a great many of us wanted to write
> about social problems. . . . Hemingway's style is so concentrated upon natu-
> ralistic detail that there is no room for social comment. One boy said that one
> way was to dig deeper into the character and try to get something that will live.
> I decided to try it. . . . I tried to conceive of a simple peasant woman, whose
> outlook upon life was influenced by natural things, and to contrast her with a
> white salesman selling phonographs and records. [10]

At the time he was putting *Native Son* together, Wright again resorted
to a close study of Hemingway's writing techniques, and discussed this
with his friend Ralph Ellison. [11] One could even say that Wright went so
far as to adopt some of Hemingway's literary attitudes, especially his
position as an expatriate and his relationship with Gertrude Stein.

Gertrude Stein was indeed another of Wright's revered writers, though
her influence was limited to her use of language. "Experiments in words,"
he noted. After finding *Three Lives* on the shelves of the Chicago Public
Library, he rediscovered "authentic Negro talk" in the lengthy, involved
sentences of "Melanctha." This meant for Wright a renewed vision of the
possibilities of folk dialect and speech rhythms. When he started writing a
review of *Wars I've Seen* [12] in 1945, the piece soon turned into a long

article entitled "Memories of My Grandmother" (unpublished), which underlined this personal revelation as much as the merits of the book *per se:*

> I had heard my grandmother speak ever since I can remember so that I was conscious of anything particularly distinctive in her speech. Then I read a sketch of Negro life by Gertrude Stein and suddenly it was as if I were listening to my grandmother for the first time, so fresh was the feeling it gave me. [13]

However, Stein's influence was elusive, except perhaps in the story "Long Black Song." Later, Wright became an eager collector and a fanatic admirer of her work (the only instance in which he really collected an author's writings). As his favorite piece for Whit Burnett's *I Wish I'd Written That,* Wright significantly selected "Melanctha." This may have been in part because "she was the first American author to treat the Negro seriously,"[14] but principally because of this linguistic revelation.

"He spent all his spare time reading Conrad, Dreiser, Sandburg, Stein, Caldwell, Hemingway, yes, even William Saroyan," an interviewer says of Chicagoan Wright in the August, 1940 issue of the *Kaputskan.* Wright liked Sandburg's *The People Yes,* which was highly praised in left-wing circles; he owned Saroyan's *Love, Here Is My Heart* (1938); by E. E. Cummings, only *Eimi* (1933) remains in his library, but he also owned *The Enormous Room* in the mid-thirties, and was attracted by its absurd, almost existentialist overtones. It is Cummings's translation of Aragon's *Red Front* (the Contempo 1933 edition, a gift from Minna and Abe Aaron) which, we must remember, inspired Wright's long poem "Transcontinental." Isidor Schneider's *The Temptation of Anthony* (a novel in verse and other poems), and Thomas Wolfe's *The Web and the Rock,* bought in 1939, were also on his shelves. [15]

Two groups of writing deserve special mention here, because they were not really represented in his early library: Black authors and American playwrights in general. In the first group, he owned *Through Sepia Eyes,* which Frank Marshall Davis, also a member of the Chicago South Side Writers Club, had given him in October, 1938. Although they later differed politically, Wright always considered him a fine poet. He also had Walter White's *Fire in the Flint;* he reviewed Arna Bontemps's novel, *Black Thunder,* which he found excellent, but surprisingly, he apparently had nothing by Langston Hughes at the time. He knew Hughes personally in the thirties, though, and even lectured on *The Weary Blues* and *The Ways of White Folks* at the Indianapolis John Reed Club on November 23, 1934. Wright's early poetry is influenced to a certain extent by Hughes (compare "I Have Seen Black Hands" and "I Have Known Rivers"), and they collaborated on the writing of "Red Clay Blues" in 1937. However, their literary relationship was rather weak and Wright was later critical of Hughes's approach to autobiography in his *I Wonder as I Wander*. Although he hardly ever refers to them, Wright certainly knew the writings of the Harlem Renaissance to a point. He never even mentions Jean Toomer's *Cane*, but it seems difficult to believe that the Toomer-like treatment of the black woman and effects achieved in "Long Black Song" are purely coincidental.

Of American playwrights, Wright only owned one volume, Eugene O'Neill's *The Emperor Jones;* he liked to say to several of his friends who feared for him during the skirmishes between Communist demonstrators and the police: "Only a golden bullet is going to get me." He liked Paul Green's one-act *Hymn to the Rising Sun* to such an extent that he tried to have the Chicago unit of the Federal Negro Theater produce it in 1936. He also defended Meyer Levin's *Model Tenements* against censorship. While in New York for the First American Writers Congress in 1935, he had seen and admired *Till the Day I Die, Waiting for Lefty,* and *Awake and Sing* by Clifford Odets, the adaptation of *Tobacco Road,* and *Black Pit* by Albert Maltx. Together with his friend Theodore Ward's *Big White Fog* (which Ward claims inspired Wright with the image of the mountain of white hate in "Bright and Morning Star" and *Native Son*) and the plays by Hughes performed at the time, this was about all he had seen of American theater. Nonetheless, his articles dealing with black theater and Federal theater during the Depression which appeared in the *Daily Worker* in 1937 and in "Portrait of Harlem" in the *New York Panorama* were accurate and well-documented up through the performance of William DuBois's *Haiti.*

## II

Wright's initiation to British literature may well have begun with his battered second-hand copy of Henry S. Pancoast's *English Prose and Verse from Beowulf to Robert Louis Stevenson,* or T. H. Ward's *The English Poets,* even before Mencken guided him with more discrimination. He was particularly well-provided with British classics, considering that he was self-taught: Bunyan's *Pilgrim's Progress,* Robert Burns' *Songs* (which he left half-uncut), Thomas Carlyle's *Past and Present* and *Sartor Resartus,* Chaucer's *Poetical Works,* Dickens's *David Copperfield, Bleak*

*House,* and *The Pickwick Papers,* Lamb's *Essays of Elia,* Macaulay's *Lays of Ancient Rome and Other Poems,* Milton's *Poetical Works* (plus *Comus, Lycidas, Allegro, Penseroso* in one volume), Shakespeare's *Complete Works,* Swift's *Gulliver's Travels,* Tennyson's *Idylls of the King,* Thackeray's *Vanity Fair,* and Oscar Wilde's *Poems.* Of these, two names only seem to have made any impression upon Wright. Shakespeare he always loved and reread, especially the tragedies, often quoting from them in his articles, finding possible titles for his novels in them, or exulting at a performance of *Othello, Macbeth,* or *Hamlet,* and naively trying to emulate these masterpieces. From Swift's satirical solution to the Irish Question, Wright stole the idea of his "Repeating a Modest Proposal (with Apologies to Old Jonathan)," a four-page letter to the President of the United States suggesting that the Negro problem could be solved economically by eating all colored Americans. The piece was unfortunately never published. Another name left unmentioned should be brought up here, since it is most likely to Byron's apostrophe to the ocean that Wright's line, "Sweep on, o red stream of molten lava," in "Everywhere Burning Waters Rise" (1934) should be traced.

Among modern British novels, Wright owned *Mr. Prohock* by Arnold Bennett, *Lorna Doone* by Richard Blackmore, *South Wind* by Norman Douglas, *The Silver Box, Strife, Justice, The Pigeon, A Bit of Love,* and *Loyalties* by John Galsworthy. However, his favorite authors were clearly Joseph Conrad, Thomas Hardy, George Moore, and H. G. Wells. Conrad came first by far, and Wright had bought *The Arrow of God* (1927 edition), *Nostromo* (1924), *A Personal Record* and *The Shadow Line* (1928), *Typhoon and Other Stories* (1929), *Victory* (1921), and *Youth* (1903) by the very beginning of the thirties. From such books, as well as from *Lord Jim* and *The Nigger of the Narcissus,* he derived what he called a "sense of mood," of atmosphere, in the same way he had borrowed from James for dialogue and scene, and from Gertrude Stein for words and language. He ranked Conrad with Dostoievsky and always spoke of him with "more than a hint of awe in his voice." Reminiscences of *Heart of Darkness* haunt *The Outsider* as well as *Black Power,* but Conradian undertones already exist in "Superstition."

Mencken, who recommended Conrad, also introduced Wright to Thomas Hardy's *Tess of the D'Urbervilles,* and he bought *Far from the Madding Crowd, The Return of the Native,* and *Two in a Tower.* His liking for George Moore may seem strange only to those ignorant of Moore's enormous success at the time. Wright owned *Confessions of a Young Man* and *Esther Waters,* and he certainly read other novels like *Sister Teresa,* which Mencken praised in *A Book of Prefaces.* H. G. Wells, whom he briefly mentioned in *The Color Curtain* with Lathrop Stoddard for having predicted the coming of age of the Third World, undoubtedly attracted him as a thinker and as the author of *The Undying Fire* and *The Outline of History,* of which he secured a 1930 edition.

Although he read some Aldous Huxley and as a budding poet was definitely influenced by T. S. Eliot, whom he quoted in *Lawd Today,*[16] Wright's contemporary British favorites were undoubtedly James Joyce and D. H. Lawrence. He still remembered Lawrence's sooty landscapes when travelling through England in 1953, but the handling of human relationships was the major interest (one might say fascination) which *Lady Chatterley's Lover,* bought in 1933, *Women in Love,* bought in 1937, and still more *Sons and Lovers,* held for him. He was not rich enough to secure a copy of *Ulysses* even in the thirties, and he borrowed the book, a part of his omnivorous readings while working at the Chicago Post Office. The structure and several episodes of *Lawd Today,* dealing with twenty-four hours in the life of a Black Chicago postal worker, show a sometimes clumsy desire to emulate *Ulysses. A Portrait of the Artist as a Young Man,* to which *Black Boy* was compared by a few critics, is another definite source, and Keneth Kinnamon has convincingly argued for the derivation of the last paragraph of "Bright and Morning Star" from the end of "The Dead."[17] Wright always admired Joyce immensely, and when *Time* quoted him as saying that *Wasteland* by Jo Sinclair had thrilled him more than anything he had read since *Dubliners,* this was no light praise on his part.[18]

When thinking of Russian novelists in connection with Wright, one at once remembers his high reverence for Dostoevsky, whom he ranked with Conrad and Dreiser after having read *Poor People* in Memphis. *The Brothers Karamazov, The Possessed,* and *Crime and Punishment* he bought upon arrival in Chicago, and only around 1934 did he buy *The House of the Dead.* In an interview for *L'Express* on November 8, 1960, he acknowledged: "Ahead of all the writers who molded my philosophy concerning modern man comes Dostoevsky. . . . Raskolnikov is one of my heroes." Wright's stories may have been influenced by those of Turgeniev and Chekhov, whose *Plays* he also owned, but certainly not in the same way his whole work was influenced by Dostoevsky. This obvious influence deserves a full and detailed treatment in the field of existential philosophy as well as in the field of literature, taking *Native Son,* "The Man Who

Lived Underground," and *The Outsider* as the main examples, but also investigating Wright's non-fiction.

The importance of Tolstoi should not be discounted either. Wright read *War and Peace* by forging notes to borrow it from the Memphis Public Library and later bought it, together with *Anna Karenina, Redemption and Other Plays,* and also *Zanine* by M. Artzibashev. This completes his Russian holdings, not to speak of the numerous revolutionary authors he may have read in translation in the pages of *New Masses* and especially *International Literature.*

Wright was also familiar with many French classics. He bought Honoré de Balzac's bizarre *Seraphita* and *Louis Lambert,* Alexandre Dumas' *The Three Musketeers,* Anatole France's bloody tale of the French Revolution *The Gods are Thirsty, Revolt of the Angels* (in 1936), Théophile Gautier's *Mademoiselle de Maupin,* Pierre Loti's *The Iceland Fisherman,* and even the works of Rabelais and Voltaire's *Candide,* most of these on the recommendation of Mencken. He read but did not own stories by Maupassant, as well as *Madame Bovary.* He long thought of Flaubert as a great master of prose, and tried to identify with Bigger as a character in the same way that Flaubert had identified with Emma Bovary.

Among more contemporary writers, Wright mentioned Henri Barbusse in "Blueprint for Negro Writing" (1937), probably because he had read his antiwar novel *Under Fire* before introducing him to the Chicago John Reed Club in 1934. I have already alluded to Wright's admiration for Aragon's *Red Front.* Gide's praise for the USSR he read in *International Lierature,* but he knew nothing of his anti-colonialist stand and his disillusionment with the Soviet Union until much later. Romain Rolland's *Jean Christophe* may have been suggested to him by Communist friends, and Wright also had a volume of Jules Romains' *Men of Good Will.* His great French love was not a progressive writer, however, but one the Communists dubbed a reactionary. He bought Proust's *Remembrances of Things Past* at great expense in the 1934 Knopf edition in two volumes, and spent his nights reading it avidly, "admiring the lucid, subtle but strong prose, stupefied by its dazzling magic, awed by the vast, delicate, intricate, psychological structure of the Frenchman's epic of grandeur and decadence," he confesses in *American Hunger.* "But it crushed me with hopelessness," he admits, "for I wanted to write of the people in my environment with an equal thoroughness and the burning example before my eyes made me feel I never could."[20]

Much more encouraging and rewarding was the reading of André Malraux's *Man's Fate*, and when he was putting *Native Son* together, of *Man's Hope*, which was suggested to him by his friend Jane Newton. Both novels he discussed at length with her and with Ralph Ellison. Although Malraux was a major influence mainly for Ellison, he was doubly important to Wright both as a politically committed novelist and as a novelist who could strike a balance between his art and his message.

There remain a few books in Wright's early library, the importance of which cannot be determined in his career. He owned Dante's *Divine Comedy*, Boccaccio's *Decameron*, the *Meditations* of Marcus Aurelius, Lessing's *Laocoon, Minna von Barnhelm, Nathan the Wise* (all in one volume), Ibsen's *Works*, and Arthur Schnitzler's *Theresa*. These were probably unimportant holdings, with the exception of the last two.

III

Compared to his holdings in fiction, Wright's books dealing with criticism and language are ridiculously few, probably because he derived much of his theoretical criticism from magazines, mostly of the Left. On the same shelf as his battered English dictionary are to be placed Phyfe's *10,000 Words often Mispronounced*, Roget's *Thesaurus*, and Edwin Wooley's *Handbook of Composition*, from which he allegedly learned nothing as a budding writer. Arthur Schopenhauer's *The Art of Literature*, S. S. Curry's *Imagination and the Dramatic Instinct*, and F. C. Prescott's *Poetry and Myth* may prove hardly more interesting. The proceedings of the 1935 *American Writers Congress* collected by Henry Hart, Frazer's *Golden Bough*, and *The Twentieth Century Novel* by Joseph Warren Beach, are of more consequence. Wright acknowledged his debt to Burrow's *Social Basis of Consciousness* for his characterization of Mann as a self-denying hero in "Down by the Riverside," and in 1937, he recommended John Howard Lawson's *Theory and Technique of Playwrighting*. His debt towards Kenneth Burke, whom he admired and whose *Permanence and Change* he bought in 1935, is still unrecorded as far as his literary philosophy is concerned. However, remembrances of his friends help us record Henry James' *The Art of the Novel* as an extremely important influence on the technique of *Uncle Tom's Children*. He owned John Dewey's *How We Think*, and he read William James and was struck quite early by his theory of the "unguaranteed existence," which he later mentioned in his preface to *Black Metropolis*. He quotes Joseph Wood Krutch's *The Modern Temper* and Van Wyck Brooks' *America Coming of Age* in *Lawd Today*. Not in his library, but read and discussed with his friend Ralph Ellison in 1937, is Miguel de Unamuno's *Tragic Sense of Life,* from which Wright may have borrowed nearly as much of his theoretical existential outlook as from Nietzsche.

However, most, of Wright's ideological perspective was derived from other sources. In 1936, he bought *The Bible Designed as Living Literature,* which shows that he was more drawn to its imagery and symbolism than to its contents, although he quoted at random from the Scriptures in *Black Boy, Savage Holiday, The Outsider,* and *Black Power.* On the other hand, he apparently did not read Marx until 1936, when he was offered his *Selected Works* by a Communist friend. When in "How Jim Crow Feels" he boasts about crossing the Mexican border with *Das Kapital* in his luggage in 1940, this may well mean that he was simply reading it for the first time, not that he used the book as his Bible. He owned Engel's *Socialism, Utopian and Scientific,* acquired after 1932, and Stalin's *Marxism and the National and Colonial Question* (1935), which he considered a key work on the Black minority in America. By Lenin, he had numerous works, including *Imperialism, the Highest Stage of Capitalism* (1938), *State and Revolution* (1935), *Woman and Society* (1938), and also Clara Zetkin's *Lenin on the Woman Question* (1936). He alluded many times to Lenin in his writings; in "Blueprint for Negro Writing," he spoke of Lenin's observation that oppressed minorities often reflect the techniques of the bourgeoisie more brilliantly than some sections of the bourgeoisie themselves; in "How Bigger Was Born," he alluded to Lenin's reflection on the workers' sense of estrangement from the monuments of the system; and Lenin's "Freedom Belongs to the Strong" gave him the final clue for "Fire and Cloud." Along with a spate of pamphlets published and distributed by the American Communist Party on political problems and current issues, his only "theoretical" book concerning the United States was James W. Ford's *The Negro and the Democratic Front* (1938),[21] while his copy of the *Report on the Court Proceedings in the Case of Anti-Soviet Bloc of Right and Trotskyites* (1938) shows his interest in the Trotsky trials, possibly in relationship with the trial of his friend Pointdexter that he had witnessed in Chicago. Angelo Herndon was a friend of Wright's, and he probably gave him his *Let Me Live* in 1937; Wright received John Strachey's *The Nature of the Capitalist Crisis* after hearing him lecture in 1936. To complete the list for this section, one should add Heinz Liepman's *Murder Made in Germany* (1938), Emil Ludwig's *Napoleon,* Mary Mc Lane's *A Diary of Human Days,* J. S. Shapiro's *Modern and Contemporary European History.* If we take into account F. M. Taussig's *Princi-*

*ples of Economy* and *How to Make Good Pictures,* distributed by Eastman Kodak, this brings to an end the meager list of Wright's library at the time he published *Native Son.* As one can easily realize, fiction and literature were predominant among his holdings, and he knew comparatively little about the theory of literature. He had to wait until the forties and fifties, not only to perfect his knowledge of psychology, psychoanalysis, sociology, criminology and philosophy, but to add significantly to his library in these fields.

1. See *Black Boy* (New York: Harper & Bros., 1945), pp. 217–223. *Resources for American Literary Study* (1971) indicates areas of future research and provides basic bibliographical help.

2. Margaret Walker, "Richard Wright," *New Letters,* 38 (Winter 1971): 182–202.

3. Michel Fabre, *The Unfinished Quest of Richard Wright* (New York: William Morrow & Company, Inc., 1973).

4. The listing is divided into several sections: literature (United States, British, and foreign); language and criticism; political and social sciences; technical. To the titles still in Wright's personal library at his death (the ones which belonged to him before 1940 are recognizable because Ellen Wright marked them "Wright" in pencil when she married Richard), I have felt free to add titles and authors mentioned in his works, correspondence, and interviews, in order to give a more complete picture.

5. *The Emergence of Richard Wright* (Urbana: University of Illinois Press, 1972), Kenneth Kinnamon identifies it as "Another Mencken Absurdity" (published May 28, 1927, in response to Mencken's editorial in the *Baltimore Sun,* May 23, 1927, on the Mississippi floods). According to May Cameron (interview with Richard Wright, *New York Post,* March 12, 1938) Wright had in mind another editorial in which Mencken derided Alabama segregationists, who had denied a black painter entrance to an exhibition of his own works.

6. See my "Black Cat and White Cat: Wright's Gothic and the Influence of Poe," printed in this volume.

7. The dates given in parentheses refer to the year of publication of the editions Wright owned.

8. Quoted in Annie Brièrre, "Richard Wright: L'Amérique n'est pas conformiste . . .," *France-USA,* September/October 1960, p. 2. See *Black Boy,* p. 219.

9. Said Wright, "[Stephen Crane's] *Maggie: A Girl of the Streets* is simply a coldly materialistic picture of poverty, while Jack Conroy's *The Disinherited* is the picture of men and women groping their way to a new concept of human dignity" (in "Writing from the Left," Yale University Library, p. 1).

10. Richard Wright, "How *Uncle Tom's Children* Grew," *Columbia University Writer's Club Bulletin* 2 (May 1938): [18].

11. See Ralph Ellison's interview in *The Paris Review,* Spring 1955, p. 57. Wright also discussed *Men Without Women* in a 1941 lecture.

12. *PM,* March 11, 1945, p. M5.

13. Interview with Joseph Gollomb, *New York Post,* February [?], 1945.

14. Interview in the *New York Sun Telegraph,* March 4, 1940.

15. Wright also mentioned Jack London in "Blueprint for Negro Writing," along with nine other American, Russian, French, and Swedish writers, as a potential part of the heritage of the Negro writer, but he hardly ever alluded to him again. One should add that from 1936 to 1940, Wright reviewed a number of books such as Arna Bontemps's *Black Thunder* (*Partisan Review & Anvil,* April, 1936); Waters E. Turpin's *These Low Grounds* and Zora Neale Hurston's *Their Eyes Were Watching God* (*New Masses,* October 5, 1937); H. B. Kroll's *I*

*Was a Sharecropper* (*New Republic,* December 1, 1937); William Rollins's *The Wall of Men* (*New Masses,* March 8, 1938); Langston Hughes's *The Big Sea* and W. E. B. DuBois's *Dusk of Dawn* (*Chicago News,* December 4, 1940).

16. Wright read T. S. Eliot intensively and some Pound and Joyce at about the same time (1934–1936). The influence of Eliot's technique can be felt especially in "Between the World and Me," "Obsession," and "Rise and Live."

17. Kinnamon, *The Emergence of Richard Wright,* p. 116.

18. *Time,* February 18, 1946. The review Wright wrote for *PM* (February 17, 1946) was quite enthusiastic.

19. *L'Express* (Paris), October 18, 1955, p. 8.

20. *American Hunger* (New York: Harper and Row, 1977), p. 24.

21. In fact, Wright probably read many books dealing with the Negro in the United States when doing research first for the Chicago and then for the New York W.P.A. Guides. He compiled a bibliography of the Negro in Illinois in 1936–1937 (see *New Letters* 39 [Fall 1972]: 61–72). In "Portrait of Harlem" in *New York Panorama* (New York: Random House, 1939), he mentions G. W. Williams's *History of the Negro Race* (1883) and Booker T. Washington's *A Story of the Negro* (1909).

# Black Cat and White Cat:
## Wright's Gothic and the Influence of Poe

I N enumerating such requirements for literary success as the ludicrous
heightened into the grotesque: the fearful colored into the horrible:
the witty exaggerated into the burlesque: the singular wrought out into
the strange and the mystical,[1] Edgar Allan Poe certainly spoke from experience. That is, he sought those literary qualities with avidity, for he felt
that to really be appreciated, one must be read. And read he was, not only
by his contemporaries but also by twentieth–century readers lured by
similar fascinations—and especially by a young black American writer
named Richard Wright. Tales of horror and imagination were the favorite
reading of Richard Wright, who had his first significant literary experience when a fearless teenager told him the tale of Bluebeard in the
household of his book–hating Seventh–Day Adventist grandmother. This
gruesome story was the first experience in his life that elicited from him a
total emotional response.[2] It certainly paved the way for his inordinate
love of melodrama, murder stories, and ghastly settings.

Among the books and magazines he read in his youth, Wright lists not
only Zane Grey's *Riders of the Purple Sage,* but also *Flynn's Detective
Weekly* and *Argosy All-Story Magazine.* One of his favorite tales is that of
"a renowned scientist who had rigged up a mystery room made of metal in
the basement of his palatial home. Prompted by some obscure motive, he
would lure his victims into his room and then throw an electric switch.
Slowly, with heart-racking agony, the air would be sucked from the metal
room and his victims would die, turning red, blue, then black." He
comments: "This was what I wanted, tales like this. I had not read enough
to have developed any taste of reading" (*Black Boy,* pp. 34–35).

Although he later developed a taste for the realistic fiction of Dreiser
and Sherwood Anderson, Wright never forgot this version of "The Pit and
the Pendulum" or "The Cask of Amontillado," brought up to date to
foreshadow the horrors of the gas chamber. The first story which Wright

27

recalls writing at the age of twelve was indebted to the dual influence of frontier romanticism and of the frail heroines of Edgar Allan Poe.

More significant is the presence of Poe's main works among the scanty hundred volumes Wright possessed before becoming the author of *Native Son*. Of the collection, Volume IV of the *Complete Works,* published by Harpers at the beginning of the century, comprised Poe's criticism. A second hand copy of *Poems and Tales,* printed in 1924 for the University Publishing Company, included "To Helen," "Annabel Lee," "Ulalume," "The Bells," "The Raven," "Eldorado," "Coliseum," "The Fall of the House of Usher," "Descent into the Maelström," "The Tell-Tale Heart," "The Pit and the Pendulum," "Ligeia," and "The Gold-Bug." It is very likely that Wright, having discovered and enjoyed Poe to the point of buying these books, did his best to secure the rest of his works in the George Cleveland Hall branch of the Chicago Public Library, where they were readily available. At a later date, he also bought Volume III of the 1876 Middleton Edition of Poe's works. We may therefore assume that he was more conversant with Poe's fiction and aesthetic theories than the average student would have been.

An early debt to Poe's technique as a storyteller is to be found in Wright's first preserved story. Written in 1930, its title is, significantly, "Superstition," and the caption reads: "Each year the family held a reunion—each year death claimed its toll—was it superstition—or was it fate?"[3] At the end of a leisurely dinner with two friends, when the conversation turned to subjects of a weird and mysterious nature, the first-person narrator relates "a baffling incident that defied explanation". The experience is simple: having to spend the night in a small Southern town, the young man has to stay with the Lancaster family, which takes guests, because all the hotels are full. The younger daughter, Lillian, has no sooner expressed her fear of the superstition which entails death to a member of a household at a family reunion when her brothers arrive for an unexpected Christmas visit. She dies in the night of acute pneumonia. When chance brings the visitor back to Koogan a year later, curiosity prompts him to stay with the Lancasters again, and, this time, Mrs. Lancaster dies of a heart attack after the ominous fall of Lillian's portrait from above the mantlepiece and a second unexpected visit of the two brothers.

Wright owes much to Poe's technique of describing the setting in order to suggest an eerie, dreary atmosphere. The beginning of "Superstition," with "houses standing out like gaunt sores against the bleak sky, . . . the

incessant rain, the cold and penetrating damp, the overhanging gloom
. . . in the far distance the mournful whistle of a departing train, the faint
and musical tinkle of a cowbell, a solitary dog, the monotonous beat of
rain", seems a clumsy attempt at recreating the opening note of "The Fall
of the House of Usher." The Usher family and their mansion are analogous—crumbling from within, stained with time; so do the Lancaster
parents and their wooden house, used up as they are, decline together.
Mr. Lancaster is "exceptionally frail, so frail that she seemed to cling to
life by bare effort . . . her eyes entirely lifeless, so sunken were they." Her
husband is "a bent and aged man, somewhat older than she, dressed in a
loose-fitting black suit, and whose head was wrapped in a black silk skull
cap." Although cozy, the room, "with an abnormally high ceiling across
which flitted fantastic shadows from a blazing log fire, seemed heir to a
blanket of decay and melancholy."

As for Lillian, she seems a sepia Ligeia, a beautiful, yet disembodied,
consumptive beauty. "Her narrow face, pale and emaciated, attracted me.
Her hair was brushed backward and revealed a broad, bulging forehead,
below which, shining in contrast to her pallid features, were a pair of
dark, sunken eyes. The most unusual thing about her was a timid and
perpetual smile, a smile that seemed melancholy and slightly cynical. A
peculiar air of resignation pervaded her whole being." Lillian is the victim, marked for sacrifice by an unseen hand.

More interesting is Wright's use of Poe's habit of blending the uncanny
and the natural by postulating hidden but rational laws governing the
action, as is particularly apparent in "The Fall of the House of Usher." In
"Superstition," the reader is left with a dual explanation: Lillian and her
mother die for natural reasons (of pneumonia and a heart attack), but the
coincidence, in place and in time, equally vindicates she supernatural
explanation expressed by the popular saying about family reunions. The
mystery here is related to chance, but mostly to a strange correspondence
between externals and psychology where the "objective correlative" takes
on an active role. The arresting attributes of both works are the creation of
the atmosphere and the disruption of mental states, the early work of
Wright being clumsier in that respect. In realizing that a situation replete
with horror is more catching by being vague, Wright tries to make fear
more terrible through ambiguity. "At that moment the coming tragedy
cast its shadow, and that shadow, like all the shadows that attend human
events, was unseen by human eyes. The causes in our lives that later
develop into glaring effects are so minute, originate in such commonplace

incidents that we pass them casually, unthinking, only to look back and marvel". Here the moralist breaks the dramatic suspense by his intrusion. Elsewhere, the same effect is more appropriately achieved to bring the reader back to the teller of the tale in his Chicago setting: "I shall never, as long as I breathe, forget that silence. In that silence, there was revealed, hideously and repellently, the stark nakedness of the fearful hearts of a primitive folk—fearful hearts bowing abjectly to the terror of an unknown created by their own imaginations. . . . The very contents of their inmost hearts were laid bare in that one moment: the unreasoning fear of death". Having pretended to share the characters' fears and feelings, the narrator now steps aside and poses as a rationalist.

Despite their differences, Wright owes his nineteenth-century master more than he admits; they are more akin than one thinks. Both share similar experiences; their imagination has measured the limits of terror in real earnest because a hostile world has assulted their souls and left them shaken; both, feeling cut off from the average man by their talent, resist authority and will concede to the superiority of no one but themselves. Art, based on firsthand data and autobiography, is for them a means of escape and self-realization. They share the same liking for psychiatric case histories, where they find valuable source material; the grim existential importance of terror, death, depression, or in Poe's case, dissolution of personality, compels them to treat these subjects other than as merely good material for a horror story in the Gothic or the melodramatic tradition. Wright's fascination for the roots of religious belief and for the unexplainable motives of human behavior brings him the closer to Poe's sounding of the malevolent powers of man's soul. Both authors deal in delusions, dread, and dreams, their work a tissue of nightmares in which symbolism takes over naturalism, although Wright concentrates more upon factual truth and Poe more on the fantasies of a cerebral logician. Their dreaming is a form of social criticism and, clearly, a way to escape from the shocks and vulgarities of life, be it a world of brutal racial discrimination or one of debts, social snubs, and petty intrigues.

Among the few American writers to whom Wright occasionally alluded, Poe's name is ranked with Hawthorne, Emerson, Melville, Thoreau, Whitman, Twain, Dreiser, Sinclair Lewis, and Sherwood Anderson as literary artists who made major attempts to deal with their times. Around 1937, Wright judges that Poe "hid in the shadows of a dream world, a region almost akin to the Heaven of the surrealists,"[4] while Melville dramatized his conflict with society in pessimistic, emotional terms.

Three years later, he thinks again of Poe, this time as the representative of horror: "We have only a money-grubbing civilization but we do have in the Negro the embodiment of a past tragic enough to appease the spiritual hunger of even a James; and we have in the oppression of the Negro a shadow athwart our national life dense and heavy enough to satisfy even the gloomy broodings of a Hawthorne. And if Poe were alive, he would not have to invent horror; horror would invent him."[5]

The last quotation could be drawn directly from the plea pronounced by Max, the Communist lawyer who tries in vain to rescue Bigger Thomas before a self-righteous court in *Native Son*. It makes use of a too-obvious Gothic imagery which immediately recalls Poesque metaphors and scenes.[6] Likewise, the comparisons of vacant houses with skulls, "empty buildings with black windows like blind eyes, buildings like skeletons standing with snow on their bones" (p. 147), or "tall, snow-covered buildings, whose many windows gaped blackly, like the eye-sockets of empty skulls" (p. 196) are reminiscent of the luminous, red-lit windows of "The Haunted Palace." An autodidact, Wright certainly first learned from Poe words like "pallid," "sunken," or, in a more obvious case, "oblong." For Wright, "oblong" inevitably alludes to a coffin and to death, as in "The Oblong Box." The word recurs with that connotation throughout his fiction, but particularly in *Native Son:* "the oblong black belt" (p. 266) on the Chicago map hems the fugitive like a cell and the "oblong, sheet-covered table" (p. 280) on which Bessie's corpse is brought to the tribunal recalls the oblong, empty mound of coals left by Mary's burned body.

Still more striking is the use of "The Black Cat" in Wright's *Native Son*. It would be too easy to speak of a mere literary finding. As we learn from *Black Boy*, his autobiography, Wright recorded two important traumatic events of his early youth: the time when he set fire to his grandmother's house, starting with the white curtains, and his hanging of a kitten with a string, apparently as a gesture of resentment against his father. Both episodes brought a strong sense of guilt to the four- or five-year-old boy. This personal psychological background may have increased the impression that Poe's tale (in which the hero hangs the cat to the limb of a tree and in which he finds the curtains of his bed in flame) made upon Wright's sensibilities. For him, the tale was linked with personal guilt, and he had no trouble recreating, half-unconsciously, a situation in which the fire, the cat, and the obsessive guilt are linked. These influences crystallized in the basement scene of *Native Son* when the white cat of Mrs. Dalton looks at Mary's murderer, and upon another occasion, jumps upon his shoulders at the very moment when Bigger fears being discovered by the reporters. Mrs. Dalton, blind as she is and dressed in flowing white robes, already seems like a ghost (cf. p. 40); her cat is the embodiment of her intuitive knowledge of the situation; it is the eye of justice looking at Bigger. Its eyes, at first "large placid eyes" (p. 41). turn into "two green pools—pools of accusation and guilt—staring at him from a white blur that sat perched upon the edge of the trunk" (p. 78).

Bigger's reaction is typical of Poe's murderer: "It was the white cat and its round green eyes gazed past him at the white face hanging limply fom the fiery furnace door. God! He closed his mouth and swallowed. Should he catch the cat and put it into the furnace too? He made a move. The cat stood up; its white fur bristled; its back arched. he tried to grab it and it bounded past him with a long wail of fear" (p. 79). This symbolicaly white (the colors are inverted) cat plays the part of the tell-tale heart in a scene destined to show the murderer's fright. To create suspense, Wright makes use of the literary culture of his reader: when the cat leaps upon Bigger's shoulder at the moment when the host of newspapermen are searching intently for clues, Bigger feels that "the cat had given him away, had pointed him out as the murderer of Mary. He tried to lift the cat down, but the claws clutched the coat. The silver lightning flashed in his eyes and he knew that the men had taken pictures of him with the cat poised upon his shoulder" (p. 171).

Here the situation and the symbolical use of the cat are unmistakably Poesque. But the central episode of the novel—once the reader can step back from the psychological suspense and the social protest—is one long, melodramatic murder story, from the unreal bower of the rich heiress's bedroom with its flowing drapes, blurred outlines, and the ghost-like appearance of the blind mother at the door, to the fiery atmosphere of the basement where Bigger performs his gory task. Equally fantastic is the icy blizzard of the Chicago night, from moldy room to empty, crumbling house, in a world of angry rats, cockroaches, clinging cobwebs, and blood trickling from Bessie's crushed head in the room "filled with quiet and cold and death and blood and the deep moan of the night wind" (p. 202).

In later novels, the influence of horror tales, of the dime novel—all most or less indebted to Poe—on Wright's fiction dwindled greatly. *The Outsider, Savage Holiday,* and *The Long Dream* evince a definite appeal for violence, murder, and blood. The treatment, however, is more psychoanalytical and far less macabre. What Wright may have learned from Poe was that his own liking for the type of abnormality which is precisely at the border between insanity and the normality of the "aver-age man"—a liking he shared with Dostoevsky, among others—could be used in literature in a way that went further than simply getting the reader involved, a way that forced him to accept abnormality as normal.

1. "Letter to Thomas White" in *Letters of Edgar Allan Poe,* ed. John Ward Ostrom (Cambridge: Harvard University Press, 1948), pp. 57–58.

2. According to Wright, "The tale made the world around me throb, live. As she spoke, reality changed, the look of things around me altered, and the world became peoples with magical presences. . . . I hungered for the sharp, frightening, breath-taking, almost painful excitement that the story had given me, and I vowed that as soon as I was old enough I would buy all the novels there were and read them to feed that thirst for violence that was in me, for intrigue, for plotting, for secrecy, for bloody murders" (*Black Boy* [ New York: Harper & Bros., 1945], pp. 34–35).

3. Richard Wright, "Superstition," reprinted in this volume. Dan McCall in *The Example of Richard Wright* (New York: Harcourt, Brace, & World, 1969), pp. 70–71, has briefly touched on Wright's debt to Poe in "Superstition" and *Native Son;* my own, more detailed, conclusions were arrived at before I had read his study. Kenneth Kinnamon first wrote about this in his *The Emergence of Richard Wright* (Urbana: University of Illinois Press, 1972).

4. "Personalism," unpublished article, circa 1937, p. 1. Wright Archive, Yale University Library.

5. "How 'Bigger' Was Born," in *Native Son* (New York: Harpers, 1940), p. 1; hereafter, page references are to this edition.

6. "We have thought to thrust a corpse from before our eyes. . . . the corpse is dead! It still lives! It has made itself a home in the wild forests of our great cities, amid the rank and choking vegetation of slums! It has forgotten our language! In order to live it has sharpened its claws!" (*Native Son,* p. 331).

# From Revolutionary Poetry
# to Haiku

WIDELY recognized as the father of the contemporary Afro-American novel, Richard Wright is now also beginning to find his place in the history of contemporary ideas. In Europe, perhaps even more than in America, he is remembered as the passionate observer of the birth of Ghana and of the Bandung Conference, and his newspaper contributions and lectures enlightened the Western world about the problems and struggles of the colonized peoples long before the emergence of the Third World became a political reality and a fashionable concept.

Less well-known is his poetry. Except for the readers of anthologies,[1] only a limited public has come in contact with his work. His early poems, few in number and not yet republished, first appeared in leftist magazines all of which, except for *New Masses,* were of short duration and narrow circulation. Encouraged by the success of *Uncle Tom's Children,* he soon turned to the novel and almost abandoned poetry after the triumph of *Native Son.* And yet the prose of *Twelve Million Black Voices* is deliberately poetic, and lyric couplets convey the wonder of childhood in Wright's autobiographical *Black Boy.* Ten years later, as shown by the notes for an unfinished work, he still saw poetry as the complementary form of the dramatic prose of his novels. Finally, on the eve of his premature death, he composed several thousand haikus whose publication would enhance his literary fame. From a purely esthetic point of view, their publication would also justify a study which, in the present circumstances, mostly seeks to uncover the major tendencies of Richard Wright's imagination by examining the evolution of his poetry.

Although symbolic, the genesis of "I Have Seen Black Hands," one of Wright's earliest poems, is significant:

> Towards dawn, I swung from bed and inserted paper into the typewriter. Feeling for the first time that I could speak to listening ears, I wrote a wild,

crude poem in free verse, coining images of black hands playing, working, holding bayonets, stiffening finally in death. I felt that in a clumsy way it linked white life with black, merged two streams of common experience.[2]

At that time his literary vocation, awakened by reading Mencken, only seemed to manifest itself in interminable stylistic exercises; under the influence of Gertrude Stein's "Melanctha", he would rewrite finely-wrought phrases, skillfully balancing the sounds of a picturesque language: "The soft melting hunk of butter trickled in gold down the grooves of the split yam," or "The child's clumsy fingers fumbled in sleep, feeling vainly for the wish of its dream," or "The old man huddled in the dark doorway, his bony face lit by the burning yellow in the windows of distant skyscrapers."[3] Lacking in these phrases (the necessary steps towards a mastery of language) is the element of inspiration, which would flow from image to image binding impressions and ideas into a vivifying whole.

It was the discovery of Communism during the most terrible winter of the Depression that provided the indispensable catalyst. Returning home after a meeting of the John Reed Club, Wright composed several poems which "blended two currents of common experience." He had just discovered an audience eager to hear his message: the great proletarian family. The Marxist demystification of the society which oppressed him racially justified his personal revolt and gave him reasons for persevering. His poetry found its inspiration in this social crusade and received its political orientation. However, as his quarrels with some leaders soon proved, Wright did not docilely conform to the party orthodoxy; his work joined the stream of proletarian literature only because it was guided there by his sense of mission.

Was Wright influenced by the numerous examples around him? As editor of *Left Front*, he read the works of Sam Gaspar or Norman McLeod; in the pages of *New Masses*, he discovered the earlier generation: Kenneth Fearing, Langston Hughes, Archibald MacLeish. At the meetings of the John Reed Club, the members criticized the works of William Carlos Williams, discussed those of T. S. Eliot and analyzed the revolutionary message of Walt Whitman. They read aloud John Reed's "America 1918." Wright's poems, however, generally do not show signs of evident imitation. On the contrary, he seems original in comparison with the secondary writers of the left.[4] His political engagement never made him lose sight of his art nor of his desire to be linked to that rebirth of Negro poetry which is associated with the Harlem Renaissance.

From 1935 to 1937 a group of black writers met every Sunday at the Abraham Lincoln Center in Chicago. The members of this "South Side Club" criticized each other's latest works and discussed the relationship between literature and the racial situation. Fenton Johnson and Frank Marshall Davis were considered the "deans" while Margaret Walker, Russell Marshall and, of course, Richard Wright were among the promising young writers. Wright attended the meetings as assiduously as those of the John Reed Club, often giving talks on the authors of the previous generation like Langston Hughes and Arna Bontemps. His belonging to a dual movement—black nationalist and revolutionary—led him to merge the two major themes of his poetry, just as the Negro's fate and the class struggle were in fact intertwined. Published side by side in the February 1935 issue of *Midland Left*, the poems "Obsession" and "Rise and Live" seem to symbolize in their juxtaposition the coexistence within Wright of an obsessional terror of lynching and a vital impatience for revolt.

The first of these two major themes is that of the suffering of the black American. One of Wright's most beautiful pieces, "Between the World and Me" ends with a cry of pain from the author who identifies with the Negro who has been lynched, and through a miracle of poetic sympathy, the reader is led to share this pain:

> Panting, begging, I clutched childlike, clutched to the hot sides of death,
> Now I am dry bones and my face a stony skull staring in yellow surprise at the
> sun . . .

Wright does not give in to the temptation of facile pathos; he quickly links the fate of the Negro to that of the white proleterian, his comrade in alienation. In "Red Leaves of Red Books" he asks the pages which bear the Marxist gospel to "turn under white fingers and black fingers." The sharecropper of "Red Clay Blues" who has migrated to the hard, side-walked city, wants to return to Georgia as much from a desire to see his former landlord overturned by the agrarian revolution as from a feeling of nostalgia for the soft clay beneath his toes. The tramp of "Ah Feels It in Mah Bones" has a coenesthesiac awareness of the social upheaval and becomes the barometer for it. The more successful "I Have Seen Black Hands" traces, in long lines of free verse, the evolution of the black community; the baby reaching with chubby hands for his mother's breast, the child with sticky and ink-spotted fingers, the adolescent able to throw dice and wield the billiard cue. In terms which foreshadow the finale of *Twelve Million Black Voices*, Wright then describes the calloused hands of the worker producing objects whose poor sales will bring on the War, while for himself there will only be poverty, street fighting, and repression. In opposition to "Between the World and Me," here there is hope in the solidarity of those who are oppressed:

> I am black and I have seen black hands
> Raised in fists of revolt, side by side with the white fists of white workers,
> And some day—and it is only this which sustains me—
> Some day there shall be millions and millions of them
> On some red day in a burst of fists on a new horizon!

Thus the theme of black suffering, in its celebration of an interracial unity, joins that of the triumph of socialism.

Out of some twenty poems written between 1933 and 1939, a dozen, in fact, sing of this triumph while others exalt the virtues of the workers. "Hearst Headlines Blues" provides us with a convenient summary of the themes of these poems. Its stanzas quote headlines taken from the pages of the Hearst press and show the decomposition of American society. Immorality and senseless violence reign; social problems are treated ineffectively or brutally. Counterpointing the famine which is decimating America, the Soviet Union suppresses rationing. This propaganda piece brings us back to the unprecedented atmosphere of the Depression years which, thanks to the editorship of the Harlem Bureau of the *Daily Worker*, provided Wright with a good opportunity to chronicle.

The other poems systematically probe the failure of capitalism: "Rest for the Weary," on a note of false pity, condescendingly addresses the financiers ruined by the 1929 panic. It is also the failure of liberal Christianity incapable of pacifying "the bitter and irreconcilable waters of class struggle" in "Child of the Dead and Forgotten Gods." "A Red Love Note," using the analogy between a love letter and an eviction notice, is an artistic failure. But the choice of its imagery is inspired by the daily scenes of eviction, the furniture spread out on the sidewalk and the neighbors' demonstrations of solidarity; with tender words the poet takes his leave of capitalism whose lease on American society has long run out.

If the poems which sing of the fall of the old order can be seen at the first panel of the revolutionary diptych, those which celebrate the unity of the workers and the rise of socialism can be said to form the second. The education and unity of the masses are set down by the poet as the essential prerequisites: "Red Leaves of Red Books" praises those who devote their hours of leisure to deciphering the volumes of new theories.

"Strength" opposes mass action to solitary protest, the latter seen as destined for defeat. The unity of the oppressed (which, as we learn in "I am a Red Slogan," it is the poet's mission to accelerate) will be realized through demonstrations, for the slogans chanted during a political march do not only express particular demands, they also serve to guide the masses, "lingering as a duty after my command is shouted." This theme of the mass demonstration, part of the traditional May First ("working class") literature, offers little that is original.[5] However Wright treats the end of "We of the Streets" in an interesting way, focusing on the exhilarating sense of strength which comes from a crowd, and this treatment is reminiscent of the ending of his novella "Fire and Cloud." The street thus becomes the organic milieu in which the worker grows conscious of his belonging to History and of his own immortality.

Enthusiasm for the Russian Revolution inspired Wright to compose "Spread your Sunrise" and "Transcontinental." In the first of these odes, he hails the arrival of a young Communist giant, applauding the liberties taken with the established order and urging him to paint the Statue of Liberty red and to frighten the millionaires cowering in their mansions.

A long fresco dedicated to Louis Aragon in praise of "Red Front," the poem "Transcontinental," published early in 1936 by *International Literature*, sings of the coming of better days in America. This six page symphony blends various themes: a criticism of the American dream, the rehabilitation of the exploited minorities, the wealth of the New World that will appear with the institution of the Soviets. These themes, evoked by a profusion of images, are carried forward by an epic inspiration.

In addition to such propaganda pieces, Wright's poetry at this time, and especially after 1937, centered on a description of the world of the workers and the poor. "We of the Streets" exalts the dignity and generosity which lie hidden in the slums; in "Old Habit and New Love" the worker is the salvation of humanity: not satisfied with just increasing the world's riches, he restores its soul, he delivers it from its fragmentation:

> There is an ache for marriage, for the sight of halves grown whole, for cactus
> land to blend with dingy dreams, for the welding of irons and bleeding
> palms.
> It is for fusion of number and nerve we strain . . .

Breathing life back into the machine and tuning its music to the harmony of the celestial spheres, the worker becomes the Demi-urge, an artist like the poet:

O Creators! Poets, Makers of Melody! Some first-shift dawn shall find us on
equal ground, holding in our hands the world's tools, drafting the hope-
prints of our vision on canvases of green earth!

Although these poems were not inspired by a particular political event,
their ideological content is closely linked to Wright's Communist faith,
and yet both his sincerity and his originality emerge more clearly in the
manner than the themes.

One is first struck by the fact that Wright is as realistic in his poetry as
he is in his novels: lynching, financial failures, strikes and police repression, bread lines, are all news items from the columns of the *Daily
Worker*. His realism—often visionary realism—extends even to urban
scenes sketched effectively in a few words:

We have grown used to nervous landscapes, chimney-broken horizons, and the
sun dying between tenements . . .
Our sea is water swirling in gutters; our lightning is the blue flame of an
acetylene torch, . . . we hear thunder when the "L" roars, our strip of
sky is a dirty shirt.[6]

Here we find the Chicago of Dreiser, of Farrell, of Algren, the blizzard on
the outskirts of Michigan and the pale glow of the street lights in *Native
Son*. There is realism in the grounding of collective lyricism on Wright's
personal experiences; however, the real world, naked and violent, is
never incorporated in its everyday form: either the Marxist interpretation
transforms it into a significant universe or else the author's imagination
recreates it through a religious, elemental, or mythical symbolism.

At this stage of its development, Wright's art already rests on a solid
culture base in which we can distinguish several distinct sources: a Protestant tradition incubated under the aegis of his intransigent grandmother; wide and eclectic reading; a vital knowledge of American
folklore; a keen sensitivity to nature and a truly elemental imagination.

A wealth of Biblical references, paradoxical component of these Communist poems, produces a two-sided effect: at times the aim is to parody,
underlining the state of confusion in American society, as when the spectator who observes the Socialist Messiah painting the belfry cross red
utters a series of pious exclamations.[7] At times the satire is directed at
Christ's liberalism; the descendant of obsolete divinities, he is shown in
"Child of the Dead and Forgotten Gods", to be incapable of repeating his
miracles. At times the metaphor is required for reasons of form: the
Marxist books become the Bible, and in "A Red Love Note" the final

notice of the proleterian to the capitalist echoes the Creator's curse on Cain's; the deluge and the destruction of the Temple are the principal symbols of "Everywhere Burning Waters Rise." Wright constantly harks back to Christian formulas which seem the most appropriate for his political designs. Above all, it is in following his inspiration that Wright, as we can see in this passage from *Black Boy*, delves into a religion-bound black culture:

> The elders of the church expounded a gospel clogged with images of vast lakes of eternal fire, of seas vanishing, of valleys of dry bones, of the sun burning to ashes, of the moon turning to blood, of stars falling to the earth, . . . While listening to the vivid language of the sermons, I was pulled towards emotional belief . . .[8]

The adolescent refused the dogmas of this religion, but its images remained engraved in his mind.

Linked to the Biblical references, the natural elements in "Everywhere Burning Waters Rise" become symbols of destruction. The blood haze that covers the empty silos and deserted workshops of the Egypt of the New World is the beginning of the deluge which, in the middle of the poem, is curiously transformed into a torrent of fire. The first section restates the theme of the water cycle: icy, viscous fog condenses into pools of water, flowing in thin streams and then in heavy torrents, to swell into a tidal wave. Water turns to fire—the transition facilitated by the ambiguity of the word "boiling"—and suddenly the glowing coals burst into flame, fanned by the poet's prophetic malediction:

> Sweep on, o red stream of molten anger
> surge and seethe like liquid lava
> into every nook and cranny of this greed-reared temple
> and blister the rottening walls with your hot cleansing breath!
> Lick and lap with your tongues of flame
> at the golden pillars of oppressive privilege . . .

Wright seems to be fascinated by the element of fire. We have no intention here of analyzing his exploits as a four-year-old incendiary, nor those of his hero Bigger who burns the body of his boss's daughter in a basement furnace, nor the fire by which Cross Damon effaces his identity, nor the blaze which destroys the dance in *The Long Dream*. But it is important to mention that in the poems under discussion, the element of fire already appears in all its destructive and purifying aspects. In "Spread your Sunrise" the Reichstag fire is symbolically evoked by a splash of red paint. In the numerous lynching scenes, the flames blend with the water and the blood of the Negro burning at the stake:

> Then my blood was cooled mercifully, cooled by a baptism of gasoline
> And in a blaze of red I leaped to the sky as pain rose like water, boiling my limbs . . .[9]

Along with his orchestrations of warring elements, the more benign aspects of nature are occasionally invoked. In "Strength" the image suggesting individual action, "a gentle breeze ineffectually tearing at granite crags," is just as successful as the sonorous metaphor for mass revolt.

> . . . a raging hurricane, vast and powerful, wrenching and dredging by the roots the rotting husks of the trees of greed.

Similarly the urban landscape of "We of the Streets" is transposed into natural terms. Wright frequently borrows from nature and nature is the touchstone of his poetic sensitivity: it was the Mississippi country that restored his strength during a childhood of struggle and deprivation. We are therefore all the more prepared for the lyrical tirades of *Black Boy* when the writer sings of his renewed wonder before the scenes of nature.

The two odes to the revolution, which represent a sharp break with his other compositions, celebrate the exploits of a mythical character or narrate a symbolic adventure. Eager to communicate the appeal of the new ideology, Wright personifies it in the giant of "Spread your Sunrise." This incarnation was perhaps suggested by some of the illustrations of *New Masses*,[10] but in fact is rather in the tradition of the rough and ready hero of American folklore:

> a bushy-haired giant child,
> Big-limbed and double-jointed,
> Boisterous and bull-headed,
> With great big muscles bursting through his clothes.

Compound words, alliterated consonants, the exaggerations of popular speech make him a mixture of Johnny Appleseed and John Henry. Wearing not the seven-league boots of the fairy tale but the shoes of the Five Year Plan, this "tall man" of the steel mills seems to come from certain pages of *The People, Yes* and clearly belongs to the legends of the Frontier.

The same informal and enthusiastic tone graces the poem "Transcontinental" in which Wright has painted the chariot of Time, slightly renovated as the automobile of History. The key to this symphony lies in the use of the idea of speed. At first a group of young men and women, enviously observe the glittering world of the rich:

Across the ceaseless hiss of passing cars
We hear the tinkle of ice in tall glasses
Clacks of crocket balls scudding over cropped lawns
Silvery crescendos of laughter
Like in the movies
On Saturday night
When we used to get paychecks . . .

Then the desire to penetrate this inaccessible world, to ride in the rich man's limousine, takes on the convincing form of reality: time is telescoped and the rigid structure of the first stanzas comes alive in a wild race of moving images. Leaving behind them a social upheaval similar to that created by the Communist giant, these new horsemen of the Apocalypse, casting down the oppressors, lifting up the oppressed (Indians, Negroes, proletarians) cross the United States in their symbolic automobile.[11]

Lyricism plays a privileged role in these early poems; it can be shaded with humour or with anger but it always assumes one of two principal forms: that of the song, and particularly the blues ballad—as in "Red Clay Blues," "Ah Feels It in Mah Bones" or "Hearst Headlines Blues"[12]—or, more frequently that of large spans of free verse modeled on Whitman's *Leaves of Grass*.

The terms used by Wright always correspond to a definite aim. At times the Negro dialect is adopted:

It's done got so bad Ah can't even beg a dime
An' mah bread-basket's a-swearing mah throat's been cut.[13]

At times, the language is that of popular speech, racy and coarse, which contrasts with the affected and somewhat hysterical phrases of the society women:

But Dear America's a free country
Did you say Negroes
Oh I don't mean NEEGROOES
You wouldn't want your DAUGHTER
and they say there's no GOD
And furthermore it's simply disgraceful how they're discriminating against the
    children of the rich in Soviet schools.

The above passage from "Transcontinental" is characteristic in many ways. It fits into the context like the fragments of polite conversation which Eliot scatters through "The Love Song of J. Alfred Prufrock." In fact Wright owes as much to "The Waste Land" as to Aragon's "Front Rouge," although it is to the latter that "Transcontinental" is dedicated. Similar to Eliot's synthesis of fragments of Western civilization (quotations, songs, references, bits of dialogue), Wright's composition incorporates all the socially significant elements of American civilization. Setting aside the lyrical movement of "Transcontinental," we would be left with a static fresco, halfway between the cubist collage and the stream of consciousness, composed of the solidified English of the upper class, the slang of the worker, the materialized language of the road sign, blended with a litany of slogans, loudspeaker addressed lines from the "Internationale" and even a radio communique. The lyricism which binds all these diverse materials to the canvas starts out as a kind of aside, a tender evocation soon embittered in reproach, which then expands and reverberates throughout the poem into a glorification of America reborn.

In his quest for a distinctive style, Wright seems to be torn at that period between two conflicting tendencies. On the one hand he admires the lyrical and rhetorical gifts of poets like MacLeish or Eliot, from whom he borrows his abrupt transitions from the serious to the trivial, his use of free association in place of a logical continuity, his succession of images without explanatory metaphors. On the other hand the robust simplicity of a Carl Sandburg or a Whitman also attracts him. Drawn both ways, he tries to create a special language:

> My purpose was to capture a physical state or movement that carried a strong subjective impression . . . I strove to master words, to make them disappear, to make them important by making them new, to make them melt into a rising spiral of emotional stimuli, each greater than the other, and all ending in an emotional climax that would drench the reader with the sense of a new world.[14]

With this purpose in mind, Wright sometimes coins new terms like "hope-print" or "five-year boots." Words explode into phonetic transcriptions and letters are lengthened into words. These inventions aim to do more than surprise the reader. When, for example, the poet gathers all the colors of the rainbow into one line in "I Have Seen Black Hands," it is not from a love of enumeration but rather in order to give the counterbalanced color black the same value as all these shades added together. Like the circumvolutions of Gertrude Stein's poetic line, the unfolding of

Wright's verse tries to exhaust all the resources of literary expression. However, more than in this typographical or structural experiments, the young poet's originality shines forth in the series of images enriched by their emotional message. We see this process at work in "Between the World and Me" where the splendor of dawn yields to the horror of a lynching:

> And through the morning air the sun poured yellow surprise into the eye-
> sockets of a stony skulll . . .
> And while I stood my mind was frozen with a cold pity for the life that was
> gone.
> The ground gripped my feet and my heart was circled by icy walls of fear
> The sun died in the sky; a night wind muttered in the grass and fumbled the
> leaves in the trees; the wood poured forth the hungry yelping of hounds;
> the darkness screamed with thirsty voices and the witnesses rose and
> lived:
> The dry bones stirred, rattled, lifted, melting themselves into my bones
> The grey ashes formed flesh firm and black entering into my flesh.

This passage alone makes "Between the World and Me" one of the most beautiful poems written by a black American.

Having made poetry the vehicle of his enthusiasm or his indignation, Wright then turned to fiction where his gift for dialogue and for tragedy, his sense of realism, enabled him to rapidly master its forms. If these qualities hinder the reader, too often fascinated by the unwinding of the plot, from paying sufficient attention to the lyric or intimate climate of certain passages, the poetry of *Twelve Million Black Voices* cannot fail to strike him.

Although Wright was beginning to detach himself from a Communist movement that then made little of the Negro's interests, his historical point of view was that of a Marxist. *Twelve Million Black Voices*, subtitled "a folk history of the Negro in the United States of America," eliminated the privileged element, the so-called "talented tenth," as not representative of the fate of the black majority, which Wright wanted the reader to feel and share intimately.

In order to create the atmosphere necessary for this empathy, the author must avoid a language that is either too erudite or too picturesque. Wright therefore translated most of his concepts into easily accessible metaphors. One of the most evident examples is the use of the opposing symbols "Lords of the Land" (landed capital of the South) and "Bosses of the Buildings" (industrial capital of the North) as characters in a mystery play surrounded by all their attributes. Elsewhere the metaphor of a shoal of fish symbolizes the rising of the black masses against the current of racial prejudice; the island represents the Negro's psychological isolation; and the state of a soldier echoes the vicissitudes of the Negro's existence. These stylistic techniques avoid the use of concepts which would destroy the poetic climate but they do not create it. Nor can this climate be evoked by the colorful idiom of the Southern Negro; even in a popular history, particularities of speech would create too much distance between the reader and the black community. Also, to make a white and a black man speak the same language is to resist the force of stereotypes as it is to demand true racial equality. The prose of *Twelve Million Black Voices* must be situated mid-stream between the picturesque Negro dialect and the concision of the historian so that the reader will open his eyes to the realities hidden by custom and ignorance and feel that pity and indignation requisite to all sincere action.

This work is poetic, therefore, because of its wealth of simple and carefully chosen images and because of its tone, at times epic, at times lyric, which links this narrative to the blues tradition. The special atmosphere of *Twelve Million Black Voices* is often the result of imagery which flowers spontaneously in the turn of a phrase: "Like black buttercups our children spring up on the red soil of the plantations" (p. 59) or "The sand of our simple folk-lives runs out on the cold city pavement" (p. 136). Simple in appearance only, these images create a continuous metaphor and give color to the prose. More essential, however, are the passages where rhythm, emotion, and lyricism harmonize into large symphonic units. This description of the seasons, for example, paired with an admirable photograph of a team of mules toiling under a lowering sky, should be read aloud to be fully appreciated:

> In summer the magnolia tree fills the countryside with sweet scent for long miles. Days are slumberous, and the skies are high with clouds that ride fast. At midday the sun blazes and bleaches the soil. Butterflies flit through the heat; wasps sing their sharp straight lines; birds fluff and flounce, piping in querulous joy. Nights are covered with canopies, sometimes blue and sometimes black, canopies that sag low with ripe and nervous stars. The throaty boast of frogs momentarily drowns out the call and countercall of crickets. (p. 32)

Here evocation and image are one; the lyricism springs from an open sympathy long considered the distinctive trait of Negro sensitivity and the psychological foundation of negritude. It is in the childhood memories of the author that this lyricism has its root, memories that will be revived in the autobiographical *Black Boy.*

The text modulates like the voice of a narrator reciting a four-act play: "Our strange birth", "Inheritors of slavery," "Death on the city pavements" and "Men in the making." The rhythms and sonorities predominate over the visual element which might have distracted from the photographs placed opposite the text. This is a narrative meant to be read aloud, recited, chanted, or declaimed. By the constant use of the pronound "we," the chorus of the black community traces for a universal public the vicissitudes of a minority about to enter the promised land of democracy. Like the spirituals, this text is a sort of plea which ends with the Biblical verses or Whitman-like couplets of a stirring hymn of hope.

A condensed version, in verse "Twelve Million Black Voices", published in *Coronet* magazine, resembles a Negro folk song. It is a succession of couplets which introduce some thirty photographs and which describe the conditions and perspectives of Negro life in the big city ghettos. The ballad opens with a nostalgic recall of the family atmosphere on the plantation:

> Gone are de days when Negro hearts
> Were ever light as air
>
> Now we ain't got nobody
> And no one gives a care
>
> Gone de black old mammies
> A-bossin' o'ver the roost
>
> Gone de old plantation
> For a filthy kitchenette. . . .[15]

Here the poet is clearly addressing a black audience. This explains the abundance of idiomatic expressions and the characteristic pronunciation. Moreover the regularity of the lines, the assonances and rhymes, help to create the rhythm of folk ballads. In the middle of the poem the lament changes into a lullaby as the mother muses on the hard future awaiting her son:

> Sleep my kinky-headed babe
> You've stormy days ahead
>
> You'll grow up doing nigger work
> In dust and dirt and grime

Your bones'll ache from toting loads
On shoulder sorely bent.

But Wright allows her a pious hope:

So on bended knees she prays de Lord
To give you half a chance

To play a bigger part than she
In America's advance.

After his break with Communism which had nourished his inspiration for some ten years, Wright devoted himself to his now world-famous autobiography. In *Black Boy* the lyrical vein is no longer collective but personal, and in two different places, free verse provides a formal contrast with the rest of the style. One passage lists the numerous superstitions which charmed the magic world of Wrights' childhood:

Up and down the wet or dusty street, indoors and out, the days and nights began to spell out magic possibilities:
If I pulled a hair from a horse's tail and sealed it in a jar of my own urine, the hair would turn overnight into a snake.
If I passed a Catholic sister or mother dressed in black and smiled and allowed her to see my teeth, I would surely die. (p. 63)

A second, more important passage describes the way the world affected his sensitivity, and the link that his imagination forged between an event and its meaning:

There was the wonder I felt when I first saw a brace of mountain-like spotted, black-and-white horses clopping down a dusty road through clouds of powdered clay . . .
There was the vague sense of the infinite as I looked down upon the yellow, dreaming waters of the Mississippi from the verdant bluffs of Natchez.
There were the echoes of nostalgia I heard in the crying strings of wild geese winging south against a bleak autumn sky . . .
There was the langor I felt when I heard green leaves rustling with a rainlike sound.
There was the incomprehensible secret embodied in a whitish toadstool hiding in the dark shade of a rotting log. (p. 7)

Here we find an echo of the experimental phrases of the young writer and especially of the hymns to nature in *Twelve Million Black Voices*. But in this passage the description is less important than the relationship between the child and the scene, or that between the sensation and the feeling it awakened, for: "Each event spoke with a cryptic tongue. And the moments of living slowly revealed their coded meanings" (p. 7). The symbolism leads to the discovery of a metaphysical reality in the scene before the poet's eyes. Poetry no longer appears as a creation—as it did in "Old Habit and New Love"—but as a revelation. The poetic moment becomes an epiphany.

Perhaps because it is a question here of childhood experience remembered, the relationship between the event and the message is made explicit as well as suggested by the poetic context. Nostalgia is openly associated with the cry of wild geese (similar to the cries which, in AS I LAY DYING, filled Addie Bundren with the desire for an impossible flight) and, at the same time, the line of monosyllables represents the birds with their shrill recurrent sound. This nostalgia rises from the immensity of the sky and from the opposition between the gloom of autumn and the warmth of the summer that only the geese will see again. The sense of universality is suggested by simply the sight of the birds' flight. This is exactly what will occur in the haikus that Wright composed in the final stage of his poetic evolution.

Ten years elapsed before Wright came back to the poetic form. During the period when he considered poetry the complement of his novels' dramatic prose, it was used more as a foil for an ideology than a vehicle for the expression of his personal emotions. In July 1955 he sent a thirty-page letter to his friend and editor Edward C. Aswell in which he outlined a future work concerning the relationship between the individual and society:

> That problem poses for me many paradoxes: society and man form one organic whole, yet both, by the very nature of their relationship are in sharp conflict . . . I have no solution to that problem. I just want to pose it in as many ways as possible, that is why I have chosen CELEBRATION as the general title of the work which I hope to do. . . . (p. 8)

Eager to avoid a repetition of the criticism which his work The Outsider attracted because philosophical commentary occasionally marred the artistic unity, Wright adopts a different method:

> I want to assume an attitude that places me wholly on the side of feeling in life. To inject this into the work without the author speaking in his own name, in order to remain outside of the work, I've invented a device which I'd call an Impersonal mood, which would, by implication, give the reader the above ideas. This mood rendered in terms of a kind of free verse prose says yes to all forms of experience which seek an outlet when the environment balks it . . ." (p. 3)

For Wright the interest of this mood was its dual effect, both poetic and impersonal. Its form would distinguish it from the dramatic prose of the novel, its tone would contrast it with the feelings of the characters, its content would be a commentary on the novels that preceded or followed it. It is the monologue of a diffuse cosmic power which both participates in and transcends the human comedy. The following extracts from this work give an idea of its remarkable breadth:

> For the fulness of time is every day and every hour; and of time I sing, time that seeks fulfilment.
> And yet no song am I; my music is unheard; there is no pulse that can feel my rhythms;
> And yet nearer to music am I than to anything amidst the millions of whirling suns;
> And no flesh am I, and no blood;
> And though I am of myself persuaded to dwell for swift moments in the breathing temples of men, I am not man, and with his ways I have I am not to be confounded.
> Yet I live; yet I have my being; yet I haunt the whole of this and other worlds without number and without end;
> At home in the rock's deep heart, in the still cold depths of the ocean's sand, on the trembling leaves of tossing trees,
> In the icy stretches of stellar spaces, on the stream of nodding flowers, in the falling columns of light imprisoning mote and beams, in the darkness and silence of swamps—
> I was, I am, I will be,
> Everywhere and nowhere, visible and invisible, felt and unfelt, there and not there, in all and in nothing, I hover, seeking to enter . . . (p. 4)

This hymn to the eternal and multiform force of life is reminiscent with it recueillement and its lyricism of certain passages of the Psalms although its human incarnation is celebrated with greater vigor:

> . . . Controlling the fluttering of a baffled and curious child's eyelids,
> Relating the heart's beats, each to each,
> Structuring the bones of men and women,
> Breathing in laughter that leaps from singing lips,
> Exulting in flexed and tensed flesh,
> And equally,
> Suffering I am, pain, the compulsive rasping in the choked throat,
> Flowing warm and red out of the fresh and stinging wound,
> Bleeding in sweat on pallid brows,
> . . . . . . . .
> Restlessly I come and go, timing myself by my time, judging by my own harshly loving standards,

Indifferently regarding life and death, joy and sorrow,
Entering all things, reshaping, spreading, scattering, dissolving, coming forth
again in dying, being born at will. (p. 5)

Although this is only "a very rough first draft version," it is evident that the lyricism with which the poet once glorified Communism is now serving the cause of a universal transformation. For Wright, it is in harmony with Nature that man will most fully realize his humanity. The cosmic and physiological manifestations of the life spirit are the very source of this humanity paralyzed or destroyed by our present materialistic society. The mood conveys the poet's message: if alienated society desires to be liberated from its sclerosed forms, this mutation will be achieved when the individual, thanks to the umbilical cord organically attaching him to nature, has established a meaningful relationship with the objective world.

Wright may have preferred to use his lectures or his prose works to explore the question of man's relationship with society, yet we find this question reappearing in the intimate poems composed near the end of his life.

He discovered the Japanese haiku by chance, although there are many traces of this poetic form in the Western literature of early twentieth century. In 1905 Paul Louis Couchoud founded a French haiku movement; in America, Ezra Pound was one of the first poets to become interested in these tercets where a landscape may comment on the whole human fate.

The haiku goes back as far as the thirteenth century to poetry contests at the Heian court. The competitors took turns composing, in a witty or amusing style, the initial tercet or the final couplet of the Tannka, a thirty-one syllable verse. The Hokkou (the first line) soon became a poem in itself composed of seventeen syllables and named a haiku or comic piece; paradoxically it flourished several centuries later as a philosopical and serious form. Three great masters gave it successively different orientations: in the fifteenth century the bonze Matsuo Basho evoked the delicate and tranquil scenes suggested by Zen Buddhist meditation; the eighteenth century painter Tanoguchi Buson brought to the haiku the impressionism of his engravings; finally the poet Issa accentuated the realism of this form and enriched it with personal experiences. Wright who scrupulously studied the history and technique of the haiku in the four volumes of R. H. Blyth, was aware of all of these aspects.

He made a particular effort to follow the rules: three lines, neither rhymed nor stressed in Japanese, number respectively five, seven, and five syllables; an implicit or explicit reference links the poem to the mood of one of the seasons; the symbolic meaning of the painting is expressed in the association of all these elements. Whereas neither the French school nor the haikuists writing directly in English generally bother about the number of arrangement of syllables within each line,[16] Wright seems to accumulate difficulties for himself. Not only does he usually follow the prescribed syllabic scheme, but he also, in the Japanese manner, condenses the essence of the poem in its first two lines. Here is an excellent example:

> The crow flew so fast
> That he left his lonely caw
> Behind in the fields.[17]

The crow which suggests autumn (as the frog, the spring, and different insects the other seasons according to the Japanese tradition) seems to symbolize by its carefree and rapid flight the selfishness of the male who, devoting all his attention to his personal ideal, leaves to his mate the drudgery of everyday life.

The painting may be more impressionistic, in the style of Buson, and the meaning less immediately accessible, as in:

> The spring lingers on
> In the scent of a damp log
> Rotting in the sun.

The seasons seem to be telescoped: spring dwells on in the summer sun and in the autumn decay. Is this the perfume of youth lingering on in old age? The association is less vague in the hurried race of the spring rain, unaware of its origin and its destination, a prey to youth's oblivious and imprudent haste:

> What town did you leave
> O wild and drowning spring rain
> And where do you go?

With this rhetorical question Wright renders a characteristic of the Japanese model which is almost untranslatable: the Kireji. This word indicates the author's state of mind and that which is desired for the reader. Thus Yara corresponds to this answerless question and Ya to the emphatic mode of this haiku:

> Keep straight down this block
> Then turn where you find
> A peach tree blooming

or, even more closely, to the wonder of this one:

> With a twitching nose
> A dog reads a telegram
> On a wet tree trunk.

Is this a surrealistic scene? The poem seems more humorous than symbolic, in the tradition of the witty poet Issa. Wright's sympathy for animal and insect can be found also in this poem:

> Make up your mind snail
> You are half inside your house
> And halfway out.

Even more often, it seems, the author prefers the serious and more personal mode of the Kara, this nostalgic sigh of man confronting his destiny:

> I am nobody
> A red sinking autumn sun
> Took my name away.

Here is a real cry of despair, the recognition that the individual can no longer define his being when the star of light and meaning disappears with his name. We are even more moved by the anguish of the writer ill on his fifty-first birthday, trying with familiar thoughts to recover his desire to write:

> It is September
> The month when I was born
> And I have no thoughts.

Rereading these poems, one finds a special quality in the evocations which at first seemed only to yield a general significance. Thus in our initial contact with the following poem,

> In the falling snow
> A laughing boy holds out his palms
> Until they are white

we feel a child's joy in receiving the gifts of nature. But does not the insistence on "until they are white" suggest that this child is black? His laughter takes on a deeper meaning if we consider it as an affirmation that there is no natural barrier between black and white. Also, the suggestion of a racial conflict gives poignancy to the innocent laughter of childhood.

It is important to underline the distinctive sensibility and particular atmosphere of Wright's haiku: the indulgent smile of the humorist, the restraint of the mature adult, the delicacy of the direct intuition of nature, the freshness of an unstaled receptivity. If he chose to obey the strict requirements of this form it is because it corresponds to an important facet of his inspiration. In some of the experimental phrases of the 1930s he was unwittingly already composing haikus.[18] Even more significant are certain descriptions from *Twelve Million Black Voices* and the quotation from *Black Boy* already discussed above: "There were the echoes of nostalgia I heard in the crying strings of wild geese winging south against a bleak autumn sky." Without changing the word order or the meaning of the image, we can feel the suggestion of nostalgia in these three lines:

> Crying strings of wild geese
> Winging south against
> A bleak autumn sky,

Nothing is missing, not even the indication of the season. The same procedure could be used as successfully with other sentences. Wright therefore did not have to twist his inspiration into the haiku form; all the necessary elements were already there: word paintings, scenes rapidly sketched, and universal emotions. At the final stage of his evolution, at a moment when nature and the individual played an increasingly important part in his thinking, the poet developed a taste for these intimate tercets in which he could condense the quintessence of his art.

Wright fell in love with the haiku at first sight, and began composing in the fall of 1959 at the beginning of his illness—the consequence of a trip to Africa five years earlier. By March 1960 he had written four thousand tercets which he began to group for publication. He wrote to Margrit de Sabloniere:

> I've so far selected 1500 haikus. I think now that I ought to boil them to about 800 and leave them. The problem of selecting them is agonizing. I'm trying to figure out a scheme.[19]

How deeply involved he had become in this phase of his poetry is somewhat surprising:

> I'm now through with the haikus. You know, I cannot let anything out of my hands as long as I feel and know there is something else to do with it. But now,

for better or worse, I'm giving the ms. to the typist. Maybe I'm fooling around with these tiny little poems. But I could not let them go. I was possessed by them . . . There are 811 in all and they will make a ms. of some 80 pages.[20]

In September 1960 Wright was to declare:

"I've finished nothing this year but those damned haikus, and I've not even looked at them since my friends in New York looked at them. I'll sit down one of these days and go over them, that is, reread them and see how they sound.[21]

Death prevented him from making this volume his poetic testament.

We hope that this volume will soon be published. It reveals a talent very different from that of the well-known vigorous novelist, but in perfect harmony with the deeper manifestations of his sensibility.

The distance separating the revolutionary poems of the 1930s, vibrant with indignation and brutal imagery, from the intimate symbolism of the haikus may seem great indeed. But the road travelled from the awkward enthusiasm of the young militant to the serene mastery of the mature artist is the sign, in the case of a writer as politically engaged as Wright, of a certain detachment. On the eve of his death, the novelist's interest in human affairs, his struggle against racism and injustice, had by no means faltered. It was rather that he had gradually reserved the poetic form, initially the sole vehicle of his social and political message, for the expression of feeling. Poetry served to paint scenes at once more personal and more universal, while his prose works reflected his ideological stands. Furthermore, it must not be forgotten that his poetic gifts, which shine most brilliantly in his final compositions, were manifest all along the course of his career. Often masked by the hard honesty or biting realism of the novelist, this poetry never stopped appearing in his prose works. At times lyrical, at times offended, at times outraged, his poetic sensibility vibrated in harmony with an imagination solidly rooted in the naturalness and wonder of childhood. Let us remember that *Native Son* was dedicated "To my mother who taught me to revere the fanciful and the imaginative."

The study of Wright's poetry brings to light an often neglected aspect of the writer's personality: his intimate sense of the universal harmony, his wonder before life, his thirst for a natural existence, all these tendencies which nourished, as much as did any ideology or faith, his courageous and incessant battle against all that prevents an individual from fully belonging to the world.

1. For example, *The Negro Caravan*, ed. Sterling Brown et al. (New York: Dryden Press, 1941); *The Poetry of the American Negro*, ed. Arna Bontemps and Langston Hughes (New York: Doubleday: 1949); or *Black Voices*, ed. Abraham Chapman (New York: New American Library: 1968).

2. "I Tried to Be a Communist," *Atlantic Monthly* 174 (August 1944): 63.

3. *American Hunger* (New York: Harper and Row, 1977), p. 22.

4. See the reviews and chronicles in *New Masses*, March 1934 to February 1936.

5. For instances of this type of literature, see Meridel LeSueur's "I Was Marching," *New Masses*, September 12, 1934, p. 16; or Clara Weatherwax's piece which won the *New Masses* competition the following year.

6. "We of the Streets," *New Masses* 23 (April 13, 1937): 14.

7. "Spread Your Sunrise," *New Masses* 16 (July 2, 1935): 26.

8. Richard Wright, *Black Boy* (New York: Harper & Brox., 1945), p. 89. All future references are to this edition.

9. "Between the World and Me," *Partisan Review* 2 (July–August 1935): 19.

10. "I stared at a cartoon drawn by a Communist artist; it was the figure of a worker clad in ragged overalls and holding aloft a red banner. The man's eyes bulged, his mouth gaped as wide as his face, his teeth showed, the muscles of his neck were like ropes." Wright admired *The People, Yes* and Carl Sandburg, but these lines almost strangely resemble "Tempo Primo" of Melvin Tolson's "Dark Symphony," which reads: "The New Negro, / Hard-muscled, Fascist-hating, Democracy-ensouled / Strides in seven-league boots." The opening lines of "Everywhere Burning Waters Rise" also recall the rhythms and associations of concrete and abstract terms in "Tempo di Marcis." "Dark Symphony" was only published in 1940 and we could not determine whether it influenced Wright's early poetry.

11. Aragon used the image of a red engine pulling the train of revolution. Railway imagery also appealed to Wright, who , as a boy, worshipped Casey Jones.

12. Wright wrote about twenty blues at different dates. The best known is "King Joe," written in praise of Joe Louis, and recorded by Paul Robeson and Count Basie in 1941.

13. "Ah Feels It in Mah Bones," *International Literature* 4 (April 1935): 40.

14. *American Hunger*, p. 22.

15. "Twelve Million Black Voices," *Coronet*, April 1942, pp. 77–93.

16. See, for instance, Miyamori Asataro, *Haiku Poems, Ancient and Modern* (Tokyo: Marizen & Co., 1940).

17. In "The Last Days of Richard Wright," *Ebony* February 1961, p. 82, Ollie Harrington quotes a number of Wright's haikus.

18. Wright had also shown interest in Imagist poetry. He had probably read Genevieve Taggard's article on William Carlos Williams ("Poet Among Imagists," *New Masses*, April 3, 1934, pp. 43–45) and Williams's "Red Wheelbarrow" with the poet's commentary as to why he considered it a perfect piece.

19. Unpublished letter to Margrit de Sabloniere, April 8, 1960. Wright Archive, Yale University Library.

20. Ibid., May 29, 1960.

21. Ibid., September 23, 1960.

# Beyond Naturalism?

THAT Richard Wright is a naturalist writer has generally been taken for granted by American critics. In his review of *Lawd Today*, entitled "From Dreiser to Farrell to Wright," Granville Hicks proceeded, not incorrectly, to show that

> . . . he could scarcely have failed to be influenced by James T. Farrell who was just beginning to have a strong effect on American fiction. As Farrell had learned something about documentation from Dreiser, so Wright had learned from Farrell.[1]

When he reviewed *The Outsider* for the *New York Times*, the same critic noted:

> . . . if the ideas are sometimes incoherent, that does not detract from the substance and the power of the book. Wright has always been a demonic writer, and in the earliest of his stories one felt that he was saying more than he knew, that he was, in a remarkable degree, an unconscious artist.[2]

Other reviewers even seemed to regret that Wright attempted to deal with ideas. In his review Orville Prescott stated that "instead of a realistic sociological document he had[d] written a philosophical novel, its ideas dramatized by improbable coincidences and symbolical characters."[3] And Luther P. Jackson outspokenly lamented that the

> words of Wright's angry men leap from the page and hit you between the eyes. But Wright can no more resist an argument on the Left Bank than he could a soapbox in Washington Park. The lickety-split action of his novel bogs down in a slough of dialectics.[4]

It is clear, then, that Wright is regarded not as a novelist of ideas or as a symbolist, but as an emotionally powerful creator who writes from his guts and churns up reality in a melodramatic but effective way because he is authentic, close to nature, true to life. Conversely, the critics's displeasure at his incursions into other realms than that of social realism proves

56

only that there are elements in his writing which cannot be reduced to their favorite image of him as a hard-boiled naturalist. The question then becomes: to what extent is he part of the naturalistic stream in American literature? Is he, in fact, sufficiently a part of it for his works to be judged, and found satisfactory or wanting, only according to that perspective? Or is his originality so strong that it cannot be adequately accounted for in terms of the Dreiser/Farrell line of succession, and does this therefore necessitate a reassessment of what is commonly held for American literary naturalism?

It is not my purpose here to reopen the long-debated question of what exactly naturalism is. In his preface to *American Literary Naturalism, A Divided Stream*, Charles C. Walcutt described it as "a beast of protean slipperiness" which, soon after it had sprung from the fountain of Transcendentalism, divided into rebellious, idealistic social radicalism on one side and pessimistic determinism on the other; consequently, the assertion of the unity of nature and spirit, the equality of intuition and reason was somewhat diminished.

If we consider naturalism as a philosophy, it is clear from the start that Wright's perspective is only very partly akin to it. He had read Darwin's *Origin of Species* but he probably did not even know of Herbert Spencer, the true philosophical cornerstone of American naturalism. If he did, his Communistic leanings set him early on the side of Marx against the Spencerian view of the "survival of the fittest." To him, the fittest were the productive workers, not the parasitic upper classes. Insofar as he was a Marxist, "the organized exercise of the social will" meant the liquidation of the bourgeoisie.

Estranged as he was from God by the oppressive religious practice of his Seventh-Day Adventist grandmother, Wright was also prone to eschew Transcendentalism as well as the very American belief that physical progress reflects spiritual progress. His childhood taught him that knowledge could indeed bring freedom, and self-education became his only means of escape from the cultural ghetto. But if knowledge can make man similar to God, he later discovered that too much knowledge can bring man beyond good and evil so that he ends, isolated from his fellowmen, in the position of a "little God" who has no right to act as one. This is the lesson in existential absurdity to be derived from *The Outsider*. Thus, at times Wright comes close to the naturalistic vision of determinism, which conceives of man as an accident, or an epiphenomenon caught in a general movement toward universal rest. This is apparent in a long (still unpublished) piece of poetry he wrote in the mid-fifties to celebrate the manifold incarnations of life. In it he deals with a force that works through man, and that inhabits him for a time, making him the vessel of a principle he cannot control. This force, though, does not tend toward static, cosmic rest; rather, it aims at self-fulfillment and unlimited expansion, it gropes toward a kind of pantheistic harmony in which matter and spirit are one. If this is Transcendentalism of a kind, it represents only a transitory stage in Wright's thinking. On the whole, he is a humanist who retains the Marxist perspective as an ideological tool, and who believes in ethical responsibility, and a certain degree of free will in a world whose values are not created by a transcendental entity, but by the common workings of mankind.

Insofar as naturalism is opposed to romanticism as a philosophy, it attacks the unscientific values of tradition and evinces a distrust of those natural forces that man cannot control; it thus corresponds to one facet of Wright's personality. If we look at an early short story, "Superstition," and at a later one, "Man, God Ain't Like That," we find that both denounce the obscene power that such beliefs—and Wright deliberately makes no difference between religion and superstition—can wield over the spirit of man. There, Wright is largely a rationalist. Similarly, when he advocates the cultural liberation of African nations, he still upholds the idea that what was good for Europe, insofar as rationalism and technology are concerned, should be good for the Third World: colonialism has unwittingly given Africa the tools for her own liberation from her religion-ridden ancestral past, and the new African leaders should seize that opportunity to step boldly into the twentieth century. Such is Wright's contention—an opinion which encountered strong opposition on the part of many African intellectuals at the 1956 Congress of Black Artists and Writers in Paris.

Where America was concerned, however, Wright held somewhat different views; he often regretted that his country had no past and no traditions (however unscientific or irrational they might be).

Like many naturalists before him, Wright feared the forces that reason cannot control, forces that lie within the darkest recesses of man's soul, and his descriptions of Africa evoke at times Conrad's sense of horror in *Heart of Darkness*. Mostly he fears the forces man has unleashed and can no longer subdue, like the overpowering social systems that stifle the development of individuality.

A brief survey of Wright's many-faceted *weltanschauung* shows him to be inconclusively close to or remote from what passes for the common denominators of the various American naturalists. His position oscillates between Marxism and humanistic Existentialism.

We ought to remember that he is not primarily a thinker but a novelist, and therefore, that whatever may be characteristically naturalistic in his fiction is more likely to have resulted from his personal experience as a poor black American or from his early readings and stands as an embattled writer. Although naturalism is as protean as a set of literary forms and techniques as it is as a philosophical view, it is, nevertheless, on these forms that the brunt of our analysis must rest.

In the often-quoted episode from *Black Boy* in which he relates how he was spiritually saved by reading a few American novelists to whom he had been introduced by Mencken's *Book of Prefaces,* Wright mentions Sinclair Lewis's *Main Street,* Dreiser's *Jennie Gerhardt,* and *Sister Carrie,* as well as Stephen Crane:

> I was overwhelmed. I grew silent, wondering about the life around me. It would have been impossible for me to have told anyone what I derived from these novels for it was nothing less than a sense of life itself. All my life had shaped me for the realism, the naturalism of the modern novel, and I could not read enough of them.[5]

Two things are important in this statement. First, the experiential basis of Wright's literary outlook ("all my life had shaped me for the realism, the naturalism of the modern novel"); second, the apparent lack of distinction between realism and naturalism; he seems to consider the two terms practically interchangeable. In this piece, written in 1943 after he had established his reputation as a novelist, Wright considers naturalism loosely, as simply another version of American realism; he is mostly interested in it because it provides an authentic sense of life and an understanding of the American scene:

> *Main Street* . . . made me see my boss, Mr. Gerald, and identify him as an American type . . . I felt closer to him though still distant. I felt that now I knew him, that I could feel the very limits of his narrow life.[6]

Such naturalistic novels convinced Wright that his life, hemmed in by poverty and racism, was not the only life to be circumscribed. Even the lives of the powerful whites that he had pictured as glamorous were restricted by uncontrollable circumstances. All men were encompassed by the same definition of the human condition. In a sense, Wright is relieved to see that white people don't escape man's common destiny; the racial gap artificially established by them tends to disappear, yielding at the same time to a more social perspective of rich versus poor, and to a universal humanistic view. Realistic/naturalistic fiction is thus defined, through Wright's own experience, as an eye-opener, in opposition to the romantic tales, the dime novels, the detective stories, the blood and thunder episodes he relished primarily because they provided him with an escape from everyday life. Romantic fiction became for him a synonym of evasion and vicarious revenge, wholly artificial because it precluded meaningful action. Naturalistic fiction provided him with a means of liberation through understanding. Although he sometimes read it, he contritely admits, as he would take a drug or dope, he generally derived from it a new social perspective.

> The plots and stories in the novel did not interest me so much as the point of view revealed. . . . I could not conquer my sense of guilt, the feeling that the white men around me knew that I was changing, that I had begun to regard them differently.[7]

That early impact upon his sensibilities was to last. Throughout his life, he considered Dreiser, his favorite American master, a literary giant nearly on par with Dostoevsky. Nothing indicates that he had read such early naturalists as Harold Frederic, Hamlin Garland, or even Frank Norris. Yet, he knew the works of Gorki, Hauptmann, George Moore, London, Stephen Crane, and Sherwood Anderson. Anderson appealed to him because of his revolt against small-town life in *Winesburg, Ohio,* and because of the essentially instinctive realism of his portrayals of domestic revolt. Anderson, like Wright, neither apologized for himself nor submitted to naturalistic despair; rather he tended to make of personal freedom a sort of mystic quest and to consider fiction as a substitute for religion—a thing in which Wright also characteristically indulged.

Later, the discovery of James T. Farrell's works and his personal acquaintance with him in the mid-thirties had some impact on his own writing, as is apparent in *Lawd Today.* True, Wright certainly derived more from Conrad or Poe with regard to the expression of moods; from Henry James and Hemingway with regard to the use of symbols; from Gertrude Stein with regard to speech rhythms; and he learned from Joyce, T. S. Eliot, and above all, Dostoevsky. Yet, the impact of the American realists was important because it came first and because it closely corresponded to Wright's own experience. There is a kinship between the lives of Dreiser and Wright that goes beyond literary theories. From the first, Dreiser was hard pressed by suffering, and the destitution of the existence to which he was born suggested to him a vision of men struggling aimlessly in a society which excluded them. American life he could thus identify as a figure of distant, capricious destiny.[8] He grew up hating the narrow-mindedness and helplessness of his family and was so overpowered by suffering that he came to see it as a universal principle to the point that he considered only the hand of fate where others saw the political and economic evils of capitalism.

Isn't that largely what happened to Wright? The sufferings due to poverty and family disruption, the narrow-minded religion practiced at home, the subservient attitudes of the family figures of authority caused him to question and to rebel against the order of things. He too hated the threadbare woof of his spiritually deprived childhood so strongly that he tended to generalize it in his oft-criticized declaration about black life.

> I used to mull over the strange absence of real kindness in Negroes, how unstable was our tenderness, how lacking in genuine passion, we were, how void of great hope, how timid our joy, how bare our traditions, how hollow our memories, how lacking we were in those intangible sentiments that bind man to man, and how shallow even was our despair . . . what had been taken for our emotional strength was our negative confusion, our flights, our fears, our frenzy under pressure.[9]

He too disliked his father who had relinquished his responsibilities; he too deplored his mother's inefficacy; he too had a brooding boyhood and the lonely joys of wallowing in books. He too came to experience destiny as an unexpected dispensation of fate, particularly brutal in the case of his mother's stroke, and he started to build up the precariousness of his own life into a philosophy. At twelve, he held ". . . a notion as to what life meant that no education could ever alter, a conviction that the meaning of living came only when [he] was struggling to wring a meaning out of meaningless suffering." He concluded:

> It made me want to drive coldly to the heart of every question and lay it open . . . love burrowing into psychology, into realistic and naturalistic fiction and art, into those whirlpools of politics that had the power to claim the whole of men's souls. It directed my loyalties to the side of men in rebellion; it made me love talk that sought answers to questions that could help nobody, that could only keep alive in me that enthralling sense of wonder and awe in the face of the drama of human feelings which is hidden by the external drama of life.[10]

If Wright followed Dreiser along the road of pessimistic determinism and stressed the helplessness of man, it also appears that the racial oppression he suffered enabled him to find the cause for his own, and his people's, sufferings in the hatred of the surrounding white world. Severed from knowledge and from the mainstream of American culture, he tried to join it. A victim of oppression, he directed his efforts toward rebellion. Thus, he partly escaped Dreiser's deep pessimism while his reverence for the invisible helped him maintain a sense of wonder and awe in front of his existential dilemma.

The fact that Wright came of age, in a literary sense, under the aegis of the Communist Party and during the Depression largely accounts for the special tenor of his naturalism. The revival of naturalism in the thirties corresponded to Wright's efforts to adapt his writing to a style he could achieve relatively easily. Among the John Reeders he found for the first time a milieu akin to, and favorable to, his preoccupations. That was the time when America was being educated by shock, and the impact of the crisis on the values of American culture was probably stronger than the repercussions of the economic crash upon the capitalist system. The rational character of the social structure seemed to disintegrate, and its existential components were revealed through the alienation of the individual from a society which did not care for him. Wright had experienced this since his childhood in Mississippi and could thus translate his own experience into general terms. His desire to use words as weapons, after the fashion of Mencken, in order to achieve some kind of liberation, had also become a nearly general tenet. The novelists of the thirties seemed heir to new obligations and were called upon to leave their ivory towers and become politically relevant. Authenticity, which had always been Wright's criterion, was rehabilitated to stand against artiness. A comparable movement had already taken place at the turn of the century, when Frank Norris supposedly declared, as he embraced naturalism out of hatred for so-called pure literature, "Who cares for fine style, we don't want literature, give us life." And in Europe, the social studies of Émile Zola had developed in opposition to the stylistic achievements of Flaubert's realism. Yet, in the thirties, a new sense of urgency was added, and Wright felt strongly confirmed in what he believed his mission as a writer to be.

> In their efforts to recruit masses [the Communists] had missed the meaning of the lives of the masses, had conceived of people in too abstract a manner. I would try to put some of that meaning back. I would tell Communists how common people felt, and I would tell common people of the self-sacrifice of communists who strove for unity among them.[11]

There was indeed a deep convergence between Wright's idiosyncratic attraction to violence (or compulsive counter-violence) and protest, and, on the other hand, the social attitude of the committed writers of the times as Alfred Kazin has analyzed it with perspicacity.[12] Of course, there did not remain much of the original philosophy of naturalism in that attitude. It was taken for granted that the writer should be a tough guy. In fact, most of the so-called proletarian writers were the sons of the bourgeoisie, but they considered themselves as starting from scratch and rejected literary traditions. On the contrary, Wright came from the lower classes, was largely self-educated, and had been kept from a literary tradition; he tried to invent one for himself, and this explains why he could endorse writers in the thirties who, like T. S. Eliot, were often attacked by the left as "decadents."

Also, the hardness of naturalism was more or less instinctive to those writers who tended to see life as oppression. Wright had really suffered oppression, so he could be vehement about what he repudiated. They all shared a common belief in social determinism, not the biological determinism of Spencer or even Dreiser, but the conviction that man is made and crushed by his social background and environment.

As Kazin further emphasizes, proletarian naturalism generally had narrow categories and ready-made prescriptions. It was assumed that the embattled novel ought to be relatively fast-paced so that the reader could be stimulated into active sympathy with the right cause; accordingly, thought was often subordinate to action, and the characters developed in a predetermined way toward class-consciousness. The novelists did not pose psychological problems whose refined variations constituted the novel proper. The strategy, Kazin argues, consisted in beginning with a state of fear or doubt which action dissipated. One always found a great deal of facts and documentation which answered for documentary realism.

This enumeration of the characteristics of the proletarian novel nearly amounts to a description of Wright's outstanding success of the period, i.e. *Native Son.*

Above all, Wright is conspicuous by his use and abuse of violence. This theme of violence was revived in fiction where it tended to become a demonstration of economic and social dislocation and a reflection of the state of the American system. Wright's own inclination to violence in fiction (in life he abhorred physical violence) could mirror the violence inflicted by American society, pass for the counter-violence of the oppressed Negro, and prefigure revolutionary violence. This was also the case for Erskine Caldwell and, to a degree, for James T. Farrell, both of whom displayed real excitement in reporting capitalistic decay. One may wonder, indeed, whether those novelists—in spite of their different political affiliations, temperaments, and styles—were not united by this coming of age in a time of catastrophe, a time which corresponded to their deep need for terror. Such terror in Wright hardly finds release except in a kind of obsession with details of utter brutality; the endings of his novels are not cathartic. Although Bigger discovers that he is what he killed for, this does not really free him from his alienation. On the contrary it fills Max with horror at the thought of his own (and the Communists') failure. *Native Son* differs noticeably from the standard proletarian novel in that the protagonist does not achieve real social and political consciousness; as a piece of propaganda, it is much weaker than "Fire and Cloud" and "Bright and Morning Star," in spite of the opinions of the reviewers and critics of the time. The writing of violent novels thus appears, above all, to be a search for emotional catharsis, maybe for vicarious fulfillment; this is what Wright meant when he said that writing "drain[ed] all the poison out of [him]."

Brutality is also, at times, deliberate and calculated to shock the reader. Because bankers's daughters had wept when reading *Uncle Tom's Children* and thereby found relief, Wright says in "How Bigger Was Born" that he wanted *Native Son* to be so taut, so hard that they would have to face it without the relief of tears.[13] This cultivation of violence often brings him closer to Dostoevsky who excels in depicting characters under extreme stress—think of Raskolnikov or Karamazov before and after the murder—than to the American naturalists. The naturalists's supposed contempt for style and their refusal of sensationalism do not apply to Wright and is certainly better exemplified by James T. Farrell's deliberate literalness of description. Farrell renounces effects to such a degree that this becomes an attribute of his writing (his writing is far more barren and clinical than Dreiser's, whose epic imagination took him, like Zola, into wild and beautiful flights). By accumulating details with detachment and also with some cruelty to his characters, Farrell achieves a sort of stonelike solidity, which is a monument in itself. Not so with Wright. There is in him a great attention to detail, but he depends much more for his effects upon the sweep and the suspense of narrative rather than upon the accumulation of revealing evidence—with the exception of *Lawd Today*.

At times, Wright's realism is quite naturalistic. He does not attempt to create simply the illusion of reality; after a careful study of life, he sometimes resorts with evident relish to nearly photographic verisimilitude. This, of course, is true mainly for descriptions and details, and is best documented by *Lawd Today*. This is also true for reactions and attitudes. For instance, while Wright was writing *Native Son*—in which he depicts in deterministic terms, "the story of a boy born amid poverty and conditions of fear which eventually stopped his will and control and made him a reluctant killer"[14]—the Robert Nixon case broke out in Chicago, and the novelist was quite happy to copy verbatim some of the *Chicago Tribune's* descriptions of the murderer and to use the brief prepared by attorney Ulysses Keys. Wright also resorted to authentic sources in order to present a view of the racist reactions of the white reporters—perhaps he did so to forestall any possible challenge by his critics. Why did he desire such literalness? One may surmise that he wanted to emulate Dreiser, who had based *An American Tragedy* on the Grace Brown/Chester Gillette case. In several other instances, however, Wright goes beyond that need for undebatable proof and documentation. As I have tried to show elsewhere, even in a novella as surrealistic and existentialistic as "The Man Who Lived Underground," Wright did not use Dostoevsky's *Notes from Underground* as a source, but used instead a glaring account of the subterranean adventures of a Hollywood delinquent he had lifted from *True Detective Magazine.* Likewise, we have to go back to actual events in order to find the origin of his humorous and imaginative "Man of All Works." "The Man Who Killed a Shadow" actually comes from the Julius Fischer case, which attorney Charles E. Houston had related to Wright shortly before his departure for France. Wright secured a transcript and nearly contented himself with narrating it: describing, for instance, the way the defendant had strangled and clubbed with a stick a librarian, Catherine Cooper Reardon, because she had complained about his work, Wright went as far as lifting whole sentences from the court record; even details which one could think came from his imagination and zest for horror, such as the use of the victim's pink panties to wipe her blood from the floor, are borrowed from the official transcript. Again and again, whether for details or plot episodes, Wright goes back to actual occurrences. Of course there is in this something of the painstaking search for documentary proof that he greatly admired in Émile Zola. An interview he gave to a Swedish newspaper in the late fifties shows how much he wanted to imitate the French naturalist master. Just as Zola, notebook in hand, jotted down information about prostitutes when he wanted to write

*Nana*, we discover that Wright, not satisfied with copying real letters from American sailors to Spanish prostitutes in *Pagan Spain*, also tried to buy similar letters from French prostitutes when gathering documentation on GI's in France for the last volume of his Fishbelly trilogy.

To Wright, the document, designed as proof, is nearly sacred. His industrious research into the facts can sometimes be ascribed to the necessity to check actual details because of a lack of personal experience: for instance, apropos of the arraignment of Tyree in *The Long Dream*, he had to learn the details of Mississippi court procedure. In other instances his journalistic zeal seems to be a carry-over from his beginnings as a correspondent for the Harlem Bureau of the *Daily Worker*. As was the case with Crane, Norris, London, Dreiser, and many muckrakers, Wright's schooling in the writing profession began partly in a newspaper office, hence his reverence for the document as objective record. Yet, contrary to Sinclair Lewis, he never turns the novel into a sort of higher journalism, and it might be truer to say that his best journalism—articles like "Two Million Black Voices" or "Joe Louis Discovers Dynamite"— derives its power from a nonjournalistic interest in time, locale, and dramatic sequence.

Among the many reasons for the importance of the authentic record in Wright's fiction, two seem to prevail: first, the obligation of a black writer to substantiate his most trifling indictments of the white system; second, but not least, Wright's naive pleasure in discovering that reality is often more fiction-like than fiction itself and in persuading the reader of this.

As far as form is concerned, a commonly held opinion is that the naturalists did not really care for the niceties of style. This may be true of a few proletarian novelists who disguised their ignorance in literary matters as a deliberate contempt for refined "bourgeois" aestheticism. This may be true of Farrell; and it may even be partly true of Dreiser, though his clumsier attempts at elegance are the result of a failure rather than a lack of care. This is never true of Wright, who always evinced a deep interest in style. His best-known pronouncement about writing, "Blueprint for Negro Writing," stresses the balance between content and expression. Indeed he takes writing seriously, sometimes awfully so; for him it is no gratuitous game, but a weapon, a vital, self-justifying activity, a means to change the world.

In his eyes, to write well was not sufficient. He did, for instance, censure Zora Neale Hurston because the "sensory sweep of her novel [*Their Eyes Were Watching God*] carries no theme, no message, no thought."[15] And he praised Carl Von Unruh because his comprehension of the problems of Fascism in *The End Is Not Yet* "lifts him, at one stroke, out of the class of fictionneers and onto the plane of writers who through the prophetic power of their vision, legislate new values for mankind."[16] For Wright, the ideal for people "writing from the Left," as he does, should be to "create in the minds of other people a picture that would impell them to meaningful activity."[17] This quest for the meaningful even leads Wright to assert that Stephen Crane's *Maggie: A Girl of the Streets* is simply a coldly materialistic picture of poverty (while Jack Conroy's *The Disinherited* is the picture of men and women groping their way to a new concept of human dignity[18]) and to find Arna Bontemps's or Langston Hughes's novels more relevant, though not better, than *Sister Carrie* because their characters are "haunted with the desire to make their lives meaningful."

The strength of true fiction comes above all from the nature of writing itself, which must achieve a nice balance between form and content; "the limitations of the craft constitute its greatest virtues. If the sensory vehicle of imaginative writing is required to carry too great a load of didactic material, the artistic sense is submerged," Wright states in "Blueprint for Negro Writing."[19] This explains why he did not hesitate to fight the attempts of CP leaders who wanted him to propagandize. He did so in the name of personal freedom and also for the validity of an art defined by intrinsic criteria; in a reply to the Jewish liberal critic David Cohn, he says:

> Mr. Cohn implies that as a writer I should look at the state of the Negro through the lens of relativity and not judge his plight in an absolute sense. This is precisely what, as an artist, I try NOT to do. My character, Bigger Thomas, lives and suffers in the real world. Feeling and perception are absolute, and if I dodged my responsibility as an artist and depicted them otherwise, I'd be a traitor not to my race alone but to humanity.[20]

Art certainly requires a "point of objectivity in the handling of the subject matter," yet, Wright will never define it through extrinsic criteria: "In the last analysis," he answers engraver Antonio Frasconi in a beautiful letter dated November 1944, "the artist must bow to the monitor of his own imagination; must be led by the sovereignty of his own impressions and perceptions; must be guided by the tyranny of what troubles and concerns him personally. There is no other true path."[21]

Wright himself spent hour upon hour trying to master the craft of fiction, experimenting with words, with sentences, with scenes; and with the help of other novels or prefaces after he had found grammar books and style manuals quite useless, he tried patiently to make his writing jell, harden, and coalesce into a meaningful whole. When he was successful, stories such as "Big Boy Leaves Home" or "Down by the Riverside" are proof that he was able to blend and to fuse elements and techniques borrowed from Joyce, Hemingway, Gertrude Stein, Conrad, and even James. His single-mindedness can, at times, be reminiscent of the efforts of Flaubert, whom he greatly admired. Proust's *Remembrance of Things Past* also filled him with boundless admiration and equal despair because he felt unable to do as well. In one of the most revealing chapters of his autobiography, Wright confesses:

> My purpose was to capture a physical state or movement that carried strong subjective impressions, an accomplishment which seemed supremely worth struggling for. If I could fasten the mind of the reader upon words so firmly that he would forget words and be conscious only of his response, I felt that I would be in sight of knowing how to write narrative. I strove to master words, to make them disappear, to make them important by making them new, to make them melt into a rising spiral of emotional climax that would drench the reader with a sense of a new world. This was the single end of my living.[22]

Here we are far indeed from the supposed naturalistic/proletarian distrust for fine writing!

The major difference between Wright's view of how fiction should depict the lives of the common people and what the believers in scientific determinism tried to achieve in fiction can be found in Wright's opinion of Nelson Algren's *Never Come Morning*. The preface he wrote for that novel considers a few of the literary strategies which could have been used for the treatment of Bruno Bicek and his friends: some writers would have resorted to satire or humor, others would have "assumed an aloof 'social worker' attitude toward it, prescribing 'pink pills' for social ills, piling up a mountain of naturalistic detail."[23] Wright, by the way, did *not* go in for such techniques and he believed that Algren's perspective excelled all of those because he "depicts the intensity of feeling, the tawdry but potent dreams, the crude but forceful poetry and the frustrating longing for humanity residing in the lives of the Poles of Chicago's North West Side."[24]

Here, the importance attributed to intensity of feeling over naturalistic detail, the insistence on the forceful poetry of commonplace lives is somewhat unexpected; yet, is this not what Wright attempted when he depicted Bigger Thomas' or Jake Jackson's frustrated longings for a movie-like world? And, at the same time, is not such a statement in the very vein of a Frank Norris who considers naturalism, as incarnated by Zola, as another kind of romanticism?

In "Blueprint for Negro Writing," Wright seems to be responding to Norris' desire that ordinary characters "must be twisted from the ordinary" when he prescribes:

> The presentation of their lives should be simple, yes; but all the complexity, the strangeness, the magic, the wonder of life that lays like a bright sheen over the most sordid existence should be there. To borrow a phrase from the Russians, it should have a *complex simplicity*.[25]

This is a way of claiming equal treatment for all in the field of literature, hence a political statement. At the same time, Wright is convinced that no literature exists without romance, without "the bright sheen" of illusion—he dedicated *Native Son* to his mother, who taught him as "a child at her knee, to revere the fanciful and the imaginative." He was convinced that art had little to do with scientific objectivity (not to be mistaken for authenticity and honesty) and that:

> An artist deals with aspects of reality different from those which a scientist uses. My task is not to abstract reality but to enhance its value. In the process of identifying emotional experience in words, paint, stone, or tone, an artist uses his feelings in an immediate and absolute sense.[26]

Literature is thus less the depiction of the actual world than the representation of emotional experience through words. The world interests Wright only insofar as it affects the individual, as it is perceived, experienced, acted upon, or reacted against. He places the emphasis on emotion, the emotional potential of the material, the emotion to be aroused in the reader, the emotion of the creator at work. It may be in that last domain that his intimate convictions about literary creation bring him the farthest from the theoreticians of the experimental novel and "laboratory creation." He does not view writing as a conscious production in which intellect and critical sense are unceasingly called upon to regulate fancy. His conception is rather dangerously close to the Romanticists' definition of inspiration. Being a rationalist and an agnostic, if not an atheist, he confesses there is something paradoxical in such a view, and he honestly admits this contradiction:

> I abhor the very notion of mysticism; yet, in trying to grasp this [creative] process in me, I encounter a reality that recedes and hides itself in another reality, and, when hunted too openly, it alters its own aspect, chameleon-like,

thereby escaping introspectional observation. I sigh, shrug, leave it alone, but still trust it, welcoming it when it comes again.[27]

Doesn't this half-reluctant admission amount to a recognition of the contingency of visitations of quasi-divine inspiration? Further on, Wright recalls that, preceding the writing of all his books, not only fiction but even travel narratives, he had been invaded by a feeling of estrangement from his surroundings, a sense of "being possessed by a slow stirring of the emotions, a sort of haunting incitation as though . . . vainly seeking to recall something long forgotten."[28] He owns that he had no power over these creative moods, that they came when they wanted, and that no distraction could dislodge them until the writing of the piece had actually drained them off. Such a perspective defines the writer as the instrument of a power which inhabits him temporarily, coerces him to express it, and then leaves him after these strange visitations. This is strongly reminiscent of Wright's description of the working of the life force in a poem of his that was mentioned previously. It corresponds to a fatalistic creation, because it becomes, in this view, a process which takes place without much actual effort on the part of the writer:

> I was aware of subjective movements . . . finally being strung out in time, of events spelling a sequence, that of interlocking images shedding that kind of meaning we associate with a 'story'. . . . Such moods . . . suck themselves into events, long past and forgotten, declaring them their personal property; then to my amazed delight they telescope alien and disparate images into organic wholes. . . . A crime story in a newspaper evokes a sense of excitement far beyond the meaning of the banal crime described, a meaning which, in turn, conjures up for some inexplicable reasons its emotional equivalent in a totally different setting and possessing a completely different meaning.[29]

Even more significant than his conception of inspiration is the definition Wright provides of a "story": it is not so much an organized plot carried out through narrative, as it is a "sequence of interlocking images shedding [a] kind of meaning." "Meaning" here is emotional rather than intellectual, and the image-pattern stands for the essential element. A close reading of Wright's symbolic, often dream-like fiction reveals that the crudely apparent three-to-five-act dramatic structure is only an external framework which supports a finely woven symbolic texture. The dramatic framework is mainly a means of prodding the narrative onwards at the hectic pace required by the narrow time limits of the classical tragedy (these time limits are actually narrow in *Lawd Today*, *Savage Holiday*, and even *Native Son*; they are made to seem narrow in *The Outsider* and *The*

*Long Dream* by the selection of important scenes and by glossing over several months in a few sentences). As a result, Wright's narrative derives its emotional unity not so much from the plot or even the breathless rhythm with which he carries the reader forward, as from the "complex simplicity" of its associational imagery. Again, this brings Wright closer to the expressionists (or the impressionists, for that purpose) than to the naturalists. But does not the power and beauty of *Sister Carrie* derive less from Dreiser's objective presentation or see-saw-like structure than from its weird and emotionally laden images? Isn't this true also of the glittering world of *Nana* or Flaubert's *Madame Bovary?*

In the last resort, can't the best naturalists be declared great *because of,* not in spite of, their diffuse romanticism or epic vision? It may well be that the tendency to weave emotion and passion into documentation and reportorial accuracy is the secret of successful naturalistic writing and that naturalism should be reassessed in that light. Rather than sheer reaction against romantic exaggeration, it would appear to be a semi-conscious attempt to rationalize the sense of doom which was so keenly felt by the romantics. Scientific theories were introduced into the naturalists' critical and conceptual views of literary creation, but did they ever turn the novel into a scientific process? On the contrary, they tended to subordinate and assimilate science to the imagination. What they considered slice-of-life authenticity, what Wright believed to be real and authentic in his novels because it rested upon documentary proof, was often only a starting point, as he admitted toward the end of his career.

> A crime story in a newspaper evokes a sense of excitement far beyond the meaning of the banal crime described, a meaning which, in turn, conjures up, for inexplicable reasons, its emotion equivalent in a totally different setting and possessing a completely contrary meaning.[30]

If the setting and meaning are thus totally "contrary," can the original reports still be considered as relevant proof of authenticity?

Wright's conception of the artistic aim is, in the final analysis, that of a technique directed at bringing the reader, through poetic ecstasy or shock treatment, to acceptance of a new consciousness. A sort of alchemistic strategy (he actually uses and abuses the terms "to blend" and "to fuse") must be devised in order to drench the reader with the sense of something unheard, a result which could not be achieved by demonstrative logic or philosophizing. It is not surprising, then, that Wright should compliment Fritz Von Unruh because his novel is:

. . . a marvellous nightmare which has the power to shed light upon your waking hours. It depends for its continuity not upon the logic of two plus two equals four but upon the blooming of opposite images, upon the linking of widely disparate symbols and events, upon the associational magic of passion.[31]

"The linking of widely disparate symbols" was the touchstone of "good" surrealistic imagery in the eyes of the French surrealists; they considered the image more successful as the symbols were more distant and unrelated. At the root of Wright's fondness for what he calls surrealism one finds not a reading of the French surrealists (although Wright liked Dali's paintings and wrote a poem in homage to Aragon) but rather the influence of his grandmother whose Seventh-Day Adventism connected in his eyes ordinary reality with remote beliefs and, even more, the influence of the blues with their typical ability to bring together seemingly unrelated elements of the American Negro's existence and blend them into a new, meaningful whole.

Another, more obvious, trend of Wright's fiction, which, at times, differentiates him from the naturalists, is his sensationalism. True, such sensationalism could pass for an answer to Norris's demand that a naturalistic tale must possess "a violent and energetic greatness," that the characters must be "wrenched from the quiet, uneventful round of ordinary life and flung into the throes of a vast and terrible drama that works itself out in unleashed passions, in blood and sudden death." Certainly, if the naturalists thrive on the appearance of power and gross effects (which might be defined as expressionistic), then Wright is very much of a naturalist because he retains a great deal of the awareness of American naturalism. Viceral writing is his forte; critics generally agree that he is "a born storyteller" with all the implications of such a definition. Yet, if he willingly resorts to suspense, melodrama, coincidence, and subjection of character analysis to plot and storytelling, does not Wright do so mostly because of his early schooling in the stock techniques of popular fiction? In his mind, rawness and brutality are associated with fantasy and the gothic, i.e., another kind of romanticism. Here, the influence of Edgar Allan Poe is prevalent; in the most gruesome epidsodes of *Native Son*, for example, Wright blends two such apparently irreconcilable trends as gothic horror and sadism and, on the other hand, matter-of-fact, slice-of-life reporting. Perhaps he was able to do so because of his early ability to live simultaneously on the level of everyday destitution and that of evasion through popular fiction. The tenets of naturalism would impose upon Bigger a passive character, one subject to the workings of determinism and fate; we are made to share in his subordinate behavior through a quasi-reportorial rendition of his physical and psychosomatic reactions, sensations, and half-formulated thoughts. At the same time he evolves, by implication, in a world which is more that of Dostoevsky's *Crime and Punishment* than that of Dreiser's *An American Tragedy*, and by indirection he is enlarged into a King-Kong stereotype (quite consistent with the Rue Morgue murderer)—all without losing any of his humanity, because the reader is compelled to see the whole scene from his eyes.

Wright's conception of fiction as a magic telescoping of disparate elements if certainly linked to his childhood discovery of the power of the written word. He read with the feeling that he was performing a forbidden act, and, indeed he was, given the reactions of his grandmother, who saw fiction as a creation of the devil, and the attitude of the Deep South, which banned Negroes from public libraries. As much as the educational power of fiction, its capacity to arouse wonder was always important to him. As a Communist, he emphasized the former without renouncing the latter. He made ready use of the naturalistic and proletarian perspective, but only among other possible ones. Only in the late twenties did the philosophy of social determinism answer his questions concerning the restrictions which had been imposed upon him: universal determinism posited the equality of the oppressed Negro and his white oppressor under the common sway of human destiny. Wright could then consider the absurdity of the world through the eyes of Dreiser, who, he wrote, "tried to rationalize and justify the defeat of the individual in biological terms; with him it was a law of the universe."[32] Yet he could no more accept subjection and powerlessness as a universal law, since subjection amounted to his own slow death in a racist setting, than he could his grandmother's attempt to explain his mother's illness in terms of his own impiety and God's ensuing wrath. Determinism provided him, at best, with only a transitional belief, soon superseded by the optimistic social revoluionism of the Marxist faith. When he could no longer believe in the irreversible progress of History in Communism, Wright had to face again the absurdity and precariousness of the human predicament but he did so in terms that were closer to Russian, German, or even French existentialism. Existentialism left a way open for the creation of values by man, for individualism, and for solidarity, in a fashion that even the optimistic Spencerian brand of determinism could not. At the same time, existentialism satisfied Wright's tragic sense of life. The novel which best illustrates this shift in his philosophy (or rather the different emphasis he placed on different philosophies at different times) is undoubtedly *The Outsider*. Its first section, derived as it is from the then-unpublished *Lawd Today*, is strongly naturalistic, not only in the piling up of documentary detail but in the fashion in which economic, family, and sexual ties determine both Cross Damon's and Jake Jackson's life. That Wright has to resort to violent circumstances and largely coincidental plot in order to break off with this materialistic setting and deterministic definition of Damon's life is irrelevant here. The break is significant because it represents a jump into existential freedom and into an absurd world beyond the laws of "normal" causation. Cross will lie, kill, burn a church, drive to suicide the woman who loves him, act like one of those "little Gods" he so vehemently condemned for their ruthless use of power, only to finally discover the necessity of human solidarity and some kind of moral law. The break in the style is itself a significant transition from naturalistic reportage in didactic, philosophical prose, somewhat in the fashion of Sartre's *Les Chemins de la Liberté*. Although Wright's contribution to that type of fiction is of historical importance, we must confess that he is not at his best as a stylist when he resorts to such long-winded arguments and that the jump from naturalism to the philosophical novel does not always suit his talents.

He, on the contrary, effected the change from naturalism into what he would call surrealism quite successfully in "The Man Who Lived Underground." It is revealing that the piece was begun as a novel, in whose naturalistic first part the protagonist was a victim of circumstances: the police arrested him and beat him up on suspicion of a crime he had not committed. This part (which was suppressed from the published novella) ended with Fred Daniels's literal jump outside reality into the underground world of the sewer. Chance allowed him to escape in the way Cross Damon later did, but necessity and a search for an emotional relationship also drove him back above ground and into the hands of his torturers. In the same way, Damon owns on his deathbed that man cannot bear absolute solitude, that he must establish a bridge with other men, that the necessity of man's determinism must, in some way, be acknowledge. As a change from naturalism into another kind of literary strategy, "The Man Who Lived Underground" is a success because surrealism, as we tried to show, better suits Wright's passion for gothic detail and violence than philosophical didacticism. It appears that Wright functions best as an artist whenever, in his own words, he is able to "fuse and articulate the experiences of man, because his writing possesses the potential cunning to steal into the inmost recesses of human hearts, because he can create the myths and symbols that inspire a faith in life."[33]

To that end, American naturalism, both as a philosophy and as a literary technique in the line of Dreiser and James Farrell, provided him only with a starting point; then either, as we suggested, a larger definition of naturalism must be given—if it is to encompass the many facets of Wright's writing—or it must be recognized that he often overstepped its boundaries. Wright's attraction to the fanciful, the mysterious, the irrational always proved too strong for him to remain attached to his self-declared rationalism and deliberate objectivity. His heavy reliance upon visceral and violent emotions may account for this inability. Far from being a limitation, it turns out to be one of the major resources of his narrative power, in the same way that his obstinate refusal to submit to authority and his insatiable curiosity concerning everything human certainly led him to ask some of the most relevant questions of our time.

1. Granville Hicks, "From Dreiser to Farrell to Wright," *Saturday Review*, March 30, 1963, pp. 37–38.

2. Granville Hicks, "Portrait of a Man Searching," *New York Times Book Review*, March 22, 1953, Sec. 7.

3. Orville Prescott, review of *The Outsider, New York Times*, March 18, 1953, p. 29.

4. Luther P. Jackson, "Writer's Outsider," *Newark News*, April 5, 1953.

5. *Black Boy*, (New York: Harper and Row, 1945), p. 219.

6. Ibid., pp. 218–219.

7. Ibid.,

8. See Charles C. Walcutt, "Theodore Dreiser: The Wonder and Terror of Life," in his *American Literary Naturalism* (Minneapolis: University of Minnesota Press, 1956), pp. 180–87.

9. *Black Boy*, p. 33.

10. Ibid., p. 88.

11. Richard Wright, "I Tried To Be a Communist," in *The God That Failed*, ed. Richard Crossman (New York: Harper & Bros., 1949), pp. 107–08.

12. See Alfred Kazin, *On Native Grounds* (New York: Harcourt, Brace and Co., 1942), especially "The Revival of Naturalism."

13. Richard Wright, "How 'Bigger' Was Born," in *Native Son* (New York: Harper & Bros., 1940), pp. 29–30. Wright's phrase certainly was an allusion to Eleanor Roosevelt's reactions; she had found the book beautifully moving and had said so in her *New York Post* column.

14. "Interview," *Bulletin Board*, June, 1950.

15. Richard Wright, "Between Laughter and Tears," *New Masses* 25 (October 5, 1937): 25.

16. Richard Wright, "A Junker's Epic Novel about Militarism," *PM Magazine*, May 4, 1947, p. m3.

17. Richard Wright, "Writing from the left," (Unpublished typescript, p. 3, Wright Archive, Yale University Library).

18. Ibid., p. 1.

19. Richard Wright, "Blueprint for Negro Writing," *New Challenge*, Fall 1937, p. 63.

20. Richard Wright, "I Bite the Hand That Feeds Me," *Atlantic Monthly*, June 1940, p. 826.

21. "An Exchange of Letters: Wright to Frasconi," *Twice a Year,* Winter 1944–45, p. 258.

22. Richard Wright, *American Hunger* (New York: Harper and Row, 1977), p. 22.

23. Richard Wright, "Introduction" to Nelson Algren's *Never Come Morning* (New York: Harper, 1942), p. ix.

24. Ibid.

25. Richard Wright, "Blueprint for Negro Writing," p. 60. Here Wright comes quite close to Ellison's opinion that the heritage of the American Negro is made of many influences. He adds that "Eliot, Stein, Joyce, Proust, Hemingway and Anderson, Gorki, Barbusse, Nexo and Jack London no less than the folklore of the Negro himself should form the heritage of the Negro writer. Every iota of gain in human thought and sensibility should be ready grist for his mill no matter how far-fetched that may seem in its immediate application."

26. Wright, "I Bite the Hand That Feeds Me," p. 826.

27. Richard Wright, "Roots and Branches," (Unpublished typescript, p. 5, Wright Archive, Yale University Library).

28. Ibid.

29. Ibid.

30. Ibid.

31. Richard Wright, "A Junker's Epic Novel about Militarism," p. m3.

32. Richard Wright, "Personalism," (Unpublished typescript, p. 1. Wright Archive, Yale University Library).

33. Wright, "Blueprint for Negro Writing," p. 59.

# Wright's South

"Southland was bad and mean
But this North is hard and cold"

$R$ICHARD WRIGHT is as much a son of Mississippi as is William
Faulkner, yet many of his readers do not think of him as a southern
writer. This is because of *Native Son,* which depicts black life in the
ghettos of the North, or *The Outsider,* which is steeped in existential and
ideological controversy, and because of social comments on continents
other than America in *Black Power, Pagan Spain,* or *The Color Curtain.*
Most readers, however, cannot escape associating Wright with the South
because the tremendous impact of his autobiography, *Black Boy,* lies in
his having managed to survive in Mississippi (i.e., one of the most desti-
tute and racist parts of the United States) and finally leave it. *Black Boy*
implied that a black youth had to escape southern destitution and discrimination to become a writer, which, being black, he was not even
supposed to attempt. As a result, *Black Boy* makes Wright a writer *out of*
the South, not *of* it.

Wright liked to see himself as an individual who happened to be born
in a poor black Natchez family and had to carve for himself not only his
own identity through rebellion but seek a chosen place—a place of freedom versus servitude, knowledge versus cultural void, action versus
apathy. Also, he would cast himself in the persona of a man forever
seeking a place where he could be more fully human, moving from Mississippi to Memphis, to Chicago, to New York, to Paris; visiting different
parts of Europe, America, Africa, and Asia; and, for a while, joining the
Gary Davis movement in order to be a "citizen of the world." At the close
of a lecture in Paris, he once told a student: "You see, the difference
between the two of us is that I am completely free, I have no roots,
whereas you are bound by European history and the tyranny of place."[1]
Beyond the metaphorical opposition between myths of the New World
and the Old, this was a defiant, perhaps heroic statement, yet literally not
a believeable one. Like others of his generation, Wright was heir to the

tyranny of the First World War and the depression, of Mississippi and the Great Migration. To begin with, throughout his life he attempted to reject what the South stood for in his mind but he also kept reaffirming, re-peatedly and compulsively, what it had meant for him and how he had been molded by it.

As a result, the few American critics who have chosen to call Wright a southern writer may have something to tell about his uneasy relationship. They are only a handful, most of them black. Professor Blyden Jackson, himself born in Kentucky, insisted upon this definition of Wright in *The Waiting Years*. During the few years I knew him, Arna Bontemps empha-sized Wright's southern heritage together with what he considered his lack of humor.[2] Jay Saunders Redding claimed Wright for the South in his 1961 obituary essay, "Home Is Where the Heart Is," defining the place as "the America that only Negroes know; a ghetto of the soul, a boundary of the mind, a confine of the heart."[3] Finally, James Baldwin somewhat unexpectedly described Wright as "a Mississippi pickaninny, mischievous, cunning and tough. This seems to be at the bottom of everything he did."[4] In "Everybody's Protest Novel," Baldwin's phrase reflected his desire to stress Wright's roots in order to claim what he saw as the black man's heritage: "Our humanity is our burden, our life; we need not battle for it, we need only to do what is infinitely more difficult—that is, accept it."[5]

However, these critics' perceptions may differ, they are right in stating that Wright's allegiance to the South (or his rejection of it) played an important role, both in his creative writing and his nonfiction, but espe-cially in *Twelve Million Black Voices*. But this role was complex, if not ambiguous. It may best be illuminated by going back to a crucial, irritat-ing scene in *Black Boy* where the South is unambiguously rejected to-gether with—or as well as or in the guise of—Wright's own father. The episode deals with the writer's return to Natchez in 1940, not a special, deliberate visit to his native land since he only stopped there on a trip to Mexico and North Carolina. His meeting a father who had deserted his home and exposed his family to want and psychological distress was clearly more a confrontation than a return of the prodigal son.

The scene culminates in chapter 3, thus serving as a closing episode, or a partial conclusion at a very early stage in *Black Boy*. It functions to slay the father symbolically, dismiss him forever or, as Robert Stepto puts it in *From Behind the Veil*, to "bury him alive."[6] The emotional tenor of the encounter hints at a personal settling of accounts of a psychological, even psychoanalytical, nature, yet it is couched in terms that evoke a more general cultural and geographical conflict. The old man is "standing alone upon the red clay of a Mississippi plantation, a sharecropper, clad in ragged overalls, holding a muddy hoe in his gnarled, veined hands . . . standing against the sky, smiling toothlessly, his hair whitened, his body bent, his eyes glazed with dim recollection."[7]

The visual effect is striking and, to whoever is familiar with Wright's and Rosskam's *Twelve Million Black Voices: A Folk History of the Negro in the United States,* the reference to several of the photographs from the Farm Security Administration reprinted in it is inescapable. Nathan Wright becomes one among thousands of sharecroppers who fell victims to the Lords of the Land during the depression. He is a helpless man, economically deprived, illiterate, whose glazed eyes cannot even fathom his own condition whereas his son, endowed with the social graces befitting a nationally acclaimed novelist and endowed with Marxist political awareness, can contemplate and gauge his plight. Strangely, Wright refrains from enfolding his father in his love since he alludes to his *mind,* not his *heart,* aching—"aching as I embraced the simple nakedness of his life, feeling how completely his soul was imprisoned by the flow of seasons, by wind and rain and sun, how fastened were his memories to a crude and raw past, how chained were his actions and emotions to the direct, animalistic impulses of his withering body" (*BB,* 30).

The South at the time thus was the place where the Negro, through racial oppression, was reduced to a body, that body being doomed to wither quickly because of economic exploitation. Wright obviously blotted out all the spiritual and cultural traditions, religious and secular, which allowed the black community to endure. He spoke in strictly economic and physiological terms when he added: "From the white landowners above him there had not been handed to him a chance to learn the meaning of loyalty, of sentiment, of tradition. Joy was as unknown to him as was despair. As a creature of the earth, he endured, hearty, whole, seemingly indestructible, with no regrets and no hope" (*BB,* 30). Evidently, here Wright was not settling accounts only with Nathan Wright, the inadequate father whom he could not forgive, but with white exploitation and racism which reduced blacks to "creatures of the earth" and with other visions of the South and the Negro. This passage calls forth echoes of other works and must be examined in an intertextual context. First, it is a response to the plantation tradition, which claimed that life in the South was idyllic even for slaves and that represented it as a pastoral haven versus the evil ways of the city. Secondly, it is an implicit response to the other southern writers' images of blacks, notably William Faulkner's statement concerning Dilsey and other Negro characters in his novels: "They endured." Here Wright refused to consider sheer survival in the face of countless horrors as a sufficient asset; he saw it in a strictly physical and economic sense and would question the notion of "cultural survival" when applied to his father, if not to southern blacks in general. He seems to have reduced his father's mental universe to that of Bigger Thomas, deprived not only of literacy but of tradition insofar as a "creature of the earth" knows neither regret nor hope. Regret and hope stand for continuity between the past and the future while Nathan Wright was condemned to a flat, repetitive present.

The statement was also geographical, asserting that in the South of Wright's childhood a black youth could not, as a rule, find food for intellectual development and spiritual flowering. Had he not left, the famous novelist would have become a sharecropper. Hence the exultation and pity in his reflection: "I was overwhelmed to realize that he could never understand me or the scalding experience that had swept me beyond his life and into an area of living that he could never know. . . . I stood before him, poised, my mind aching as I embraced the simple nakedness of his life." What a proud, God-like stance on the part of Wright! He had succeeded where his father had failed, "in the same city which had lifted me in its burning arms and borne me toward alien and undreamed of shores of knowing" (*BB*, 31). Again, here Wright described his own intellectual journey out of the South, whose precise function it was to deny knowledge to blacks, in one of the major themes, or tropes, of Afro-American literature. Just as he refused to define the South as the new Eden of the "plantation tradition," he responded to the black tradition in which integrity and freedom must be won through flight to the North and the acquisition of literacy. Freedom thus became defined as the power to write one's own story—*Black Boy*—and the history of one's people—*Twelve Million Black Voices*. But, by insisting upon the cultural gulf between his unreconstructed father and his enlightened self, Wright was cutting off his roots symbolically. In *Black Boy*, he claimed that when he tried to speak with his father, he soon realized that "though ties of blood made us kin, though I could see a shadow of his face in my face, though there was an echo of his voice in my voice, we were forever strangers, speaking a different language, living on vastly distant planes of reality" (*BB*, 30). Describing the same encounter in his essay, "How Jim Crow

Feels," Wright similarly asserted: "I discovered that blood and race alone were not sufficient to knit people together in a community of feeling. The psychological gap between us which had been wrought by time made us regard one another with tension and forced smiles and I knew that it was not the myth of blood but of continuous associations, shared ideals and kindred intentions that made people one."[8] Significantly Wright's refusal to undergo the tyranny of origins took place as he was reporting his inability to get a birth certificate; all the records, if any had existed, had burned and he "could not obtain any objective evidence that [he] had been born at all."[9] What more adequate symbol could he find for his lack of roots?

Nowhere more eloquently than in the final pages of his autobiography did Wright clarify his quarrel with the South and acknowledge his incapacity to rid himself of it. In those pages one is especially struck by Wright's definition of the South as the "white South." When taking leave of one of his fellow workers in Memphis, Wright made it plain that he could never be held back, concluding: "This was the culture from which I sprang. This was the terror from which I fled" (*BB*, 225). "Culture" was clearly the equivalent of "terror"; in other words, white culture was hostile and black culture was no "supportive environment by itself"; the "sheer thin margin of Southern culture," black and white, was not sufficient to nourish a personality battered by "the shocks of Southern living." For Wright, the South was, first and foremost, overwhelmingly white and hostile:

> The *white South* said it knew "niggers," . . . Well, the *white South* had never known me. . . . The *white South* said that I had a 'place' in life. Well, I had never felt my 'place', or, rather my deepest instincts had always made me reject the 'place' to which the *white South* had assigned me. . . . No word I had ever heard fall from the lips of *southern white* men had ever made me really doubt the worth of my own humanity. . . . True, I had lied, I had stolen, . . . I had fought. . . . But in what other ways had the *South* allowed me to be natural, to be real, to be myself, except in rejection, rebellion, and aggression?
>
> Not only had the *southern whites* not known me but, more important still, as I had lived in the *South* I had not had the chance to learn who I was. The pressure of *southern* living kept me from being the kind of person that I might have been . . . I had slowly learned that the *South* could recognize but part of a man, could accept but a fragment of his personality. . . .
>
> I was leaving the *South* to fling myself into the unknown, to meet other situations that would perhaps elicit from me other responses. . . . I was not leaving the *South* to forget the *South* but so that some day I might understand

it, might come to know what its rigors had done to me, to its children. I fled so that the numbness of my defensive living might thaw out and let me feel the pain—years later and far away—of what living in the *South* had meant.

Yet, deep down I knew that I could never really leave the South for my feelings had already been formed by the *South*, for there had been slowly instilled into my personality and consciousness, black though I was, the culture of the *South*. So, in leaving I was taking a part of the *South* to transplant in alien soil, to see if I could grow differently, if it could drink of new and cool rains, bend in strange winds, respond to the warmth of other suns, and perhaps, to bloom. . . . And if that miracle ever happened, then I would know that there was hope in that *southern swamp* of despair and violence, that light could emerge even in the blackest of the *southern night*. I would know that the *South* too could overcome its fear, its hate, its cowardice, its heritage of guilt and blood, its burden of anxiety and compulsive cruelty.

With ever watchful eyes and bearing scars, visible and invisible, I headed North. (*BB*, 227–228, emphases mine).

Within a couple of rhetorical paragraphs, "South" or "southern," generally associated with "white," recurred a score of times like a refrain or a burden—a burden on Wright's consciousness. By contrast, the single, final utterance of "North" took on cumulative force. Later, Wright always insisted that he worked and lived in France because he felt free there but that the United States was his country. He did not go so far as to add that the South was his home, because he still considered it a place of oppression. In *Pagan Spain*, he compared Catholic repression of the local Protestants under Franco in the 1950s with racial oppression in Mississippi. Again, at the first Conference of Negro Artists and Writers in 1956, he warned his audience: "I was born a black Protestant in the most racist of all American States . . . I lived my childhood under a racial code, brutal and bloody, that white men proclaimed was ordained of God."[10] And his very last lecture for French radio also referred to Mississippi in terms of racial oppression. His whole novel, *The Long Dream*, could even be seen as a compulsive fictional elaboration of the inability to escape a culture of white supremacy from which Fishbelly could not even free himself after residing in France. The theme of the South as a prison thus coincided in his fiction and nonfiction when Wright said in an interview shortly before his death: "Mississippi is only an immense black ghetto, a vast prison where the whites are the jailers and the Negroes are the prisoners."[11]

In the same interview, Wright spoke at length about *The Long Dream*, stressing black absorption of southern values and their disturbing effect on the psychology his protagonist. Significantly, the novel was only the first volume of a trilogy that would have taken him to Africa in search of his roots and back to Mississippi, his real home. A summary of the novel prepared by Wright speaks for itself:

> *The Long Dream* is a novel woven of the materials of a black boy growing up in the American South. It shows how a person, be he white, black, yellow or brown, absorbs the values of such a society. When that person happens to be black and the son of a rich black father in Mississippi, then the absorption of the values of the society in which he is born assumes fantastic forms.
>
> Fishbelly's place in the society of the white American South compels him to see life from a unique angle of vision. *The Long Dream* deals with a black human plant that has to draw its nourishment from abnormal conditions of life.
>
> Men not only take their cultural and economic values from the society in which they live, but they also take the direction and the pitch of their sexual attitudes and drives. *The Long Dream* is an intimate description of how black boys in the American South react to what is taught them at school, in the press, in church, in their homes. Though black, they react positively to the dominant values of the white world in which they live—that is, sex and money—and their conditioning takes place in an atmosphere charged with greed, lust, betrayal, a world in which justice is bought and sold, where money means love and love means money.
>
> Here is the portrait of a black boy who longs to be an American and, if he prefers money to honesty, it is because he has seen his corrupt father become rich through corruption. If Fishbelly has an attitude of contempt for other blacks, it is because he has seen that that is the way to success. If Fishbelly has suppressed and confused dreams of possessing white girls, it only proves that he has read his daily newspaper and has seen too many movies.
>
> Fishbelly is an American, mangled, frightened, timid, aggressive, ignorant, generous; he confronts you with his love and his hurt, wanting to live and not knowing how, as much a danger to himself as to others.[12]

How deeply Wright's creative imagination was stimulated by his childhood environment should be apparent by now. It sometimes brought him compulsively back to early experiences where pain mixed with pleasure, racial oppression with the discovery of individual possibility, familial deprivation with the joys of living in a rural world. Going over the many occasions when Wright used the South as a theme or locale would be revealing, but we must limit ourselves to a few cases. Wright's first recorded piece of writing, "The Voodoo of Hell's Half-Acre," was set in Jackson, Mississippi, and his first published short story, "Superstition," treated black folk beliefs in a small southern town. Much of his early poetry, such as "Between the World and Me" and "Obsession," used lynchings as a theme, while other poems were southern in topic and form;

"Ah Feels It in Mah Bones" and, especially, "Red Clay Blues" employ black dialect and stress the emotional link of the ghetto immigrant to his Deep South home as he complains of the lack of human warmth in the North while remembering with sensuous delight the feel of the red dust between his toes. The long revolutionary fresco called "Transcontinental" embraces Kentucky, Mississippi, and Tennessee in its sweep, noting the rich brown soil and the lynch mobs, and celebrating the Negro sharecroppers.

Wright's major fiction dealing with the South would deserve special treatment—not only the superb novellas in *Uncle Tom's Children* but also "Silt" (or "The Man Who Saw the Flood") evoking a desolate farmstead after a flood and the black tenant's resolve to go on, and "Almos' a Man" ("The Man Who Was Almost a Man"). Taken from the still unpublished novel "Tarbaby's Dawn," it told of the routine life and frustrations of a farmer's son who decides to ride the freights northward, much like Big Boy after the obsessive lynching, contrasting with the edenic innocence of southern nature at the opening of "Big Boy Leaves Home." During the same period, several books dealing with the South attracted Wright's attention as a reviewer: Erskine Caldwell's *Trouble in July*, Zora Neale Hurston's *Their Eyes Were Watching God*, Waters E. Turpin's *These Low Grounds*, as well as Harry Harrison Kroll's *I Was a Sharecropper*.

*Black Boy*, which was originally subtitled "A Record of Southern Childhood," did not take Wright farther than Memphis, Tennessee. In the same autobiographical vein, "How Jim Crow Feels" evoked a South that stood in contrast to the early impressions of the Mississippi countryside in *Black Boy* as well as to the poetical evocation of it in *Twelve Million Black Voices*. There, after taking potshots at continuing manifestations of racism in Mississippi, Wright turned to the economic slumber of the region, to the death-in-life of what he called a "swamp of black life":

True, the tall moss-hung oaks were still there, but somehow they reminded me now of cheap picture postcards. The broad yellow Mississippi still flowed, but its majesty no longer impressed me; indeed, it looked like a big, lazy ditch. . . . Fat pigs wallowed in the filthy front-yards of Negro laborers. Sparrows flounced in the dust of gutters. People moved and spoke slowly as if lacking bodily energy. . . . There was a persistently sour smell of earth around the backs of houses where dishwater was thrown out of windows, for there was no plumbing. Over the stench of outdoor privies came the scent of magnolia. The cooking was heavy and greasy and stayed on one's stomach for an ungodly number of hours. It rained often and the damp smell of vegetation always hung in the air. By day flies hummed, at night mosquitoes sang."[13]

The static quality of everyday life, including the landscape, offset the lyrical catalogues of Wright's early childhood discoveries of the natural world in *Black Boy:* "There was the vague sense of the infinite as I looked down upon the yellow dreaming waters of the Mississippi River from the verdant bluffs of Natchez. . . . There was the teasing and impossible desire to imitate the petty pride of sparrows wallowing and flouncing in the red dust of country roads. . . . There was the aching glory in masses of clouds burning gold and purple from an invisible sun. . . . There was the languor I felt when I heard green leaves rustling with a rainlike sound" (*BB*, 7) and "There was the love I had for the regality of the tall, moss-clad oaks" (*BB*, 8) and again: "There were the long, slow, drowzy days and nights of drizzling rain" (*BB*, 40). Moss-hung oaks, the broad, yellow Mississippi, sparrows flouncing—the happy connotations were all inverted in "How Jim Crow Feels" and flies and mosquitoes replaced bees and fireflies. Destined to prove that the poverty of Southern blacks should be no picturesque fare for the casual visitor, this negative picture also counteracted the most lyrical pages in *Twelve Million Black Voices:*

The land we till is beautiful, with red and black and brown clay, with fresh and hungry smells, with pine trees and palm trees, with rolling hills and swampy delta—an unbelievably fertile land. . . .

Our southern springs are filled with quiet noises and scenes of growth. Apple buds laugh into blossom. Honeysuckles creep up the sides of houses. Sunflowers nod in the hot fields. From mossy tree to mossy tree—oak, elm, willow, aspen, sycamore, dogwood, cedar, walnut, ash and hickory—bright green leaves jut from a million branches to form an awning that tries to shield and shade the earth. Blue and pink kites of small boys sail in the windy air. . . .

In summer the magnolia trees fill the countryside with sweet scent for long miles. Days are slumberous, and the skies are high and thronged with clouds that ride fast. At midday the sun blazes and bleaches the soil. Butterflies flit through the heat; wasps sing their sharp, straight lines; birds fluff and flounce, piping in querulous joy. Nights are covered with canopies, sometimes blue and sometimes black, canopies that sag low with ripe and nervous stars. The throaty boast of frogs momentarily drowns out the call and counter-call of crickets.

In autumn the land is afire with color. Red and brown leaves lift and flutter dryly, becoming entangled in the stiff grass and cornstalks. Cotton is picked and ginned; cane is crushed and its juice is simmered down into molasses; yams are grubbed out of the clay; hogs are slaughtered and cured in lingering smoke; corn is husked and ground into meal. At twilight the sky is full of wild geese winging ever southward and bats jerk through the air. At night, the winds blow free.

In winter the forests resound with the bite of steel axes eating into tall trees as men gather wood for the leaden days of cold. The guns of hunters snap and crack. Long days of rain come, and our swollen creeks rush to join a hundred rivers that wash across the land. . . . Occasionally the rivers leap their banks and leave new thick layers of silt to enrich the earth and then the look of the land is garish, bleak, suffused with a first-day stillness, strangeness, and awe.[14]

In this "Folk History of the Negro in the United States," which he wrote in 1940 and 1941, Wright could indulge in beautiful evocations of the southern countryside in general terms, because he was celebrating the days and works of the black farm workers, who then represented a vast percentage of the black American population. Yet he was well aware of the economic oppression they were undergoing. In fact, he evoked it in terms that are quite close to the image of his father as sharecropper and victim of a feudal system: "So our years pass within the web of a system we cannot beat. Years of fat meat and corn meal and sorghum molasses, years of plowing and hoeing and picking, years of sun and wind and rain— these are the years that do with us what they will, that form our past, shape our present, and loom ahead as the outline of our future" (TMBV, 41). Here Wright did not consistently depict southern whites as hostile potential lynchers prone to violence and hypocrisy. Although writing as a poet, he espoused a Marxist analysis of the economic situation: "Sometimes, fleetingly, like the rainbow that comes and vanishes in its coming, the wan faces of the poor whites make us think that perhaps we can join our hands with them and lift the weight of the Lords of the Land off our backs. But, before new meanings can bridge the chasm that has been long created between us, the poor whites are warned by the Lords of the Land that they must cast their destiny with their own color, that to make common cause with us is to threaten the foundation of civilization" (TMBV, 46).

Wright always tried to keep a balance between opposing representations of the South and of the North; the former was no charming, idyllic Eden and the latter no Canaan for the immigrants shocked by differences in customs or speech, "clipped Yankee phrases, phrases spoken with such rapidity and neutrality that we, with our slow ears, have difficulty in understanding (TMBY, 98). Only in retrospect could the South seem sweet to those who had left it for "Death on the City Pavements." The narrator of "Red Clay Blues" complained: "Pavement's hard on my feet, I'm tired o'this city street." Although city life offered unheard of racial and social freedom, the black migrants suffered from the colder relationships in the urban North, a theme Wright explored in *American Hunger,* the sequel to *Black Boy,* and in his early novel *Lawd Today* as well as in little known lines written in 1942:

Gone are the days when Negroes' hearts
Were ever light as air
Now we ain't got nobody
And no one gives a care
Gone de happy hours
—Someone give de pot a boost?—
Gone de black, old mammies
A-bossing o'er the roost
Gone de old plantation
For a filthy kitchenette.[15]

This was no return to the "plantation tradition" in literature but a humorous and disillusioned criticism of ghetto life. In the third section of *Twelve Million Black Voices,* Wright made plain the differences between North and South, not in terms of his own successful flight as a writer, but of the transition from rural or urban environment for the Negro masses: "We live amid swarms of people, yet there is a vast distance between people, a distance that words cannot bridge. No longer do our lives depend upon the soil, the sun, the rain, or the wind; we live by the grace of jobs and the brutal logic of jobs. We do not know this world or what makes it move. In the South, life was different; men spoke to you, cursed you, yelled at you, or killed you. The world moved by signs we knew. But here in the North cold forces hit you and push you. It is a word of *things*" (TMBV, 100).

It is necessary to dwell upon *Twelve Million Black Voices* for two reasons. First because it would be superfluous to consider extensively works that have attracted abundant critical study, like *Uncle Tom's Children, The Long Dream,* or *Black Boy.* Secondly, because nowhere else does Wright speak so authentically and so convincingly of his people as a community with cultural traditions and many faceted activities. When one turns to the oft-cited single paragraph in *Black Boy* that describes Wright's family (and implicitly the black community) in terms of cultural deprivation, one may well wonder whether he was not unfairly insensitive to black folk culture. Not so in *Twelve Million Black Voices,* where one arrives at the *global* idea of what he considered his racial cultural heritage. Though he was quick to see that Wright overlooked black traditions in *Black Boy,* Ralph Ellison was never mistaken as to where his friend really stood. He wrote, upon reading the book in 1941:

After reading your history—I knew it all already, all in my blood, bones, flesh; deepest memories and thoughts; those which are sacred and those which bring the bitterest agonies and most poignant remembrances and regrets—after reading it and experiencing the pictures, I was convinced that we, people of emotion, shall land the most telling strokes, the destructive-creative blows in the struggle. . . . I have known for a long time that you have suffered many things which I know, and that the truths which you have learned are Negro truths. . . . This past which filters through your book has always been tender and alive and aching within us. We are the ones who had no comforting amnesia of childhood, and for whom the trauma of passing from the country to the city of destruction brought no anesthesia of consciousness, but left our nerves peeled and quivering. . . . The book makes me feel a bitter pride which springs from the realization that, after all the brutalization, starvation and sufferings, we have begun to embrace the experience and master it.[16]

"Embracing the experience and mastering it," as Ellison phrased it, meant much more, although in a different way, to Wright the artist than it did to Wright the spokesman—the spokesman he had wanted to be in *Black Boy* "for the voiceless Negro children of the South" and the spokesman for the Afro-American group he would later become through the French press and the African and West Indian intellectuals around *Présence Africaine.*

Wright had embraced his southern experience mostly in the role of "The Man Who Went to Chicago" (as he called a short story derived from his autobiography), which was another way of saying "The Man Who Left the South." Yet he was not only a fugitive. In the cultural field, he did much to reclaim the southern heritage of blacks and made it known abroad. One such attempt was the synopsis for a film on the Fisk Jubilee Singers on which he collaborated with Arna Bontemps in the early 1940s; another minor instance was his blurbs for Leadbelly's blues records or his "Introduction to Some American Negro Folksongs" in *Présence Africaine* in 1949. He wrote:

The following examples of American Negro folksongs can still be heard today in many parts of the American Southland. They represent, together with the spirituals, the richest and most original fund of musical expression to be found in the New World. Many misguided authorities seek to explain these songs in terms of their obvious African heritage, thereby overlooking the strains and stresses to which the harsh environment of slavery in America subjected the personality of the Negro. . . . The history of the Negro in America is the history of an intensely practical people endowed with an extraordinary capacity for emotional expression; and an intense study of the story of the American Negro reveals how music and poetry came to be on this earth. As you read these lines you are hearing not only words of sorrow and joy from men who labor hard in the fields and mines for the bread they eat. It is no wonder, then, that 'John Henry' is one of the world's great ballads.[17]

Another of Wright's constant interests was the depiction of black life in the media and literature. Among the reviews he wrote, that on Caldwell's *Trouble in July* commended the novel for its treatment of the Negro as a victim of racist violence in the South.[18] He was even more appreciative of another southern writer rising above the pressures of her environment in her portrayal of the Negro. He commended Carson McCullers' *The Heart Is a Lonely Hunter* for "the astonishing humanity which enables a white writer, for the first time in American fiction, to handle Negro characters with as much ease and justice as those of her own race."[19] When Wright called McCullers "the first in American fiction to depict blacks with as much humanity as whites," he did not omit William Faulkner out of ignorance but for a reason. He had some reservations about Faulkner's definition of black humanity as "enduring," a notion Wright had opposed (possibly because he restricted it to physical and economic survival) in the episode in *Black Boy* concerning his relationship with his own father. When Faulkner was awarded the Nobel Prize in 1950, a Paris newspaper printed the following comments by Wright, which are quite revealing of his own vision of the South in American literature:

The achievement of Faulkner is all the more arresting as he is a southern white man, the product of a section of America which has withstood and nursed the stings of a Civil War defeat which it could never accept, and misinterpreted that defeat in the most infantile and emotional manner. The literature of the white South, as well as its public life, has been for almost a century under a pressure as intense and cruel as that under which the Negro was forced to live; and it would be a great mistake to feel that the Negro was the only victim of the white South's proud neurosis. The almost atavistic clinging to the "aristocracy of the skin"; the reduction of all life's values to the protection of white supremacy crippled not only the Negro but the entire culture of the whites themselves. . . . Southern American art fell under the interdiction of "protecting the reputation of the South" and no man save the hardiest dared challenge this standard. Talented and sensitive Southerners fled the section and those who remained brooded and accepted a scale of values which killed their souls.

But the South could not remain isolated forever; wars and convulsions of social change were bound to engulf it; industrialization induced such impersonal social relations that controls loosened and allowed a certain degree of negative freedom; and it was in this transition period of confusion that the genius of Faulkner leaped and presented itself to a startled world.[20]

Intent upon making Faulkner a product of his environment and, even by reacting against it, of southern ideology, Wright by no means begrudged universality to Faulkner's vision. In Wright's opinion, many of Faulkner's characters exerted efforts that led to no end "because so much of the energy of the South is spent fighting ghosts." Thus Popeye stood for "the rising tide of the soulless and industrial men who are beginning to swarm over the Southern scene"; thus Joe Christmas represented "the violence of the Southern Negro reacting against social pressures too strong for him." Yet, because of his themes as well as his technique, Faulkner's art could not be restricted to the South, due to the universality of violence, fear and confusion: "Faulkner in showing the degradation of the South, affirmed its essential humanity for America and for the world."[21] Somewhat surprisingly, Wright concluded by contrasting Senator Bilbo, the Mississippi politican who had inveighed against *Black Boy* in 1945, with the creator of Yoknapatawpha: "A Bilbo's hate-charged utterances will be forgotten but Faulkner's gallery of characters will live as long as men feel the need to know themselves."

In Wright's opinion, writing creatively about the South was a matter of art but it was also, because of its topic, a matter of human, moral and social concern. Wright could not forget he was black, which probably accounted for Faulkner's guarded comments on Wright's achievements:

> "There was one [Negro writer] who had a great deal of talent, named Richard Wright. He wrote one good book and then he went astray, he got too concerned in the difference between the Negro man and the white man and he stopped being a writer and became a Negro. Another one named Ellison has talent and so far he has managed to stay away from being a Negro he is still first a writer. And I think that he will go far, . . . but Wright, as I say, became more interested in being a Negro than in being a writer and that destroyed him. And the writer has got primarily to be a writer first, everything else must go by the board. Let him be a writer first; let him be honest, brave or whatever, but let him be a writer first."[22]

Being a Negro first, Wright was neither able nor willing to carve his own Yoknapatawpha out of a South that remained, at the time, predominantly under white rule. In other words, black culture in the South, although it had nourished southern culture for centuries, was far from being recognized on an equal footing. Thus Wright found it hard to speak of a black South except in terms of oppression undergone, exploitation, and bare survival. Out of the deliberately accepted constraints of place and time, Faulkner could invent a fictional world in which Mississippi became a threshold leading towards universality. But Wright's Mississippi offered no such possibility; it had been preempted by white supremacy and could only be, if not a living hell, a threshold towards a freedom to be achieved elsewhere—at best a territory to which Wright would return in imagination and fiction, albeit compulsively at times, but not in reality. Defining Wright as a writer "who left the South" (although he could never flee the private South in his own mind) makes him a literary relative of the Fugitives, those "talented and sensitive Southerners who fled the section" because they refused to accept "a scale of values which killed their souls."[23] This also makes him a black American writer, i.e., an embodiment of the archetypal black quest for freedom and literacy to be found in the early slave narratives, which probably consitutes the most resilient core of Afro-American literary tradition.

1. Interview with Michel Terrier, August 1969. The remark was made after a lecture at the Cité Universitaire in Paris in the late 1950s.

2. Interview with Arna Bontemps, March 1972.

3. *New Leader,* December 11, 1961, p. 24.

4. James Baldwin, *Nobody Knows My Name* (New York: Delta Books, 1962), p. 184.

5. James Bladwin, *Notes of a Native Son* (Boston: Beacon Press, 1955), p. 23.

6. Robert Stepto, *From Behind the Veil* (Urbana: University of Illinois Press, 1979), p. 138.

7. Richard Wright, *Black Boy* (New York: Harper & Bros., 1945), p. 52; hereafter all references are given in the text as *BB*.

8. Richard Wright, "How Jim Crow Feels," *True Magazine,* November 1946, p. 27.

9. He wanted to secure a birth certificate in case he should be drafted during World War II; *ibid.,* p. 28.

10. Richard Wright, *White Man, Listen* (New York: Doubleday, 1957), p. 86.

11. Richard Wright, interview in *L'Express* (Paris), August 18, 1960, pp. 22–23. Translation mine.

12. Richard Wright, summary of *The Long Dream,* Wright Archive, Yale University Library.

13. Wright, "How Jim Crow Feels," p. 27.

14. *Twelve Million Black Voices* (New York: Viking Press, 1941), pp. 32–34; hereafter cited as *TMBV.*

15. Wright was asked to write captions for the photographs reproduced with an extract from *Twelve Million Black Voices* published in *Coronet,* April 1942, pp. 77–79.

16. Ralph Ellison to Wright, November 3, 1941, unpublished letter quoted with the permission of the Beinecke Rare Book and Manuscript Library, Yale University. In the review he wrote for the *Antioch Review* in 1945, Ellison was rather critical of Wright's depiction of black cultural life in *Black Boy.* Reprinted as "Richard Wright's Blues" in *Shadow and Act* (New York: Signet, 1964), pp. 83–104.

17. Richard Wright, "Introducing Some American Negro Folksongs," *Presénce Africaine,* January 1949, p. 70.

18. Richard Wright, "Lynching Bee," *New Republic* 102 (March 11, 1940), p. 351.

19. Richard Wright, "Inner Landscape," *New Republic* 103 (August 4, 1940), p. 195.

20. Richard Wright, "L'Homme du Sud," *France-Etats-Unis* (December 1950), p. 2. Al-

though Wright's text appeared in French translation, he kept a carbon of the English original, now in the Wright Archive, Yale University Library.

21. *Ibid.*

22. William Faulkner, "William Faulkner in Japan: Their Questions and His Answers," *Esquire* (December 1948), p. 142. Wright had just published *The Long Dream*, but Faulkner was not necessarily referring to that work when he spoke of Wright being "more interested in being a Negro."

23. "L'Homme du Sud." Until the end of his life, Wright spoke of the traditional opposition between black and white Southerners. In a lecture, "The Negro Artist and Intellectual," delivered in Paris in November 1960, he noted:

I recalld the first day in my life when I, a Negro writer, sat in the office of a white publisher in New York. Edward C. Aswell, a Southerner from Nashville, had called me in after he had read an article of mine called "The Ethics of Living Jim Crow." A Southern black was facing a Southern white. A traditional enemy faced a traditional enemy. I sat, tensely waiting to hear my work castigated, waiting to be told that what I had written was only the product of a morbid Negro imagination. Mr. Aswell, one of the sharpest editors that America ever produced looked at me and smiled and said:

"Never has anybody spoken of this as you have."

I clamped my teeth. What was that? Praise? No, it couldn't be. Doubt assailed me. What had I done wrong in that article? What slip had I made? You see, never in my life had I dreamed that a Southern white man would openly admit that the reality of life of Negroes in the Deep South was a horror. And when I did hear it, I suspected a trick. I wondered if I had said something that was of a detrimental nature to my people: . . . . The first gesture of trust that ever came my way from a Southern white man almost scared me to death. Aswell gave me a contract for the book and I left the office with a check in my pocket. But my emotional check was almost dreamlike. (Unpublished typescript, Wright Archive, Yale University Library).

# From Tabloid to Myth:
## "The Man Who Lived Underground"

### I

ALWAYS interested in new ideas and conscious of his responsibilities as a black intellectual, Richard Wright must nevertheless be considered, when one delves into his fiction, primarily as a storyteller for whom a good narrative is valid for what it relates as much as for what it signifies. One constantly finds traces in him of the poor black child who owes his spiritual survival in racist Mississippi and, in part, his vocation as a writer to detective stories, popular fiction, and dime novels. Indeed, he was always drawn towards stories in which truth is stranger than fiction; and after bringing unlikely events into his novels, he took a sly pleasure in disclosing the authenticity of episodes which his bewildered readers had taken for wild fabrications.

We can easily imagine his delight when he came across, in the August 1941 issue of *True Detective*, "The Crime Hollywood Couldn't Believe," written by Hal Fletcher from the account given by Lt. C. W. Gains of the Los Angeles Police. One night in November, 1931, the sub-manager of the local branch of the Owl Drug Company had deposited eleven thousand dollars in the safe of his store, and, on opening the intact safe the following morning, the director had not found a trace of the money in it. As the two men were above all suspicion, and there was no sign of burglary, the mystery remained unsolved. Two weeks later, the safe of a clothing store—to which only the owner possessed the key—was emptied in the same way. Then there was an epidemic of thefts; linen, jewelry, typewriters, food, blankets, books, etc., disappeared by magic always in the same neighborhood. In the spring of the following year, the field of those mysterious thefts was transferred a few streets. Incredibly enough, the manager of the Baker Shoe Company, who had left two thousand dollars and twenty-six cents in his safe one fine night, found the two thousand dollars there but no sign of the twenty-six cents. Police rounds and surveillance produced no results until the following year, when, at the end of nine consecutive nights of watching in a store, a policeman saw an arm coming up out of the floor to turn the lock on a trapdoor. The arm disappeared when he tried to grab it, but this time a search of the basements revealed a hideout, which was well furnished with blankets, canned goods, and alcohol. At last in February, 1933, the police arrested Herbert C. Wright, white, thirty-three years old, and from a good family. He had seen sewermen at work and had decided to solve his problem of unemployment by building his world from their underground universe. He did not harbor any particular grudge against society, the magazine specified, and was perfectly sane.

Intrigued, the novelist immediately became interested in the motives of his strange namesake, who was still serving a ten-year sentence in the penitentiary. On October 27, 1941, he asked the governor of California for the record of prisoner number 55836, the details of which did not make the situation any clearer. The thief claimed to have been guided at times by his dead mother's voice when undertaking his burglaries and was seemingly proud of the names given to him by the press ("the human mole," "the tunnel burglar"). But he had done his best to help in returning the stolen objects and had not incurred any punishments in the penitentiary.

With these facts in hand, Richard Wright set to work, using as his guide the account in *True Detective*, which stressed the ingenuity of the burglar and the fact that he was perhaps motivated more by challenge than by gain, and which delighted in using images of dripping, dark labyrinths. In the autumn of 1941, he rapidly wrote 150 pages of a novel—since it was then a brief novel and not a short story—which he immediately turned over to his agent and friend, Paul Reynolds. On December 13 he wrote thanking him for having looked through the manuscript and emphasized the fact that it was "the first time [he had] tried to go beyond stories in black and white."

At that time, the narrative included a first section of seventy typewritten pages, which have remained unpublished: on his way home one Saturday night, a black servant finds himself arrested by policemen who drive him to the police station, take away his money, and by all sorts of brutal means and tortures try to make him confess to the murder of Mrs. Peabody. Fred Daniels can think only of his wife, who is about to have a baby, and of his great weariness. He signs a confession at dawn despite the fact that he is innocent. After the so-called reconstruction of the crime, he is brought back home where his wife, who is surprised and terrified, must be taken to the maternity hospital. Fred is taken there as well, and that is where he manages to escape through a window, running in the rain, hiding in entrance-halls until the providential opening of a manhole cover leads him to the underground world. Then followed the pages which make up the short story in its present form.

Reynolds attempted in vain to find a spot for the narrative in several magazines after Harper and Brothers had found it to be too short for a novel. In the spring of 1942, Wright allowed his friend Kerker Quinn to publish two excerpts of about ten pages—describing the scene in which Daniels papers his cave with dollar bills, rings, and watches—in *Accent*, a little magazine he was launching. Edwin Seaver, after trying to interest Harry Scherman of the Book-of-the-Month Club in it, finally published "The Man Who Lived Underground" in his anthology *Cross Section* in April of 1944. But it was then a novella of forty-six pages rather than a novel. The first two chapters and a part of the third had been cut out in order to have the story begin under rather mysterious circumstances after the descent into the sewers. The narrative was most likely cut down in that way to enable it to fit into the format of the anthology, but we do not know who cut it. Wright does not refer to this alteration in his correspondence, and Edwin Seaver confesses that he no longer has any recollection of it. The novelist was probably not opposed to this cut, since the symbolic significance of the narrative "beyond stories in black and white" was heightened by deleting the police brutalities inflicted on the innocent Negro.

The critics generally saw this short story as the most striking one in *Cross Section*, though not as the best. Sterling North wrote in the *Chicago Sun* of June 4, 1944 (sec. 5, p. 2): "As an enthusiastic Wright fan of several years standing, I may perhaps be permitted to point out that Wright is still doing variations on the same theme and is dangerously near J. Farrell's cul de sac." In the *New York Times* of May 28, 1944 (sec. 1, p. 14), Thomas Lyle Collins emphasized, without giving an opinion, "the morbid and disturbing analogy between the way white oppression forces the Negro psyche underground and this frightening narrative." Harry Hansen, who was more discerning, observed in the *New York World Telegram* of May 31: "No doubt Richard Wright had more in mind than the story of a criminal's escape. His Negro had a symbolical mission in his wayward flight from the inevitable. . . . But," he adds, "Wright is not a symbolist and [his] story stands or falls on the narrative, not on the suspected implications."

A large majority of the newspapers echoed the review by the American Negro press in which the critic saw the short story as a "denunciation of the white race" which he thought was to be found in Wright. The importance of the short story in Wright's career as a novelist was not felt at the time, partly because of the publication of *Black Boy*. This work created an image of Wright that was to become popular in the United States. His existentialism as it existed in the short story was neglected, and when it strongly reappeared in *The Outsider* in 1953, it was then considered, and wrongly so, more as being taken from the European literary fashion than as an original and strong tendency of Wright's. "The Man Who Lived Underground," which was reprinted once in 1945 and twice in 1956, had to appear in *Eight Men* in 1961 to reach a wider public which was capable of considering it in its true perspective.

## II

The short story is therefore situated in the heart of a culminating period in Wright's production, between the adaptation of *Native Son* and the composition of the unpublished novel *Black Hope* and *Twelve Million Black Voices* on one hand, and the birth of *Black Boy* on the other. All of these undertakings were more or less intermingled in Wright's mind at that time, and we can find slight or strong traces of these preoccupations in the short story. Thus, Daniels's employment as a servant and his relationship with his employer were certainly inspired by the research carried out for *Black Hope* in employment agencies or at the Domestic Workers' Union. The Clinton Brewer case afforded Wright with details of police brutality. Several elements seem to be drawn from *Native Son:* the running from the police, the feelings of the hunted man, the importance of food, the symbolic role of the rat and of the religious hymns, the basement furnace, the newspaper in which the fugitive reads about his case, his imitating the way people act in the movies, his precarious victory which is expressed as a defiance, and his final need to establish contact with the outside world. The dream about the drowning woman and baby the protagonist is unable to rescue is taken from the unpublished *Tarbaby* and is perhaps the echo of personal phantasms similar to those depicted in *Black Boy*. There is too close a resemblance between the jewelry shop and the optical company where Wright was humiliated by the white workers for the diamond theft not to seem like a transposed revenge. The situation of the underground man also comes from the satirical episode entitled "What You Don't Know Won't Hurt You," which expresses the bitter segregation experienced by Wright as an employee in the Michael Reese Hospital in Chicago in 1933.

Apropos of this experience of the underground, one wonders if Robert Bone is justified in seeing Dostoevsky's *Notes from Underground* as one of the sources of this short story and of Ralph Ellison's *Invisible Man.*[1] Wright was familiar with the Russian novelist's work; nevertheless, any influence from Dostoevsky's narrative proves to be negligible and limited to the situation of the man underground in the case of his short story. The Dostoevskian figure is endowed with acute sensitivity, and he is consumed by a burning hate at the memory of the humiliations he had suffered, but his dreams of revenge crumble because he is certain they are doomed to fail. Fred Daniels could not be characterized in this way, and Wright never uses his hero as a mouthpiece against the industrial society, nor does he consider him to be mad. The Dostoevskian man withdrew from the world out of spite; Wright's escapes from it by accident and wishes to return. He experiences no resentment at the memory of the cruelties he has suffered, but rather a feeling of superiority which is awakened in him by his metaphysical discoveries underground. Instead of seeking revenge, he tries to share them with his tormentors in an outburst of generosity. As for the situation of the man underground symbolizing that of the Negro in American society (and here Wright refers to his own experiences), the novelist has painted it in a perspective which is exactly opposed to Dostoevsky's: rather than brooding over past humiliations, he sees his exclusion more as an opportunity to scrutinize his culture from the outside.

Therefore, the underground rather clearly represents the marginal character of the black man's existence and his ambiguous rapport with American civilization. This short story stands at a kind of philosophic crossroads in the evolution of Wright's thinking, midway between *Native Son* and *The Outsider.* This appears in the intrigue as much as in the resonances of the narrative: Fred Daniels runs away from the police as does Bigger Thomas, and, in this sense, he does not voluntarily withdraw from society. But he prefers to "stay away" for the duration of the story in the same way as Cross Damon, when accidentally liberated from his past, chooses to remain on the fringe. And the gesture made to return is identical in both cases: Daniels does not succeed any more than does Bigger in securing the ties which anchor him to society. Nor will he succeed any more than Cross Damon who, on his deathbed, proclaims his fear of complete solitude. "The Man Who Lived Underground" has many features and details in common with *The Outsider:* their existentialist philosophy; the symbolic role of the church; the theme of the innocent victim; the criminal who needs the policeman, and their deep resemblance; and, above all, man's feeling of horror when, like Kurt, in *Heart of Darkness,* he examines the depths of his soul and his mortal state.

### III

Out of the authentic adventure in *True Detective* Wright has retained, along with the general plan, the disconcerting details which take the narrative out of the commonplace and not just the characteristics which would heighten its interest as a detective story. The novelist borrows the vicissitudes, suspense, and violence from this genre, but he transforms the questioning of the system which the theft represents into something more basic than questioning the aspects of ownership. Daniels is not a common thief. When he sees a trembling hand slip a roll of bank notes up a sleeve, he becomes indignant because "he felt that his stealing the money and the man's stealing the money were two entirely different things. He wanted to steal the money merely for the sensation involved in getting it, and he had no intention of spending a penny of it; but he knew that the man who was stealing it was going to spend it, perhaps for pleasure" (p. 53).[2]

The thief who wants to get rich quickly conforms to widely accepted social imperatives, breaking certain rules at the same time. But Daniels is a kind of revolutionary since his action is aimed at breaking social conventions. In this and many other passages, Wright's commentary sets the narrative in such a perspective. The action unfolds as in a detective film, but it is entirely different from a cops-and-robbers story, since the supposedly guilty person (not a criminal, only an amateur burglar) has discovered a new metaphysical rule in the social game, which enables him to define himself as being neither more nor less guilty than other men, who are often mere amateurs in comparison.

Such are Daniels's reactions to the punishments that his own malfeasance brings to other persons. He has absolutely no scruples about letting the shopboy be accused instead of him; at most he feels a vague contemptuous pity for him: "Perhaps the beating would bring to the boy's attention for the first time of his life the secret of his existence, the guilt that he could never get rid of" (p. 69).

It is the same for the watchman who "was not guilty of the crime of which he had been accused, but guilty just the same, had always been guilty" (p. 70). Thus the watchman appears as a reflection of Daniels, who felt guilty not only for having given in to the police brutalities, but for an original crime as well, for the same sin as the congregation singing in the basement church:

> He felt that their search for a happiness they could never find made them feel that they had committed some dreadful offense which they could not remember or understand. He was now in possession of the feeling that had gripped him when he had first come into the underground. . . . It seemed that one was always trying to remember a gigantic shock that had left a haunting impression upon one's body which one could not forget or shake off, but which had been forgotten by the conscious mind, creating in one's life a state of eternal anxiety (p. 68).

Here we reach the heart of Wright's metaphysical anxiety, the feeling of precariousness, of a diffuse and obscure guilt which he has strongly experienced since his childhood, and which he constantly seeks to interpret through the tools of Marxism or psychoanalysis.

In the framework of the narrative, we discover that this guilt is not within the province of the police or the law; on the contrary, it is such a basic psychological fact that it represents (in the Kantian sense) one of the forms of the human mind, the mark of our condition.

The terrestrial universe and the world underground are in fact posed like two sides of the same reality, separated by the thickness of a wall, a partition, or even a clouded window. We cannot suppose for an instant that the fugitive will be able to organize his universe independently of the other, nor that the everyday world will escape his searching look. Alone in his cave, Daniels tries to elaborate his universe in an ironical antithesis to what is considered the normal world. He would simply have to take it apart and invert the relationships. But whether he takes apart or reconstructs, Daniels is nonetheless prisoner of the preexisting relationships, because reversing a signification implies accepting its priority. It is impossible to create *ex ninilo,* to attain an independent, asocial perspective; the individual cannot elude his human and cultural heritage, since the metaphysical reality of the human condition seems to deny solitary existence.

After the lyrical episode where the cave is transformed by Daniels's artistic imagination and culminates in an assertion of his autonomy and defiance against society, the protagonist finds himself unsatisfied, burning with a strange fever, and prompted to return to the world. For the first time, he feels smothered by the walls which protect him from others. He has understood the necessity of human solidarity, not as much from a pragmatic or moral point of view as from a philosophical or existential perspective. This interdependence is the foundation of personal identity.

Indeed, life on earth is absurd, and it confuses appearances with a rational order. Its habits replace authentic perceptions to such a point that identity is continuously mistaken. A similar kind of logic leads the policeman to consider the night watchman's suicide as proof of his guilt. The truth of the imagination or of the unusual is constantly rejected, and Lawson (the son of the Law) concludes that it is necessary to shoot Daniels and "his kind. They'd wreck things" (p. 92).

The polarization of the two universes and their complementary elements thus functions on the moral and metaphysical levels simultaneously. From the first episode in the church, a change is operating on the hero's values. At the beginning of his action as a voyeur he feels embarrassed and guilty. But why? The juxtaposition of the foul-smelling sewer and the worshippers seeking God suggests a revolting contrast. Wright uses the term "obscene." There is an obscenity in the disparity between the actual situation of man and his aspirations, between the beast and the angel.

By going down into the sewer, Daniels was freed from his past. He was a victim, an innocent man who was declared guilty by the police and the law. Down below, through his gradual experience of irresponsibility associated with the invisibility which makes him omnipotent, he has, paradoxicaly enough, a deep feeling of guilt. He feels guilty for existing like any other man, but he is also guilty because he is apart and unable to remain a superman, beyond good and evil. Thus his return to the world above ground is justified on the moral level.

On the metaphysical level, his progress reflects a difficult acquisition of identity and poses the problem of the definition of man. We can see how gradually this identity appears. At first, the protagonist is designated simply as "he" by the omniscient narrator. His appearance is slowly defined; his race is given by contrast to the white man who looks at him; his physical strength is measured against the water's; his composure is seen against the sights he encounters—the rat, the dead baby, and the filthy sewer; he gives us his name by writing "freddaniels" on the typewriter; finally, when he returns above ground, his image appears in a mirror. However, a name has no meaning in the world underground, and the hero forgets his so completely that he is unable to state his identity when he turns himself in to the police. He has literally lost it, thereby becoming "the man who lived underground," a modern version of Everyman.

The identity that Daniels was seeking was neither personal nor racial, but rather a definition of man as a member of the human family. This is even more important than the rather obvious symbolism of the rebirth of man. We can surely find the myth of the old man and the new, which is transposed into images of childbirth. The sewer resembles the womb with its dripping dome and its multiple drains into which body fluids spout forth, and the newborn baby is carried. Returned to the maternal womb, man is recreated, charged with a new force, and then ejected. The image of man as the son of the earth remains less essential, however, than his definition as a gregarious animal. Daniels can acquire his identity only through others. A reflection of himself is not sufficient, nor is the fugitive replica found in the figure of the watchman. Daniels's one-sided view is ineffective, like words without dialogue. As Cross Damon says, man must "throw bridges between men." Even though we have deliberately held off from using the term until now, this is a brand of atheistic existentialism. Wright will bring it more clearly to light in *The Outsider.* He will explore its concepts in his introduction to *Black Metropolis,* borrowing from William James the notions of an "unguaranteed existence" and of hell as the supreme punishment because of its complete isolation. By this indirect manner "The Man Who Lived Underground" is related to *No Exit.* Sartre's words "Hell is others" are literally reversed, since, for Daniels, damnation is the absence of others.

Here we should point out the secondary nature of the racial situation. The protagonist's race most certainly plays a part in the plot. If his skin had not been dark, Daniels would not have been arrested and falsely accused, and, at the end of the story, the policemen would not have treated him in such a scornful manner. However, as in *The Outsider,* Wright is less interested here in the condition of the American Negro than in that of the individual in modern society. It is true that in the eyes of many the Negro is thought to be one of the last incarnations of authentic individuality and that the two categories tend to blend together. Nevertheless, an essentially racial interpretation of "The Man Who Lived Underground" as a fable of the Afro-American situation strikes us as being, if not exaggerated, at least too restrictive. Robert Bone starts correctly with the marginal situation of the black man but interprets too exclusively the sights viewed by Fred from behind the scenery as a series of vignettes depicting this racial situation. He sees the black congregation as representing religious segregation, the dead baby as the Negro rejected by American culture, the dead body on the embalmer's table as the black man emptied of his substance and transfused with the stereotyped vision of the white world.[3]

Wright is careful, however, not to indicate the race of the baby and the corpse, and it seems to us that such visions express, primarily and respectively, the irrational and shameful aspect of any religion, and the purely materialistic values of a pitiless society which kills its children and turns death into an industry. It is, above all, the situation of Daniels himself, who is followed and chased in a dark world (a dirty, evil-smelling character such as the white man imagines the Negro) and who is finally eliminated by the oppressive system, which is a parable of black life in America. Everything he sees constitutes more a view of Western civilization from behind the scenes than a picture of the black segregated world.

This is tantamount to saying that the protagonist's situation remains constantly existentialist as opposed to that of the other characters—existentialist because it is situated in the middle ground where the critical and exterior viewpoint merges with direct, immediate access. Excluding the black man from American society or putting Daniels between brackets in the sunless world places them in this situation at the outset. Here, the lower or underground position is less important than the exclusion or marginality. Setting the individual apart allows him to pass judgment in a more detached and perhaps objective manner on whatever he is excluded from. At the same time, it implies a certain invisibility of the individual whose personality is unrecognized. If he is not actually seen, he does not exist. The metaphysical bearing of this image of the black outsider is thus double. It presupposes superiority in his vision over the common vision, also the agony in his exclusion and the necessity to return, as Ralph Ellison in his turn admirably asserts in *Invisible Man*.

## IV

Without stretching the structure of the narrative, we can easily construe the underground adventure of Wright's hero as an existential parable, but also as a quasi-mythological quest that uses certain techniques such as are found in myths or folk narratives. We find obstacles to be overcome, a "sesame" or magical instrument, a guarded treasure, infractions and punishments, adverse destiny and protective divinity, going beyond the human condition and the fall that occurs after such hubris. It is even possible to show how certain episodes relate to the weird vision of the future as found in science fiction. The story makes us think, for example, of the beginning of H. P. Lovecraft's *Demons and Wonders:* by entering the cave, the imprudent person risks entering a different world where time takes on another dimension and whose rules defy those of his own. Here, the detailed, careful description of certain happenings (such as the slow burning of a match or the description of a hymn as a "feathery cadence") is enough to make everyday events appear out of the ordinary: this type of description is also effective in creating a constant state of suspense, the latter being more a question of feeling outside the natural sphere and incessant bewilderment than of intrigue. We often find ourselves on the other side of the mirror and think of Lewis Carroll; sometimes an insidious metamorphosis brings us even closer to Kafka. In this obscure world, eyes can no longer see, but fingers take on sight in such a way that Daniels's "fingers toy[ed] in space like the antennae of an insect" (p. 35). This abnormal perception of an environment, which seems unnatural to man, further increased the general impression of strangeness. Indeed, there is something monstrous, something fascinating, about the surroundings, such as the many-colored, muddy slime that swells up like boiling lava on another planet. Similarly, faced with the rites of the underground world, the spectator finds himself becoming vertiginously mesmerized by a vision of bottomless obscenity. In this world, the human voice is insignificant: the baby floating in a foamy halo that has blossomed out like a sinister bouquet utters a silent cry. However, on the other hand, things can speak. Thus, the objects hanging on the wall of the cave convey an angry message. In the end, the distraught man can no longer even understand the meaning behind his own desires and sensations: "His mind said no; his body said yes; and his mind could not understand his feelings. A low whine broke from him and he was in the act of uncoiling. . . . Like a frantic cat clutching a rag, he clung to the steel prongs . . ." (p. 73). The unnameable has reduced the rational being to a mere animal.

Strangeness, bewilderment, the supernatural—most of the elements of the fantastic are combined in this narrative. It would only require striking out several descriptions that are too explicit for us to imagine ourselves on another planet. But, just when we find ourselves being attracted to and summoned by the unreal, the author reintroduces realistic notation which prevents us from going off into an imaginary world. He compels his hero to rationalize things, to bring what seemed bizarre back down to familiar ground. When Daniels discovers a metal pole, some sewerman had to abandon it for its presence to be justified. When he finds himself in what he thinks is a cave, it is just an old, unused sewer. We might expect that the author was disciplined for too long a time in the realistic tradition to be able to free himself from it, but then, after reading several pages, we understand that the appeal of the narrative lies in this continual alternation between the mysterious and the commonplace (and an examination of the writer's successive drafts reveals, moreover, that such was his intention). Once we have accepted this imaginary world, we are not shocked by the strangest of episodes. Because we are continually obliged to question whether the fantastic is taking place, our sense of criticism cannot let up; Wright uses this tension to lead us to question the familiar, something we would refuse to do when reading a dreamlike tale.

## V

Thus, the narrative, having hesitated on the edge of the fantastic, wanders away from it. There is only one world, not two; what appeared at first to be out of the ordinary is really, on close view, just the reverse side of the everyday and made out of the same material. Clearing up the mystery amounts to the same thing as creating the world, and, by this indirect means, the underground exploration represents the process involved in developing a culture. This makes us think of Robinson Crusoe, for, after his drowning fall, Daniels resembles the castaway equipped with a few matches and his own ingenuity who first ensures his own survival and then builds up a civilization. Like Crusoe, Daniels is a kind of pioneer, a *homo faber*, the latter owing to the fact that tools are the key to the evolution of man: a metal pole, which becomes the extension of his arm; a rusty pipe, which turns into a crowbar and drill; and finally the precious toolbox, which he discovers in a basement. By way of engaging in conversation, Crusoe had his parrots; Daniels has a radio. Crusoe trimmed his quilled pen; Daniels patiently learns the necessary, ritualistic movements so that he eventually masters the technique well enough to type a single sentence. By typing this line, he has reinvented language and literature. Typing, here, represents more artistic creation than functional writing, for solitude allows one to do what one wants in a life which, in the beginning, consisted of merely ensuring one's survival and making use of the resources of one's surroundings. Daniels experiences both a Machiavellian and an innocent delight when handling precious objects: dollar bills smelling of fresh ink; the watches, now just something to look at because the hands no longer point to any real time; the rings, glittering in the light cast by the bulb; and the diamonds, sparkling like stardust fallen to the ground. Like a potentate and aesthete, Daniels enjoys a luxury that represents more than just the eccentricities of a millionaire, for he has forgone his desire to possess things in a world rid of economic value.

Thus, the hallucinatory scene in the cave, which is the climax of the short story, can be seen as the epiphany of artistic creation. Our underground Robinson Crusoe plays a game of scattering the diamonds by kicking the heap in which they are arranged in order to feel equal to God; mathematical certitude tells him that, as he walks back and forth in measured and blind pace, his shoes will, at a moment determined by the law of probability, hit the heap—hence demonstrating a freedom contingent on chance. Looking down in all his glory upon his universe, he reminds us of Bigger, the successful murderer, contemplating Chicago. But this Nietzsche-like Crusoe, who finds himself metaphorically on the opposite side of the starry dome above, has already made a tour of his island and its possibilities. Alone in his eerily lit cave, he mumbles the fateful words "Anything's right." Whereas Crusoe clung to the laws of the country he had lost, Daniels breaks all ties and comes to the conclusion that there is no providence. However, his solipsism horrifies him to the point that he will eventually return to civilization and expose himself to its dangers.

## VI

Whether studied as a detective story, myth, fantasy, or history of the creation of human values, this short story, owing to its cyclic, uncoiling action in which each projective stage calls for a similar retrograde stage, presents us with the same humanist message that says that man acquires his identity from other men. Alone, the individual can superimpose various masks and define himself by his aptitude in leading a protean type of life and in histrionics; however, he would not know how to define the criteria necessary to differentiate reality from roles and appearances. He plays his parts in succession. When the occasion arises, the hero, from his well-positioned perch, contemplates not only the nudity of the corpse but the nudity of souls as well. He is continually the invisible, transparent man. Eyes are so used to looking at him without seeing him that one person mistakes him for someone else and another can distinguish no more than his outline. When the couple comes into the grocery store, he sells them grapes, and his guise as salesboy hides him. He is the ghost that the young girl thought she saw. In the jewelry shop he becomes a thief. Finally, in the cave, he is actor and artist, listener and spectator, poet and God. But he plays his role so well and is so good at becoming or staying invisible that he is reduced to a mere apparition, and even his most creative ventures cannot give it form. The shift between what is real and what is imaginary lasts so long that we no longer know if reality actually exists or if it is reducible to a succession of appearances. Perhaps the ultimate question that Wright wanted to ask is not "Does man survive outside a society which forms and defines him while all the same oppressing him?" but rather "Does a reality exist in each person which is eternal and unalterable and which some call God?"

In this interplay of illusions, the story in all its ambiguity seems to be at the same time both its own subject-matter and an aim in itself. Appearing as a parable representing man's identity, the writing in fact becomes its own story and its reality exists as it unfolds before us. Almost everything that "The Man Who Lived Underground" relates about the nature of mankind could be applied to the nature of literary works. Just as Daniels needs a spectator in order to exist, so does fiction need a reader. Likewise, an individual reaches out towards his fellowmen, and a written work towards a public, and also towards all works in general, for it is by relation to them that the individual work is defined. It is at the heart (literally the geometric center and dramatic climax) of the narrative that we find a work written "en abyme." The short sentence "It was a long hot day," correctly and neatly typed, seems to be chosen out of the air, but it takes up again the beginning sentence in the first unpublished version of the novel and creates a strange feeling of infinitude by suggesting that a fictitious character writes his own fiction, creates his own being. Just the simple fact that man's assertion as an artist has been placed at the center of the work would be enough to prove how important the creative process and the result (here the short story) by which he becomes incarnate are in the eyes of Wright. Daniels's expedition is a literary trajectory "par excellence." His transformations and wanderings underground reflect the winding becoming of a work in the subconscious. Constrained by time, both come to find solipsism, which shatters their existence and hurls them towards others in order that they may exist. "The Man Who Lived Underground" thus also appears to be a parable of a literary work, since its narrative becomes a discourse on the narrative in general and, by implication, a discourse on literature in general. It is woven of this fluctuation between the known and the unexplored, so well illustrated by the protagonist's scuttling route. Like his acts, the work is gratuitous and disputable; like them, it bursts into fireworks and iridescently burns away as each facet sends out flashes that answer other flashes. Like the underground labyrinth, it is made up of uneven surfaces and reversals in direction, of obstacles and sudden illuminations, of premonitory visions and imperceptible cadences, of the familiar and the fantastic. Above all, it is like a periplus that comes around back to itself after being unwound by thin, successive, and transparent layers which reveal converging perspectives, unwound until alpha coincides with omega and a perfect circle is formed. While making this short circular journey, the narrative is being symbolically written—not as a genesis, but as a brief fulguration between life and death. Fred Daniels literally exists the duration of a short story, the span of a reading of forty-odd pages. During this passage of time, the various levels of the narrative are superimposed upon each other and mirrored ad infinitum. Then everything returns to the sphere of potentiality. The story ends with the image of man unjustly vanquished, carried away into the solitary entrails of the earth, like a dead, wandering planet. But we have only to again start reading for the narrative to resume its fleeting existence. And thus "The Man Who Lived Underground," owing to its splendid polyphony of meanings and its balanced precision, may be said to represent Wright's richest short piece, one woven of the same exacting pefection as a poem.

1. *The Negro Novel in America,* Rev. ed. (New Haven: Yale University Press, 1965), pp. 201–02. See also Robert Bone, *Richard Wright* (Minneapolis: University of Minnesota Press, 1969), p. 26. See n. 3.

2. All references are to Wright's *Eight Men* (Cleveland and New York: World Publishing Co., 1961).

3. Bone, pp. 26–29.

# "The Man Who Killed a Shadow":
# A Study in Compulsion

Throughout his career, Richard Wright appears to have been fascinated by psychology as well as the cultural determinants of violent criminal behavior. From the accidental shooting of the white cracker in "Big Boy Leaves Home" to the beheading of John Franklin by Babu, the African who wanted to see a white man rise from the dead, in "Man, God Ain't Like That," his fiction may be approached as an effort to explore man's homicidal impulse. As a consequence of his association with two psychiatrists, Dr. Fredrick Wertham and Dr. Benjamin Karpman, Wright's interest grew into a sort of passion in the 1940s. He spent days poring over case studies and gained enough knowledge about specific forms of deviance among blacks to anticipate present–day ethnopsychiatry, at least in the form practiced by Frantz Fanon who was, incidentally, an eager reader of Wright at the time he completed *Black Skin, White Masks.*

Written in 1946, "The Man Who Killed a Shadow" appeared in the Spring, 1949, issue of *Zero Magazine,*[1] which places it chronologically between "The Man Who Lived Underground" and *Savage Holiday,* two other stories based on criminal cases. "The Man Who Lived Underground" included many details from the Herbert C. Wright burglaries, using them as a springboard towards a superb surrealistic and existentialist fable.[2] *Savage Holiday* was inspired in part by the story of Clinton Brewer, a black jazz musician whom Wright had helped parole out of the Tombs prison where he had already spent decades for the murder of a woman.[3] It was attorney Charles H. Houston who drew the novelist's attention to the Julius Fisher case—on which "The Man Who Killed a Shadow" is based—in 1945. Fisher, a black janitor, had killed a white librarian, Miss Catherine Cooper Reardon, on March 1, 1944, in Washington, D.C. Indicted on six counts, he was found guilty of first-degree murder and robbery of a ten-dollar graduation ring. On June 29, 1944, he was sentenced to the electric chair. Houston, who represented him, immediately presented a motion for a new trial, and the case came before the U.S. Court of Appeals for the District of Columbia in early 1945. Engrossed by details of the crime, Wright at once set out to analyze Fisher's motives and to reconstruct the murder as a consequence of the traumas inflicted upon the black mind by white racial oppression.[4]

Wright wanted to make the story factually true. As a realist he felt this was requisite but he also felt that fact would surprise the reader. Thus, he reproduced documented material in order to substantiate fictional developments whose truthfulness might be questioned, as he did when the newspapers "questioned" Bigger's murder in *Native Son*. In "The Man Who Killed a Shadow," he scrupulously adhered to sequence and detail for the clinical, nearly scientific progress of his demonstration. Wright worked from some hundred pages of testimony and cross-examination records,[5] and it is possible to compare his sources with the fictional version. By so doing, I shall attempt to reveal Wright's method to assess how well he succeeded in accounting for the murderer's motives.

Obviously, Fisher's violent reactions were excessive when Miss Reardon had complained to him that he had not dusted her desk and then apparently called him a "black nigger." Not content with slapping her, Fisher reacted by breaking her skull, strangling her, and thrusting his knife into her throat. He took home her gold graduation ring, which had slipped from her finger but that would not have made robbery a motive since he had left her purse and belongings intact. His failure to conceal the crime or to flee, and claiming afterwards that he only wanted to silence her screams, not to harm her, led Houston, a competent lawyer, to look into the case from a psychiatric angle. Wright in turn tried to answer the question: why would a man like Fisher murder a white woman so savagely with so little provocation? He accordingly made choices which proceeded from his desire for rational hypothesis but which were also dictated by his desire to endow the case with an exemplary value.

Concerning the circumstances of the killing itself, most of the altercations were introduced by Wright in order to make Fisher's testimony more explicit and his (or rather, Saul Saunders's) motivations more coherent. From Fisher's initial testimony recorded by police officers in Government Exhibit 33, to his long retelling of the events after three counts of the indictment had been dropped, to his answers during the redirect and cross-examinations, Fisher's version did not much vary. Although the sequence of events became clearer under the prodding of his attorney, his motives seemed paradoxically more baffling.

Fisher, a janitor at the Washington National Cathedral in charge of cleaning the library, did not as a rule have much contact with Miss Reardon. About a week before the murder, she had complained about him to their employer, Mr. Berkeley, who had apparently told Fisher not to mind, that she was "half-cracked." On March 1, Fisher was dusting the shelves when she came in and, he said, "fooled around the desk for a few minutes."

> Then she asked me if I had dusted her desk and I said "yes." Then she said: "It certainly doesn't look like it." I walked out from behind the stacks and in front of her desk. I said: "I have dusted the desk. I always try to keep the place clean." She said: "No," that she had seen dust and dirt around her floor. Then she spoke up and said: "You black 'nigger,' you should be able to keep this place clean. That is what they are paying you for." I got angry at what she said. Then I smacked her. I felt like I got angry inside . . . No white person had ever called me a nigger before. I had been called that by my own colored people. I had never been called that before in an opprobrium, anger, or criticism. She ran out from behind her desk, down toward the back, screaming. I started upstairs to run up. The screaming seemed to have gotten on my nerves. I got scared and nervous. (Rec., 59)

It appears that Fisher did not even know the librarian's name before his arrest. Although they would occasionally speak to each other, he had not said anything to her about her complaint. Nor is there any allusion to her being "the crackpot" she becomes in Wright's story. Berkeley's testimony specified that he had described her to Fisher as "peculiar" and "hard," not "half-cracked."

In the short story, the tragedy reaches a point of no return when Saul slaps Miss Houseman's face and she starts screaming. From then on, his feelings and actions are but half-mechanical responses to the uninterrupted, shrill, nearly inhuman, noise which he attempts to stifle at all costs. By reiterating the word "scream" (some twenty-five times within a couple of pages), as well as related words like "shrill," "holler," and "yell," Wright vividly impresses upon the reader the effect the sound produced on Saul's nerves, frayed as they were after a night's drinking. Although it seems Wright is at his imaginative best here, he is only readly drawing heavily from Fisher's own account:

I started upstairs to run up. The screaming seemed to have gotten on my nerves. I got scared and nervous. I was running up the stairs with her all the time screaming. I got up to the top of the steps, the noise got so loud, it kept scaring me. I ran into the library, got the stick of wood, ran back downstairs and started to strike her with it. The stick broke. She was still screaming and I began choking her then. . . . When I struck her with the stick I was not trying to kill her, I was just trying to keep her from making a noise. When I began choking her, I was not trying to kill her; she started hollering and I tried to stop her from hollering . . . She stopped finally and I did not strike her anymore after the noise had ceased . . . While I was up there with the tissue paper cleaning the spots up the floor, she started hollering again. She kept hollering, seemed like to me. She kept trying to holler. I took out my knife and stuck it in her throat. My idea was just to keep her from hollering; is all I can think about. The noise kept on getting on my nerves. (Record, 59–60)

According to Fisher, he only wanted to stop the screaming. As the redirect examination made clear, Fisher tried at first to flee, but the scream brought him back: "I was moving all the time [running upstairs, then walking away in the main floor] but the noise kept seeming to pull me back . . . I got to the Library floor door first and it seemed that the noise got so loud I ran into the library and grabbed the stick of wood . . . and ran back downstairs." (Rec., 82)

Wright's problem lay in explaining Fisher/Saunders's panic in both cultural and psychoanalytical terms. He did so by viewing their personal conflict (she had called him a "nigger" and he had slapped her) in the context of the larger racial situation.

Any reader of *Native Son* will immediately remember that Bigger killed Mary Dalton without consciously meaning to. He smothered her in her bedroom because he was afraid of being caught in a situation already defined by racial and sexual taboos. He feared his presence would only be interpreted as a desire on his part to possess her (and this desire does exist, at least potentially). Bigger's reaction is logical in the context of his characterization, but Fisher evidently did not desire Miss Reardon nor feel any guilt before her; rather, he had reacted with proud indignation to her racial insult. His fear of the librarian's screams could not apparently be explained unless Wright resorted to another motive in his fictionalized version of the scene. Thus, the narrator of Saunders' story makes it quite clear that a white woman screaming in the presence of a black man could only mean trouble for him since it amounted to accusing him of attempted rape.

This generalization is introduced in a key paragraph in the story when the omniscient narrator's voice has faded into the protagonist's, so that the third-person account is no longer descriptive but evokes Saunders's half-formulated fears:

> Oh God! In her scream he heard the sirens of the police cars that hunted down black men in the Black Belts and he heard the shrill whistles of white cops running after black men and he felt again in one rush of emotion all the wild and bitter tales he had heard of how whites always got the black who did a crime and this woman was screaming as though he had raped her. (*Eight Men*, 202)

It should be noted that most of this theme had already been introduced eight pages earlier in an effort to build up Saul's background. Saul already knew that "if you were alone with a white woman and she screamed, it was as good as hearing your death sentence, for though you had done nothing, you would be killed" (EM, 196). As a result, Saul's predicament in the library is only the awful actualization of an ever-present possibility.

Both in terms of characterization and of the sequence of actions, Wright therefore endowed his protagonist with a psychological make-up that accounted for the killing more convincingly than Fisher's baffled assertions ever could. To that effect Wright constructed a black character who would respond appropriately to the dramatic confrontation while sticking as much as possible to Fisher's life story. What he did in effect was lower Saul's general emotional response, making him an automation of social responses, prone to compulsive outbursts of violence, rather than a person with complex and contradictory motives.

Admittedly, some of the discrepancies that exist between Fisher's story and Wright's short story are partly accounted for by the genre itself. Firstly, the record Wright had access to was not the stenographer's verbatim transcript of the trial but a condensed publication reporting answers often without their questions and sometimes summarizing the proceedings. Yet, it contained two key sources: the defendant's signed testimony, known as Government Exhibit 33, and his oral testimony at the trial, providing a resumé of his life and a detailed account of his actions on March 1–3, 1944. This was an invitation for Wright to pattern the novella as a life story, not as a constant dialogue as he did in "Man, God Ain't Like That." Fisher's own story began thus:

> I am thirty-two years of age, was born in Alexandria, Virginia, and my mother's name was Martha Bigsby Fisher. I do not remember her because I was too small when she died. My father's name was Norman Fisher and I do not

remember him because I was too small when he died. I was reared in King Street, Alexandria, by my grandmother. I have two sisters and five brothers. We did not all live with my grandmother; just a couple of them. I went to third grade in school, not all the way through it. (Rec., 57)

This probably did set the tone of Wright's narrative, yet Saul's story received a different emphasis:

Saul Saunders was born black in a little Southern town, not many miles from Washington . . . It so happened that Saul's mother was but a vague, shadowy thing to him, for she died long before his memory could form an image of her. And the same thing happened to Saul's father, who died before the boy could retain a clear picture of him in his mind . . . He had five brothers and sisters who remained strangers to him . . . It fell to Saul to live with his grandmother . . . Saul was not dumb but it took him seven years to reach third grade in school . . . it was quite normal in his environment . . . and Saul liked to be normal, liked being like other people. (EM, 194–95)

As befits the genre of the short story as well as Wright's desire to make this individual case into a representative example, place names are blurred.[6] In order to increase Saul's separateness, he is made a stranger to his siblings while his failure to remember his parents is expressed in terms of a kind of imagelessness, i.e., he perceives them as shadows. Moreover, Wright steps in to attribute to the protagonist some childhood experiences and feelings that he had reconstructed in *Black Boy*.[7] Indeed, Fisher's grandmother did not "move constantly from one small Southern town to another," and nothing indicated that "physical landscapes grew to have but little emotional meaning for the boy" (EM, 194)—but these phrases do apply to the Wright of *Black Boy*. The omniscient narrator also intrudes to explain that Saul's alienation stems from his being black in a world "split in two . . . the white one being separated from the black by a million psychological miles" (EM, 193). Here, the schizoid, social context serves to account for the protagonist's perception of the whites as "shadowy outlines," unreal to him and thus more easily obliterated. Saul is also endowed with Wright's existential fear: "a deprivation that evoked in him a sense of the transitory quality of life which always made him feel some invisible, inexplicable event was about to descend upon him" (EM, 194). Conversely, while Wright identifies with the protagonist, he projects him, as he did himself in *Black Boy*, as a typically deprived southern Negro youngster as far as his schooling is concerned (EM, 195).

As a result, there gradually emerges a type of personality consistent with Saunders's behavior at the critical moment and also with the way blacks as a whole can be brainwashed into accepting a white definition of themselves. Saunders learns to accept his subservient role, to check his suicidal tendencies, and to find release in heavy drinking; he represses his aggressive impulses and laughs off his tensions in the company of friends. Forced to underplay emotional attachment from the start, he casually marries a pretty girl who also likes to drink (this latter detail does not explicitly aply to Fisher). By stifling his feeling of being hemmed in and his anxiety about the unexpected, he maintains a precarious equilibrium under a rather complacent mask.

Admittedly, all this does not make Saul Saunders significantly different from Julius Fisher, whose life Charles Houston tries to save precisely on the grounds that chronic alcoholism had lowered his emotional response to people and that his psychopathic schizophrenia attenuated his full responsibility for the killing. But Wright deliberately describes this pathology as the alienating effects of oppression and racism. The story is therefore a didactic demonstration, which entails appropriate modifications in Fisher's career: when Fisher simply said he quit his job as a chauffeur and butler because Colonel Kellam refused to increase his ten-dollar-a-week salary, Wright adds a paragraph to stress the lack of understanding between the races. Even though they occasionally shared a drink, whisky only lured Saul into defining his employer as "a no good guy, a shadow" (EM, 197). Fisher's job as an exterminator is similarly manipulated: he was a "household fumigator," but he made no reference to killing rats nor to his satisfaction in destroying pests. Wright claims that Saul liked "seeing concrete evidence of his work and the dead bodies of rats were no shadows. They were real. He never felt better than when he was killing with the sanction of society" (EM, 198). Saul is made to resemble Bigger Thomas, the rat- and woman-killer who finds some degree of self-realization in murder. This vindicates the slaying of Miss Houseman but is rather inconsistent with Fisher's psychology. Also, there is no reference in Fisher's testimony to a dispute with his boss at the Capital Chemical Company, but Wright, creates this past history for Saunders in order to make him more likely to jump at the librarian when she abuses him.

By rendering Saunders predictable, by turning him into the end product of years of alienation and training, Wright does weaken his story, since the appeal of the case lay in its crude outbursts of puzzling violence. The suspense remains to a certain extent, but the sense of bafflement disappears in a rather too pat demonstration. Indeed, the narrative shapes

Saul's story into a sort of parable. Already summarized in the title, "The Man Who Killed a Shadow," the plot holds little surprise in store, apart from the circumstances of the killing or the nature of the shadow. The opening sentence itself answers the latter part of the question by defining the boy's shadows as "the shadows of his fears" and, a few lines later, as "the unreal white world" (EM, 193).

Since Wright planted enough hints in the narrative to announce a possible white female/black male confrontation, one may wonder whether it was really necessary for Wright to alter, as he did, so many details of the librarian's behavior.

Although the librarian is called "a little shadow woman" at the start, the story does not really cast her as such for the reader. She is very real, and aggressive. Calling her "a crack-pot" only foreshadows her somewhat neurotic behavior as well as endows it with possible sexual connotations.[8] By repeatedly staring at Saul (a fictional detail introduced by Wright), as though she were burning to ask him something, she makes Saul wonder "what the hell is wrong with that woman" (EM, 199). Wright also provides Maybelle Eva Houseman with the exact height and the approximate weight of Catherine Cooper Reardon and takes pains to further describe her as a blue-eyed blonde, i.e., the sterotyped glamorous American female.[9] He also changes her age from 37 to 40 in order to increase the likelihood of sexual repression supposedly attached to a quadragenarian spinster. Her Christian names are presumably selected as enhancing her feminine appeal: Eva recalls the Biblical temptress far more than the innocent child in *Uncle Tom's Cabin*. Maybelle, as everywhere else in Wright's fiction, connotes a sensuous, enticing, even promiscuous female.[10] In short, Wright deliberately makes the librarian into a protagonist both driven and inhibited by sex. The web of sexual connotations even extends from description to dialogue, when the librarian reproaches the janitor for not cleaning under her desk: her allusion to dirt and dust under the table not only serves to define her own behavior, but by asking Saul to check and look under it, she is implicitly inviting him to become a voyeur.

In short, Wright acts as though he were deciphering clues which might have been left out of the Fisher testimony. Or rather, the text appears to perform the trick of revealing a sort of Jamesian "figure in the carpet," a hidden, ugly design in this case, by weaving terms in a carefully connotative fashion rather than by straight denotation. The words employed to describe Miss Houseman's uneasy exhibitionism are carefully selected: her eyes are round, not so much in feigned innocence (although she pretends not to know what takes place below her waist) as in owl-like fascination while she sits with "her knees sprawled apart and her dress drawn halfway up . . . her white legs whose thighs thickened as they went to a V clothed in tight, sheer, pink panties" (EM, 200). The alliterative sequence of "thighs," "tight," and "thickened," the reptition of "thighs", "legs," "knees," and the recurrence of "apart," "naked," and "spread wide" all make Eva into a sexual object. She is reified, not by Saul's look, but by her own overwhelming desire which compels her body to act against her better judgment. The same petrified fascination unites Miss Houseman— "rigid, as though she was being impelled into an act which she did not want to perform" (EM, 200)—and Saunders, whose "mind protested against what his eyes saw." In other words, the white woman is driven by her body to act against (transgress) her cultural code while the black man is forced by the cultural code to act against (negate) his body. Here, transfixed, both of them meet in a sort of ecstatic stare. Both are compelled, though in opposite directions. Even if this is not deliberate on their part, their physical closeness makes their exchange a double entendre. When Saul says: "You're making trouble for me," he refers explicitly to her "complaining that I do not clean well" and implicitly to "provoking me sexually." He is also anticipating the trouble to come and indicating his responsibilities. On the other hand, when she says: "Why don't you do your work . . . that' what you are being paid for, you black nigger," she is explicitly refering to the janitor's duties but is implicitly telling him to play out the role of the supersexual black man. "Dirt and dust" are here ironically reversed since Miss Houseman seems to point to her own behavior as the dirt under the desk, while the paradigmatic opposition—white/clean/virgin versus black/nigger/dirty/sexually impure—also works as a satirical inversion. True to stereotypical white behavior, the librarian projects the darker part of her repressed self upon Saul. Even more than the suggestion of emotional intercourse when their eyes meet, Saul's reactions are somewhat surprising: of course, he is expected to have internalized the taboo concerning white women and to be afraid. Yet, like Bigger Thomas, Fishbelly Tucker and other Wrightian protagonists, Saul is expected to manifest some degree of sexual excitement and desire, which he never does. In the episode which precedes the killing, the black man's fear-without-desire is linguistically suggested by the description of the woman's open thighs; supposedly provided by the omniscient narrator, it really reflects the protagonist's narrowing range of vision. As the librarian sits with "her knees sprawled apart and her dress drawn halfway up," her legs appear to be "so wide apart that he felt that she was naked" (EM, 201). Then he realizes that "her legs were still spread wide and she was sitting as though about to spring upon him and throw her naked thighs about his body" (EM, 201). She is clearly the sexual assailant here, and the janitor a voyeur. Her assault is only verbal when she calls him a "black nigger," yet it is perceived as physical and rendered so. "As the insult sank in [is this a metaphor for the rape? Is the psychic wound a substitute for the sexual penetration Saul might want to commit but is forced to forego?], as he stared at her gaping thighs, he felt overwhelmed by a sense of wild danger" (EM, 201). Baffled, humiliated, and frightened to the point of having grown angry, Saunders responds only by slapping her "flat across her face." This is exactly what Fisher had done in response to the same insult, but his testimony and the court records contain no sexual undertones.

One wonders whether Wright's introduction of an episode so explicitly sexual is warranted. He is only of course making explicit the racial/sexual taboo. In a sense, then, the scene achieves greater dramatic force than a mere hint at its sexual connotations would have provided. As a result, it is easier for the reader to believe that the actual effect of the taboo was sufficient motivation for Fisher to have committed the murder. On the other hand, by placing too much stress on his sexual fears, Wright would be impairing his image as proud black man. Accordingly, Wright is careful to emphasize Saunders's own indignation by making the racial insult occur first. The insult thus coalesces with the sexual threat to evoke his violent reaction—in fact, he voices his indignation before slapping the librarian.

The text, however, simultaneously weaves a different chain of half-conscious reactions: first Miss Houseman violates Saul spiritually by as-serting her white female superiority while insulting him and mutely daring him to transgress the taboo. Second, Saul's fear of the *white* woman somewhat unexpectedly coincides with his fear of *woman*. Her "gaping thighs" threaten to swallow him; her scissorlike legs threaten to castrate him as if in a vivid dramatization of Freud's hypothesis about the "vaginal castration complex."[11] Although Saul's terror is ascribed earlier and later in the story to possible reprisals by white men who would castrate or lynch him for alleged rape, the actual episode describes it explicitly as sexual dread of the female. This evocation comes disturbingly close to certain traumatic experiences of Wright's childhood, suggesting how phantasms infused his writing, deliberately or unconsciously. If the

latter, we perceive how Wright used his subconscious creative imagination.[12] In either case, the episode bears the stamp of the author's idiosyncratic, semi-conscious responses to women rather than expressing
culturally imposed terrors of castration.

In other respects, too, Wright exaggerated certain details in Fisher's
testimony, obliterating others in order to suit these aims. In the coroner's
report Miss Reardon was described as clad in a pink dress, pink brassiere,
pink slip, and stockings. In the story "pink" always occurs in alliterative
couplings with "panties" (a more intimate term than "underpants," which
Fisher used), and there is no mention of the librarian's bra and stockings,
thereby implicitly enhancing her nakedness. When Saul's first impression—that "her legs were so far apart that he felt she was naked" (EM,
200)—becomes one of "naked thighs" (Em, 201), the result is that the very
real "tight, sheer, pink panties" also turn into "gaping thighs," i.e., her
wide open female organ.[13] Wright probably got the idea of the explicit
sexual confrontation—lacking in the court record—from Fisher's own unexpected use of his victim's underpants to swab the bloodstains on the
library floor. The impulse seems to have hit Fisher by chance:

> While I was taking her down, her dress flew up, ran up to her chest. I saw her
> underpants. I thought that would be a good thing to clean up that blood with. I
> got her down, pulled upside the wall and left her there. I came up, wet them
> under the faucet, went around cleaning the spots of blood on the floor. I threw
> her things back underneath there, where I left her body. (Rec., 61)

This may also have spurred Wright to stress the fact that the librarian
had not been raped, although the janitor saw her half-naked when he
pulled off her underpants.[14] Wright was apparently less interested in why
Fisher had used the panties as a swab (was it because of their texture?
their color? of the association between a woman's sex and bleeding? or a
way of marking the murder as a substitute rape?) preferring to emphasize
the fact that the forty-year-old librarian had died a virgin by placing the
coroner's statement at the end of his narrative. This served to explain her
sexual frustration *a posteriori* as well as to exonerate the black man of the
customary accusation of rape.

A close comparison between the records of the Fisher case and its
fictional rendering makes abundantly clear that Wright attempted a socio-
cultural motivation for the janitor's compulsive killing of the librarian.
The sort of parable he turned the case into suggests, however, a number
of somewhat conflicting lessons. On the one hand, the theme of the

shadows, consistently developed, leads to the conclusion that dehumanized and alienated individuals will cease to consider others as human beings and that their low emotional make-up easily leads them to bloody extremes. This conclusion adds little, however, to the message already delivered in *Native Son*. The obsessive reiteration of the words "shadow," "shadow-like," and "shadow world" (which, clustering in the opening and in the climactic scenes, recur more than thirty times) may be an effective metaphor to express Saul Saunders's schizophrenic tendencies, but it is hardly more effective than his dream of watching a film after the killing.[15]

As the narrative gathers dramatic impetus during Saunders's violent confrontation with the librarian, another message comes to the fore, which had already been didactically hinted at in an earlier episode: given the sexual/racial taboos, any white woman means danger for a black man, and it is not surprising that black men react erractically in the presence of a white woman. Moreover, towards the end of the story, still another lesson (implied in an earlier scene) emerges: the black man, in fact, cannot perform effectively the role of the rapist into which white lust and guilt have cast him; rather, he feels castrated. This in essence is Wright's major theme. Although the psychological distance between the races is emblematically stressed and made an essential component of the protagonist's background, the "shadow" motif soon yields to a didactic debunking of the racist stereotype of the black male as sexual aggressor. Whereas the shadow motif is evoked largely through allusion and inference, the dramatic climax forcefully establishes the compelling image of the white woman as a siren: she stands both for the mythological temptress and the shrill symbol of modern police repression; in either role, she means trouble. This is the point in the powerful central scene, yet it does not elucidate Fisher's real motivation. Wright simply creates a fictional character who embodies one possible logic of motivation, emphasizing sexual fear to the detriment of the racial insult. In so doing, Wright's creative imagination molds Fisher's story into yet another variant of his major (should one say, "compulsive"?) themes: fear and flight; the white world as a nonhuman force, be it fog, mountain, sea, or a shadow world; black self-realization through violence and within the context of a typical black man/white woman confrontation; female sexuality as a threat to man. It is no mere coincidence that such a confrontation appears consistently throughout Wright's fiction: we observe, for example, the accidental predicament of Big Boy in *Uncle Tom's Children* develop into a trap set by the police to frame Fishbelly in *The Long Dream.* Given such a perspective, "The Man Who Killed a Shadow" represents a negative step to psychological liberation, not unlike the attitude of the protagonist in "Down by the Riverside," who believes that he cannot escape white power. Later, *The Outsider* and, above all, *The Long Dream* will suggest flight and double-dealing as alternatives to white violence. In this story, however, the murderer is simply another innocent victim—the victim of a cultural code built into his very personality by the society which shaped him and for which this society is ultimately responsible.

This story is no sequel to the heroic perspective of black activism envisioned in "Bright and Morning Star" but another exploration in social pathology or ethnopsychiatry somewhat akin to "The Man Who Lived Underground." It does not aim at building up ethnic morale but at exploring the mysteries of criminal conduct. That it should contain so much compelling power is not due to Wright's reliance on the details of an actual case but to the unexpected fashion in which his prose manages to affect our buried consciousnesses with puzzling, intermingling, archetypal figures of men and women, blood and terror, sex and death.

1. A French translation was published in *Les Lettres Françaises* as early as October, 1946.
2. See my "From Tabloid to Myth: The Man Who Lived Underground," reprinted in this volume.
3. See Michel Fabre, *The Unfinished Quest of Richard Wright* (New York: William Morrow, 1973), pp. 236–37, 377–78.
4. A hand-written draft in the Wright Archive at Yale establishes such an intent.
5. This was printed under the title, "District of Columbia, U.S. Court of Appeals, Case No. 8809, January term, 1945."
6. In the original version, Wright retained the actual date, "March 1, 1944," probably to emphasize how persistent the effects of the racial/sexual taboo still were at the time. The date was changed to "19—" when the story was collected in *Eight Men* (Cleveland and New York: World Pub. Co.) in 1961.
7. Compare this with the following passage in *Black Boy:* "My mother's suffering grew into a symbol in my mind, gathering to itself all the poverty, the ignorance, the helplessness; the baffling, hunger-ridden days and hours; the restless moving, the futile seeking, the uncertainty, the fear, the dread; the meaningless pain and the endless suffering. At the age of twelve I had an attitude towards life that was to endure." *Black Boy* (New York: Harper & Bros., 1945), p. 87 Whether or not Wright's autobiography conveys an accurate picture of his state of mind at the age of twelve, he clearly applies this re-creation of his own psychological make-up to a protagonist who is both as real and as fictional as the young Wright.
8. "Crackpot," which is never used by Fisher, does indeed have a sexual connotation through "crack" and such compounds as "fleshpot" or "honey pot."
9. The blue eyes, white skin, and beet face connote the national tri-color and make the woman into a symbol of white America. Ralph Ellison's use of a blond strip-teaser in the Battle Royal scene of *Invisible Man* is close to Wright's, but more complex. The wealthy (white) American nation is equated to an enticing bitch, a symbol LeRoi Jones develops in his turn in *Dutchman.*

10. The wife of a Communist leader, herself a white liberal artist and the somewhat naïve lover of the black protagonist Cross Damon (who always alludes to her as "woman as the body of woman"), is called Eva in *The Outsider*. The promiscuous white female protagonist in *Savage Holiday*, whom Erskine Fowler accuses of being a whore, although he ardently desires her, is called Mabel Blake. There is a sensual Negro girl, Maybelle, in *The Long Dream*. Houseman may have been inspired by John Houseman who helped produce *Native Son*. A more revealing and satisfactory accounting for the choice of these names is provided by their Freudian associations. Eve is the first woman, the incarnation of womanhood and the perpetrator of sex as original sin; Ma(y)-bel(le) easily means "ma"/"belle," i.e., beautiful mother, whose meaning is made clearer by "house-man": the house/home/haven of man, i.e., the womb when he came and where he aspires to enter. The womb of the sex, of woman/the mother is both threatening and appealing, forbidden and desired. In his study, "The Man with the Wolves," Freud speaks of the mother as symbolized by a house.

11. Wright was conversant enough with the Freudian theory to have attempted an allusion to the castration complex and *vagina dentata*; on the other hand, even if he consciously alluded to such concepts, much of the force of his description seems to come from deep-seated, semi-conscious impulses rooted in his own past.

12. Wright described comparable childhood experiences in some detail in an earlier version of his autobiography. He was about eight when a cousin of his mother's asked him to look at her sex and touch it; this evoked in him, he claims, an indescribable terror. He also relates an episode in which, at the age of twelve, he could not take his eyes off the crotch and panties of a Negro girl exposing herself to a bunch of youngsters in a train carriage (see Fabre, *The Unfinished Quest of Richard Wright*). These remembrances were deleted from the final version of *Black Boy*.

13. "Sheer" primarily means "translucent," "transparent" giving the illusion of naked sex. It also means "abrupt," "clearcut," and this "cutting" undertone, reinforced by the homophonic "shear(s)," an equivalent of "scissors," also connotes castration.

14. Both in the Court Report and in the story, it is stressed that the "decedent had not been criminally assaulted or attempted to be entered" and that her "hymen ring was intact." Thus, in the story, the castration of Saul and the rape of Eva are symbolic. Yet, through close association with the word "ring" (the ring Saul takes with him and the hymen ring), the woman seems to lose more than her life.

15. "When at last the conviction of what he had done was real to him, it came only in terms of flat memory, devoid of all emotion, as though he were looking when very tired and sleepy at a scene flashed upon the screen of a movie house." (EM, 205) In "The Man Who Lived Underground," Fred Daniels's feelings of unreality in the movie house he crossed like a sleepwalker echo Bigger Thomas's feelings about the unreality of his own life as he watched films on the silver screen.

# Fantasies and Style
# in Wright's Fiction

JUST after the publication of *Native Son*, Richard Wright accepted, on the request of his friend, the psychiatrist Frederic Wertham, an analysis permitting, by means of free association, recovery of some unconscious elements which had played a determining role in the novel's genesis. Wertham published the results of his work under the title "An Unconscious Determinant in *Native Son*," in *The Journal of Abnormal Psychology*, July, 1944.

One of Wertham's discoveries serves us as a point of departure, not so much to explain certain writing processes by reference to the novelist's traumatic past as to investigate the symbolic and stylistic structure of certain episodes by connecting them to scenes of comparable configurations lived by Wright.

Just as in the tragedy of *Hamlet*, where one of the crucial scenes is the appearance of a paternal spectre in the room of Queen Gertrude, the key scene of Wright's novel is the accidental death of Mary, brought about by Bigger in the presence of her mother. In the course of his analysis, some associations became available to Wright, referring back to an episode that he had experienced as a fifteen-year old. But it was only some months later that Wright recollected fully those experiences and recognized them. In other words, these fundamental experiences, intimately tied to the key scene of the novel, were not available to Wright's consciousness at the time when he wrote *Native Son*, nor even at the beginning of the analysis specifically focusing on the sources which had inspired his creation of the fictional Dalton family.

At the age of fifteen, Wright worked before and after school for a white family which he called Bibbs in *Black Boy*. Mrs. Bibbs, who lived with her husband and her mother, was a beautiful young woman who showed Richard a certain affection, so that his employer's house was almost a second home to him. Like Bigger in the Dalton house, Richard took care of the heating, cut wood, carried buckets of coal, lit the fire and stocked the fireplace. But one morning as he was carrying some fuel, he opened the bedroom door without knocking and surprised the mistress of the house in the process of dressing. She was greatly annoyed and she reprimanded him severely, demanding that he knock before entering.

It is easy to see how this scene relates to one where Bigger, charged with taking care of the heating, goes into the "forbidden" room of Mary. But in the analysis, that scene itself was related to others occurring quite a bit earlier: in particular, Wright uncovered the memory of a trip in the company of his mother across a park reserved for whites; the young boy saw a young nude Mexican in the middle of a group of children. The severe commentaries of his mother immediately associated nudity with guilt. Other memories of the same kind, which Wertham does not mention, date back to the fourth year of Wright's life.

In light of these underlying experiences, it appears that Mrs. Dalton plays a crucial role; she is blind but guesses that something unusual happens when Bigger tries to keep Mary from crying. Even blind, the eye which scrutinizes the secret actions of the protagonist is that of the mother. Mrs. Dalton is incapable of perceiving differences between the races or refusing to do so; but what dominates is the mother's face, omniscient and reproachful, when the adolescent violates a sexual/racial prohibition.

This analysis scientifically establishes connections between the author's life and the inspiration for his fiction; yet we will not attempt a disguised psychoanalysis of Wright. Instead we will explore associations which structure, in certain key scenes of his novels, some situations of confrontation that resemble traumatic episodes. If we consider some scenes which occur near a fireplace, fire, or furnace, we see that they bring together some elements and characters and place them. The scene often takes place in the presence of a woman, often young, beautiful, and normally friendly, but whose compassion becomes transformed into reprobation or indignation when a black adolescent accidently violates her intimacy; sometimes a maternal figure appears in the background, symbolizing prohibitions, but this figure sometimes coincides with that of the woman. On the other hand, the scene establishes some specific roles: the mistress of the house, the colored domestic charged with the fire. It defines the places: the house, the bedroom, the room where the fireplace is located. It involves certain details: fluffy feminine clothes, white colors, etc. It also creates an affective tonality which connects, among other things, voyeurism, nudity, guilt, racial and sexual prohibitions, and woman and mother as objects of desire and as authors of disapproval.

Starting, therefore, from the fireplace or the furnace, we notice that the presence of a fireplace in the room reveals a curious similarity between an episode in *Black Boy* and one in *The Outsider*. In *Black Boy*, Wright describes his father laughing while standing next to his mistress when Wright goes, in the company of his mother, to ask him for money. That this more authentic than fictional scene, drawn from the autobiography, depicts an infantile trauma is of only relative importance. What is stylistically striking is the connection between the fire, which flames in a semidarkness, and a feeling of mysterious obscenity, which is not accounted for by the possible connotation, at the symbolic level, of an infernal context.

In the rough draft of his autobiography, Wright is content to write, "I heard vague phrases of another woman but I was too young for them to mean much," (Wright Archive, Yale University Library. Wright 2) but in *Black Boy* we read:

> My father and a strange woman were sitting before a bright fire that blazed in a grate. My mother and I were standing about six feet away. . . . The woman laughed and threw her arms about my father's neck. I grew ashamed and wanted to leave. . . .
>
> We left. I had the feeling I had to do with something unclean. Many times in the years after that the image of my father and the strange woman, their faces lit by the dancing flames, would surge up in my imagination so vivid and strong that I felt I could reach out and touch it; I would stare at it, feeling that it possessed some vital meaning which always eluded me (pp. 29–30).*

A blaze in the fireplace, a dark-red glow, and dancing shadows are found together again in *The Outsider* when Blount, the reactionary, and Gil, the communist, fight: "Gil . . . . fell headlong towards the fireplace where flames danced and cast wild red shadows over the walls." (p. 208) But Cross, witness to the scene, "had stood amidst those red and flickering shadows, consumed with cold rage" (p. 212) and, shortly after, he felt a sensation of disgust: "Their brutal strivings had struck him as being obscene." (p. 218) Is this a simple coincidence? Even momentarily illuminating flames in the subterranean half light of "The Man Who Lived Underground" are enough to transform water into blood; these are the same flames which, in the Daltons' basement, turned Mary's decapitated body into a purple shroud. The red and the black, or the dark red, thus clothes a violence involved in the unbridling of forbidden sexuality. In

"Tarbaby's Dawn," this is exemplified by the crackling fire in the fireplace and the taking of Mary by Dan in the dark living room to a rhythm alluded to in terms of "dark red." In *Savage Holiday,* these terms translate the excitement which mastered Fowler just before he kills Mabel Black: "His face flamed dark red" (p. 199), because he just caught a glimpse of her thigh and her bare breast. The flame which roars and casts crimson reflections connotes the rising of desire in the face of surprised nudity like the rise of indignation against obscenity.

In the broadest symbolic system, fire often appears tied to prohibition, for example in the Promethean myth, implied by the presence of the fire on the first pages of *Black Boy:*

> One winter morning in the long-ago, four-year-old days of my life, I found myself standing before a fireplace, warming my hands over a mound of glowing coals. . . . I crossed restlessly to the window and pushed back the fluffy white curtains, which I had been forbidden to touch. . . . I was dreaming of running . . . . but the vivid image of Granny's old, white, wrinkled, grim face lying upon a huge feather pillow, made me afraid (p. 3).

In some previous drafts we find "a hot red fire glows in the grate" and: "A coal fire burned in the room, red embers glowed with powerful heat. I would look out of the window a while at the bleakness of the southern winter day, and then stand again in front of the fire, fascinated by it." (Wright Archives, Yale University Library. Wright 2.) As much as the fascination, what matters here is the constellation of details (a coal fire, a red glow, a white woman in a bed, a fluffy screen, a prohibition) which echo the scene in Mrs. Bibbs' house, the scene in Mary's bedroom, and the scene in the Daltons' furnace room.

Whether it is coal which burns in *Black Boy,* "Tarbaby" or *Native Son,* or some other substance, makes no difference. Those little black pebbles which Wright was collecting between the rails at Memphis connote at the same time the color black, the cave or the underground, and the railroad, among others. This image appears in the central dream of Bigger and in one of the numerous nightmares evoked in *The Long Dream:* having surprised his father in the process of playing "train" with a female customer, Fishbelly dreams of trains that puff and blow showers of sparks and he becomes frightened: "Papa! Papa! and he crouched in a corner of the cab nestling into a heap of glistening coal feeling that he had done something terribly wrong and was going to be whipped for it" (pp. 27–28). After having lost his virginity in the arms of Maud, Fish again dreams that he is a train-stoker:

> He was shoveling coal into a roaring firebox and feeling the runaway locomotive rocking, careening . . . . he shoveled the shining lumps throwing them onto the glowing seething bed . . . . and when he scooped up coal the lumps rolled away and he saw the legs body face of a naked white woman smiling demurely at him . . . . he scooped coal being careful not to touch the naked white woman and he was terrified as she seized hold of his shovel and smiled at him (p. 158).

Then Fish dreams that he is going out of the cabin when he sees Maud, smiling, who says to him: "Honey, you know better 'n to try to hide a white woman in a coal pile like that. They was sure to find her" (p. 159). Certainly the references to ethnic folklore, like "the nigger in the coal pile" or all the quasimythical attraction of the railroad are at the base of these symbols in this narration, but, at the subconscious level we really witness the resumption of the furnace episode in *Native Son*. After the murder, Bigger dreamed that he was running on a street paved with coal:

> His shoes kicked tiny lumps rattling against tin cans and he knew that very soon he had to find some place to hide but there was no place and in front of him white people were coming to ask about the head. . . . and he gave up and stood in the middle of the street in the red darkness and cursed the booming bell and the white people and felt that he did not give a damn what happened to him and when the people closed in he hurled the bloody head squarely into their faces *dongdongdong* (p. 141).

The coal and the red half-light are associated with desire and with the white woman who is forbidden or who is violated by murder. In the constellation of sensory impressions, the rhythmical beating of a clock or the puffing of a train also will connect many scenes of this type. This broken and rhythmical movement can be found in almost all of Wright's fiction: it is the chouchou of the train that carries Daniel north in "Tarbaby" or "Almos' A Man." It is, in *The Long Dream*, "that pounding sound, charged with an urgent significance, beating out of the darkness upon his ears: *bumpbump, bumpbump, bumpbump*" (p. 23) which leads Fish to ask his father what he was doing with the woman and to dream of "parting trains that roared yammeringly over farflung, gleaming rails only to come to limp and convulsive halts" (p. 27). In *Savage Holiday*, little Tony's drum rolls on the neighboring balcony prevent Fowler from sleeping and inspire erotic and terrifying dreams.

In "Long Black Song," the slow rhythm of Sarah's life, modeled on natural cycles, accelerates like the blows which her little girl strikes on the old clock when desire wells up in her veins: "till a red wave of hotness drowned her in a deluge of silver and blue and boiled her blood and blistered her flesh *bangbangbang.*" (*UTC*, p. 135) The blood beating in the temples, the broken hammering, and the ebb and flow of desire are thus tied to the clacking of bogies on rails (we will see how the trip on the railroad in the autobiography or *The Outsider* or in the subway in *Lawd Today* are connected to another traumatic scene). They are tied to the beating of a drum: to that of little Tony in *Savage Holiday*, to that which his father forbids young Richard to play (unpublished episode of *Black Boy*. J. W. J. Wright 2–3), to that of the Garveyist parade which Jake watches in *Lawd Today*, as well as to his work at the post office and to the rhythms of jazz in the nightclubs where he lets go: "Round black inkpads scentered the air with a sharp, fresh, smell like that of raw meat . . . He began stamping . . . Bompbomp, bompbomp, bompbomp." (p. 129) and "Black and across the room, they swayed like trees bending in strong winds. Feet went thrumpthrump, thrumpthrump, thrumpthrump. "Shake that thing!" somebody yelled (p. 169).

Returning to the key scene which was our point of departure, the connotations of the log (let's not forget that Richard was charged with cutting the wood and stocking the wood-house) are as important as those of coal. In the dreams of the protagonists, a log and an ax are often found tied to some actions corresponding to a violent invasion of a room. In "The Man Who Killed a Shadow," the reality of the Fisher case corresponded, even beyond the expectations of Wright, to his own fantasies and how little he had to modify the facts (see " 'The Man Who Killed a Shadow:' A Study in Compulsion, reprinted in this volume). Saul, the murderer, is a handyman in charge of sweeping and preparing the fire: when the immodest white librarian unleashes in him terror which compels him to kill her, he immediately seizes a log in the fireplace. Note that the broken foot of a table will furnish Cross with the same type of weapon to finish off Gill and Herndon in *The Outsider*. An ax appears in some identical contexts: at the opportune moment, Bigger discovers one in the basement in order to decapitate Mary. In "Down by the Riverside," it is disturbing to see how much Mann repeats, in some fashion, the intrusion of the black servant: he breaks into Mrs. Heartfield's bedroom with the rescue team to pull the family out from the flood, but the scene is really one of violated intimacy:

> He saw a broken chair: strewn clothing: a smashed dresser: a tumbled bed: then a circle of red hair and a white face. Mrs. Heartfield sat against the wall, her arms about her two children. her eyes were closed (*UTC*, p. 110).

When the Heartfield son recognizes him as the murderer of his father and begins to shout, Mann raises his weapon to strike, just as Saul does in "The Man Who Killed A Shadow," in order to obliterate the denunciating cry, but the house collapses and is carried away by the flood.

The ax-man appears in the nightmare in which Fowler hears the most beautiful trees of his forest fall—"whack, whack, whack, someone was in the forest chopping down one of his trees," (SH, p. 36) the sound of the ax being induced by Tony's drum. The woodcutter is transformed into a "cleaver-man" in "The Man Who Lived Underground": after having seen a butcher's aid cut up his meat, Daniels secures a bloody chopping-knife which fascinates him. And the weapon immediately seems to give birth to the imaginary situation: a little later, a white employee perceives the fugitive just opening the door of the office and a cry freezes at once in her throat. The chopping-knife, finally becomes a knife in other scenes of aggression to which we will return.

Let's return to our beginning key scene and to the suffocation of Mary in her bedroom in order to emphasize the role of descriptive details. Whether cave or basement, the place where combustibles are stored corresponds to the lower regions of the subconscious, to the deepest instincts; the bedroom (the woman's room) is a sanctuary defiled by Bigger's intrusion at Mary's house and by Richard's at Mrs. Bibbs' house. In most of the scenes of this type the intrusion is really a violent invasion of the bedroom and emphasizes the voyeuristic position of the intruder. Leaving aside for the time being the child who sees a couple making love, note that to surprise a nude white woman (or inversely, to allow oneself to be surprised nude by her as in "Big Boy Leaves Home") signifies the risk of being accused of rape and being lynched. The narrator explicitly makes this known in Native Son, "The Man Who Killed A Shadow," and The Long Dream—and the plot often corroborates their fears. In The Long Dream, the sheriff goes so far as to employ a white woman to accuse Fishbelly of rape. This fear is always present in the protagonist's mind as it is in the novelist's. Other fictional confrontations are only in some way variations of this situation where the black man is put in danger by the white woman. The reaction of the latter is infallible: she holds back her breath before crying, and the cry, when it is uttered, sounds like an inhuman howl signing the black's death warrant. "The Man Who Killed a Shadow" offers the most typical example of this:

> She sucked in her breath, sprang up, and stepped away from him. Then she screamed sharply, and her voice was like a lash cutting into his chest. She

screamed again and he backed away from her. He felt helpless, strange. . . . In her scream he heard the sirens of the police cars that hunted down black men. . . . This woman was screaming as though he had raped her (pp. 201–6).

The same reaction occurs in "The Man Who Lived Underground" when the office-worker perceives Daniels: "He tiptoed to a door and eased it open. A fair-haired white girl stood in front of a steel cabinet, her blue eyes wide upon him. She turned chalky and gave a high-pitched scream." (p. 50)

If, in *Native Son,* Mary is drunk and cannot cry out, her mother could, which causes the crazy terror of Bigger, who suffocates the girl. Other situations invert or vary the context of the episode. In "Down by the Riverside," it is the Heartfield son who, the symbolic protector of his mother, cries out in recognizing the murderer of his father. Although Mann merely defended himself, this murder entailed a potentially sexual menace toward white women, and Mann's bursting into the Heartfield house, even if to save the survivors, connotes rape. Equally, in "Big Boy Leaves Home," the situation seems inverted since it is black adolescents who swim nude. Their astonishment can be read, in fact, like a reflex of modesty: "It's a woman, whispered Big Boy in an underbreath, a *white* woman. They started, their hands instinctively covering their groins. Then they scrambled to their feet. The white woman backed slowly out of sight" (*UTC*, p. 36). Some lines later, it is the woman who is afraid: "The woman, her eyes wide, her hand over her mouth, backed away to the tree where their clothes lay in a heap" (*UTC*, p. 27). Though justified by the narrative context, these descriptions also serve to reproduce the trauma of young Wright's unintentionally breaking the prohibition which surrounds white women, to such an extent that the writer seems committed, whether by conscious recourse or at a more symbolic and almost archetypical level of black/white confrontation, to reproduce this situation. Beyond race, the encounter is anchored in a sexual taboo. In fact, the racial prohibition which surrounds the white woman is coupled with the social prohibiton which surrounds the mother, whose form, as we have seen, seems to be divided in two: she is at once the young woman whom the little boy dreams of possessing and the older person who incarnates the voice of conscience.

For Wright, the mother in this second sense is associated with the character of the grandmother. Mrs. Dalton is not an old woman, but her white hair, hieratic bearing, and carefully measured walk evidence an already aged woman. One thinks of Mrs. Bibbs' mother, a background presence in the house, but also, quite evidently, of Richard's grand-mother who seems to reappear periodically, for example, in the character of Granny in "Down by the Riverside." This ancestor, the voice of the conscience, is associated so much more easily with whiteness and with prohibition since, in reality, as stated in the beginning of *Black Boy*, "Mrs. Wilson was white as any 'white' person," (p. 21) as revealed by her "white grim face framed by a halo of tumbling black hair" in her bedroom of long muslin curtains.

Whiteness, authority, and frozen purity are associated. In any case it seems that a moral crime against a woman is often framed in curtains, feathers, and light fluffy immaculate fabric. We are thus tempted to take as significant the decor of the grandmother's bedroom, "long fluffy white curtains. . . . huge feather pillow," (*BB*, p. 3) which corresponds to a transgression of a major prohibition (to play with fire) and to a traumatic, long-lasting and far-reaching reprimand received from Mrs. Wright. In one of the crucial scenes of *Native Son*, the importance of a fluffy decor in the unreal light of dawn was so evident that it inspired the production of Orson Welles: "shadowy form of a white bed. . . . hazy blue light. . . . the furtive gleam of her white teeth. . . . a white blur was standing by the door, silent, ghostlike" (pp. 73). In this episode, the pillow is going to play a role as essential as in *Othello;* but whether or not the reference to Shakespeare is certain, the pillow will be found in similar contexts. When Bigger goes out on to the street to confront the blizzard, it seems that an enormous pillow was opened out of which snow swirls in the cold wind. As a correlative object, the blizzard outside is a transposition of a sack of feathers which, like Bigger in the room, were "ready to explode." In a rough draft of the autobiography, the grandmother's room is not only garnished with white curtains but full of pillows, those on which grand-mother rests and those in a clothes closet: "I go to the clothes closet, climb on top of a soft pile of pillows and quilts, curl up and try to sleep" ("Black Yesterdays," Wright Archives, Yale University Library). In an unforgettable way, the pillow, like the whirlwind of feathers turns out to be tied to Bobo's lynching in "Big Boy Leaves Home": "He shrank vio-lently as the wind carried, like a flurry of snow, a widening spiral of white feathers into the night. The flames leaped tall as the trees" (*UTC*, p. 62).

Feathers connote all that which is light and fluffy, such as smoke or fog, and also that which is white, an indistinct menacing mass, or a mountain of racial hate. Symbolizing purity and celestial freedom, they seem at the same time to invoke the opposite—defilement and constriction. This appears perhaps all too evidently in a premonitory detail of *Savage Holiday* where the symbolism serves to announce tragedy. Hearing the telephone ring, Fowler thinks of Mabel's lovers and, "in a hot fury," he seizes a pillow:

> He grabbed hold of the pillow of the bed and, in a hot fury, balled it tightly in his long, strong hands; his fingers squeezing at the soft batch of feathers until the fingers of his left hand touched the fingers of his right, penetrating the fluffy bunch. Then his face flushed almost a black red and he ripped the pillow in two, tearing dense, thick clouds about the room, floating and hovering slowly in the still, hot air.

In his rage, Fowler opened a light wound that he had on his hand, and a blood spot stained a feather:

> A large white feather floated slowly down to the puddle of blood, hovered about it for a second, then settled lightly upon its surface, its edges fluttering futilely, as though trying in vain to escape the clinging viscousness of the bright red liquid. . . . (pp. 165–166)

"Fluffiness" here is caught in a trap, stuck just as it will be burned or torn to pieces elsewhere, a sign of murder to come.

"Fluffy" is the opposite, in Wright's vocabulary, of "hairy" and "fuzzy," words which constantly represent animality and sexuality in their most menacing senses.

An example, quite often cited, of utilizing a white mass as an element of negative symbolism is found in the visions that Richard had when his mother wanted to discourage his incendiary tendencies with a good thrashing:

> wobbly white bags, like the full udder of cows, suspended from the ceiling above me. . . . I was gripped by the fear that they were going to fall and drench me with some horrible liquid. (*BB*, p. 6)

These representations of the maternal breast turned hostile and menacing, milk whose color is also that of the opposite race, need no explanation.

One encounters a similar detail associated with another element in the spider which appears in Fishbelly's nightmare. Here again, a young boy submits to a trauma tied to fire, since he burns his neck falling against the stove. His visions are more frightful than Richard's:

> In a corner of the room stood a giant, magically luminous spider whose thin, frizzly legs curved downward into blackness, its baglike body seemingly filled with a dangerous fluid held precariously in a delicate transparent membrane.

> Stricken, he watched the spider's roving, glowing eyes and saw the long, fuzzy legs beginning to move and the trembling, sacklike body, weighted with liquid, inching implacably forward, heading for him (*LD*, p. 57)

By means of the spider the connection is established between pubic hairs and a liquid which is sperm as well as milk, the latter evoking more the maternal womb than the beast.

Impure liquid contained between transparent walls will be found diversely associated, by the discoveries of Fishbelly, first to some fish that his father brings back from fishing. His father shows Fishbelly how to inflate the swimming bladders ("a translucent, greyish ball swelled slowly") which the child insists on calling bellies, having in mind a pregnant woman: "In his mind there was a dim image of Mrs. Brown who had a baby and her belly had been big, big like these balloons." (*LD*, p. 13) By smell, the fish are associated with the mother: "that odd smell associated itself somewhat with her body." (p. 11) But they return above all to the condom as disclosed in a nebulous memory which emerges in an adolescent's nightmare:

> There was a big white clock . . . and under the little bench mama sat upon there was a little thing he stooped yes it was a fish belly wet stinking crumpled with fuzzy hair and he laughed nervously and suddenly he started for the clock began a loud striking like somebody beating a drum TICK TOCK (p. 81).

The condom refers back to an episode of the novel where Fish plays innocently with a white rubber tube that he wound around the handle of his baseball bat. It concerns, moreover, Richard's childhood when he was playing with condoms, filling them up with sand, until his mother scolded him without explaining why. In the manuscript of the rough draft of his autobiography where he speaks of this episode, dropped thereafter, Wright connects this to a game—a dead snake dragged on the end of a string, which he will use in *The Long Dream.*

Without insisting on the bestial connotations of pubic hairs, note that it is enough for Fowler simply to stand nude on a balcony, shaggy like a bear ("[a] matting of black hair. . . . [a] dark forest. . . . [his] legs spider-like by hirsute coating," (*SH*, p. 41), to cause little Tony, terrorized, to fall from the tenth floor. Likewise let us drop for the time being the connection between whiteness and impure liquid. It will be often quite consciously exploited because of its racial symbolism: the episode of the white inflated sacs like some udder that Richard sees after the maternal reprimand appears in "The Ethics of Living Jim Crow" where Richard has a similar nightmare attached to another reprimand due to a battle with some white kids: "All that night I was delirious and could not sleep. Each time I saw monstrous white faces suspended from the ceiling, leering at me." (*UTC*, p. 11) Elsewhere, the face of a white woman is found incarnated on the dial of a clock, in particular in the Daltons' kitchen and in the previously cited dream of Fishbelly inspired by the lynching of his friend Chris. Instead let us return to the motif of the bag or of the inflated belly which, by the way, appears implied in *Native Son:* his crime committed, Bigger "felt that there was suspended just above his head a huge weight that would soon fall and crush him." (p. 185) This fear is connected to that of Fishbelly, who is sick and has visions of spiders suspended over his head.

Again it is Fishbelly who in his nightmare will serve to explain the trauma of the belly that bursts:

> The locomotive stack pipe touched the fish belly HUMPFF HUMPFF and the fish belly began swelling. . . . and getting like a balloon like Mrs. Brown's stomach before she had her baby and glowing yellow. . . . it grew so big that it began filling the room blocking the door windows he could not get out. . . . and the fish belly pressed hard against his face and he felt he was smothering. . . . and the belly burst PUFF! and out of the collapsing balloon ran a flood of blood and he saw the naked bloody body of Chris. . . . and when he opened his mouth to scream he was drowning in blood (*ID*, p. 82).

Castration, menstruation, childbirth: blood flows from the torn away sex of Chris like it is discharged from a woman. In "Tarbaby" the vision of menstrual blood leads the child to vomit at the thought of maternal impurity. Later, during a sermon which mentions the curse of God (the word "curse" also designates menstrual periods), Daniel will tie physical repulsion to the idea of divine vengeance, the bloody events of the story to the flow of women's blood.

The inflated belly is full of fluids or of air; it is disgusting and obscene. Birth, coming out of the belly, is the same. In "The Man Who Lived Underground," the sewer becomes transformed into a sort of womb viewed from the interior:

> He saw to either side of him two streaming walls that rose and curved inward some six feet above his head to form a dripping, mouse-colored dome. The bottom of the sewer was a sloping V-trough. . . . (*EM*, p. 29)

The polluted, foul water carries, among other things, the body of a baby ("the mouth gaped back in a soundless cry"—*EM*, p. 34) and, further on, the current creates an enormous bubble like a quivering organ: "a balloon pocket rose from the scum, glistening a bluish-purple, and burst." (DM, p. 55)

This ballooned belly which swells up enormously, suffocating Fish in his dream, was directly tied, in "Tarbaby," to the snake bite. When, after school, Dan shows his private parts to his friends he is reminded of the menace which stigmatizes masturbation: "You'll swell up and die." His next nightmare reactualizes this theme in connecting the snake to the conflagration: the captain of the Kate Adams takes the child to a dark room where he perceives a snake. He thinks: "If he bites me I'll swell up and die." He seizes a knife to kill the reptile, accidently knocks over the lamp and sets the boat on fire. ("Tarbaby," unpublished manuscript, Wright Archives, Yale University Library. J.W.J. Wright 907–908)

The snake explicitly represents the penis. Not content, in his games, to drag a dead snake around on the end of a string in order to frighten female passers-by, Richard certainly lived the episode of "Tarbaby" where the boys "played snake" at dusk: a passerby flees screaming; another falls to the ground. It is pregnant Sister James who suddenly gives birth in the Morrison's house. Later, in The Long Dream, the scene takes on all its meaning: hidden in a basement, the boys play in the same way to scare passers-by by their screams, stimulating in a white woman a surprising orgasm:

> The woman came forward, her heels going clackclackclack on the sidewalk. . . . They began sucking air into their lungs. . . . Their chests felt like taut - balloons. . . . 'BAAAAAAAW!' The woman jerked stock still, her hands flutter-ing; then she gave a piercing frantic scream, that was followed by a breathless, orgiastic whimpering. . . . (LD, p. 53)

Note in passing that certain details of the scene, by no means necessary to the story, originate from a semi-conscious source which united several scenes of this type. Thus the broken and repetitive noise of shoes on the sidewalk echoes back to the sexual act, and the comparison of lungs inflated with air to a balloon reproduces the enormous belly of the preg-nant woman.

Blackness is associated with the snake ("the low-bellied black snake" one reads in "Fire and Cloud"), with the belly, with the smoke-stack of the locomotive, with the virile member, with all that which, in customary symbolism, calls for religious or moral censure. But it is from Wright's phantasmal world that the connection between birth and death seems to issue, in the form of the childbirth and the dead baby. There is a sort of anguish (or is it a desire?) concerning both impossible childbirth and paternity. In the sewer of "The Man Who Lived Underground," Daniels sees a floating corpse of a new-born; in "Tarbaby," Dan is haunted in his nightmares by a black and slimy baby suggested to him by the unexpected pregnancy of Mary, who cannot manage an abortion. In *The Outsider,* the child that Gil and Eva have not had echoes, in *Lawd Today,* the one Jake killed in Lil's abortion. In "Down by the Riverside," childbirth is impossible for Mann's wife and she will die from it.

The child refused or destroyed is found tied to a violent possession of a woman, which is more a sacrifice than a rape since it implies a purifying cruelty which justifies sterility and non-procreation at the same time that it actualizes some fantasies of destruction. Of all these images of ferocious copulation barely consented to by the woman, Bigger's behavior with Bessie is the most benign, whereas the slaughter by Fowler, who pierces through the womb and not the sex remains the most insupportable in *Savage Holiday:*

> She flicked on the light and stood nude against the white refrigerator, the white gas stove, the gleaming sink, the white-topped table. . . . As she opened her mouth to scream, he brought the knife down hard into her nude stomach and her scream turned into a long groan.
>
> With machine like motion, Erskine lifted the butcher knife and plunged it into her stomach again and again. Each time the long blade sank into her, her knees doubled up by reflex action. . . . The blood was running from her body to the table top and drops began to splash on the shining tiles. (pp. 214–215)

In "The Man Who Killed a Shadow," Saul finishes off his victim with a knife's blow much in the same way that Bigger decapitates Mary Dalton with an ax; but in these two cases, and in the case of Fowler, the victim had first been suffocated or strangled. In *Black Boy* it is a little cat that Richard strangles in a hanging, but, like Fowler, he brandishes a kitchen knife against a woman in order to avoid an unjustified punishment from his young aunt Addie: "I leaped, screaming, and ran past her and jerked open the kitchen drawer; it spilled to the floor with a thunderous sound. I grabbed up a knife and held it ready for her" (p. 94).

The locale of the kitchen connotes confrontation and death and it seems that an association is quickly established between table and kitchen, white walls and stretched-out woman, as in the scene where Fowler stabs Mabel. The same associative context appears when, in the Daltons' bare, white-walled kitchen, Peggy speaks about the furnace to Bigger, who is eating lunch on the white table ("a white topped table"—*NS*, p. 47). In "Down by the Riverside," during a stormy night, Mann sees for the last time his wife lying down on a white marble hospital table, as in the words of "Saint James Infirmary." This table (of a kitchen, butcher shop, operation) is also the mortician's where bodies are laid out. In "The Man Who Lived Underground," the fugitive looks through a keyhole and sees "the nude figure of a man stretched out upon a white table. . . . He crouched closer to the door and saw the tip end of a black object lined with pink satin. A coffin, he breathed." (*EM*, p. 36) In *The Long Dream*, Fishbelly often sees in the warehouse "the long white table upon which bodies were drained of blood," (*LD* p. 21) which brings to mind that, in some way, Fowler only "drains Mabel of her blood" in *Savage Holiday*. On this table, Fishbelly will later see the mutilated body of his friend Chris under the cruel light of the electric lamp.

The table is related to the bed, stretcher, bier and coffin. The sick bed is that of grandmother Wilson, that of the paralyzed Ella Wright, the mother being transported on a stretcher in the luggage van to the Clarksdale hospital, whom Richard declares he dares not touch: "Two men who carried a stretcher. . . . brought out my mother. She lay with closed eyes, her body swathed in white. I wanted to run to the stretcher and touch her, but I could not move" (*BB*, p. 86). Likewise in Bigger's trial, the accused sees the body of Bessie being carried: "He looked and saw the two white-coated attendants pushing an oblong sheet-covered table through the crowd and down the aisle." (*NS*, p. 280).

The violent possession of or aggression against a woman by a man, which structures more than one fictional episode, is elaborated in Wright's imagination in contrast to the situation where a masculine character finds himself menaced by a devouring, if not castrating, woman. Dizziness and fascination are the characteristics. Usually the man recoils, full of fright before a woman's invitation to transgress. In the key scene at the Bibbs' house the untimely but innocent intrusion of a young black upsets the intimacy of the feminine place; in the antithetic scene a young black is upset by a sexual request which he perceives as a risk, whether it is because possession implies a penalty for breaking a taboo or because of an inexplicable connection between women and impurity.

Concerning Saul Saunders in "The Man Who Killed A Shadow," the description established that a man fears being devoured by the gaping sex, caught in a trap where jaws are going to close around him. When the librarian asks him to sweep under her desk:

> She was sitting with her knees sprawled apart and her dress was drawn halfway up her legs. He looked from her round blue eyes to her legs whose thighs thickened as they went to a V clothed in tight, sheer, pink panties. . . .
> 'There's dust there now," she said sternly, her legs still so wide apart that he felt she was naked. . . .
> Her legs were still spread wide and she was sitting as though about to spring upon him and throw her naked thighs about his body.. . . .
> As he stared at her gaping thighs, he felt overwhelmed by a sense of wild danger. (*EM*, pp. 200–201)

His reaction is attraction and fright, incapacity to turn away from the cause of dizziness and the perception of evil which attracts him. Wright deliberately exaggerates the image of woman as sexual temptress in order to justify better the strange behavior of Saul. And here he employs some terms which evoke other fictional episodes. Thus, in "Tarbaby," after the visit of his seductive Aunt Lulu, who overflows with femininity, Dan, grappling with his puberty, finds himself prey to some voracious fantasies: he dreams of a dragon who opens wide his yellow mouth to swallow, of an enormous snake's mouth, of cold quicksand which sucks him in and swallows him up. Wright will modify the context in *The Long Dream*. There he creates first the vision of the spider with a transparent belly whose mouth menaces to suck in Fish: "Through the spider's gaping mouth he glimpsed nauseous vistas of thin, red teeth." (p. 53) Further on, vagina is likened to mouth in the significant description of Chris' mutilated body after the lynching. The castration makes of his lower abdomen, in effect, a sort of lack, a double of the vagina in the form of a gaping mouth:

> The mouth, lined with stumps of broken teeth, yawned gapingly, an irregular black cavity bordered by shredded tissues that had once been lips. (p. 75
> Fishbelly saw a dark coagulated blot in the gaping hole between the thighs and, with defensive reflex, he lowered his hands nervously to his groin. (p. 77)

The following nightmare of the adolescent connects the castration of his friend to a scene of intercourse and a view of a distended belly—thus to a woman and specifically his mother at her dressing table. At this stage, an episode that Wright eliminated from *Black Boy*, but which was part of an intermediary stage of the autobiography, seems to furnish an incontestably primordial scene. Wright recounts that at California Flats, he was often confined, quite young, with some adolescents who cajoled him and whose emotional displays, full of repressed sexuality, frightened him a little. A scene comes back to him in great clarity, he says, when he calls up this memory. A cousin of his mother, abandoned by her husband, sometimes watched over Richard and she tried to use him for erotic satisfactions. He was traumatized by this experience, and the attitude of his mother, to whom he told all, increased tenfold his feelings of shame and prohibition:

> Laura was holding me in her lap, kissing me. I recall being vaguely frightened and struggling to escape her. I ran to the other side of the room and stood looking at her.
> "Come here, Richard," she said.
> I did not move. I saw her pull up her dress and was startled at the gaping hole and the abundance of hair.
> Lured, it seemed, by dread, I crept closer and stared. I don't know why I was so frightened. Being between three and four years of age I had not to my knowledge encountered such before. I know that my fear was all out of proportion to what was actually happening. Perhaps sex carries with it some racial memory; perhaps my underdeveloped body was trying to summon up from the depths of me an answering response. I don't know. When I was close to her, she grabbed me and clutched me fiercely between my legs. I struggled; she caught my arm and I stood still, my puny weight balanced against her strong grip.
> "Touch it," she said.
> I stared at her.
> "Go ahead and touch it," she said.
> "No," I said trembling.
> "You know what this is," she smiled.
> She put her fingers in her vagina and pulled the flesh apart, revealing red depths.
> "Put your hand in," she said.
> I ran out of the room. She caught me and told me not to tell anyone. I promised, feeling a dark threat in her words. Next I remember babbling the story of what happened to my mother. I also remember a loud commotion in the home. I remember finally being told to forget it, not to mention it ever again. (Early draft of *Black Boy*, Wright Archives, Yale University Library. J.W.J. Wright 2.)

To this scene, which seems to model the "seduction" of Saul by the librarian in "The Man Who Killed a Shadow," we should add the following, equally censored in *Black Boy*. The episode takes place at the time of a trip that Richard, an adolescent, took by train with his mother:

> What was happening? My mother had been sitting silent for a long time and she gazed strangely with tight lips. Black men were rising and going to the end of the car and walking back again with no apparent aim or object. And then I saw it and something gripped me and at once I knew what the men were feeling. I felt guilty and ashamed. About twenty feet away from me and facing me was a young beautiful mulatto woman, laughing, talking, her head tossed back, her large eyes flashing and her legs propped up upon the bench before her, reveal-

ing a full sweep of firm yellow thighs and legs and a tight strip of what served for a wide G string. I had never before felt so keenly, so achingly the dark terror of beauty of woman.

In spite of his mother's remark—"That woman should be whipped"— Richard cannot get her out of his mind. And, he adds:

> Years later, in Chicago, in the main public library, I was one afternoon standing with my library card and my list of books in my hand when a white woman came to the counter, her head down, and took my list . . . . She lifted two full sky-grey eyes for but an impersonal moment and turned away and I felt again the sense of physical shock. I held still for a moment and then the mulatto in the Jim Crow coach of the Mississippi train surged up out of the layers of years of memory and stood sharp and clear before me . . . . I was profoundly disturbed as though some great memory was about to come to me, some recollection of tremendous importance, and then the mood passed and was forever gone, leaving but an incredible wonder. I do not know what those two experiences meant but I had, on both occasions, the feeling that I was reacting to something beyond life. (Wright Archive, Yale University Library).

Even before Wright had "recovered" this impression during his sessions with Frederic Wertham, this scene was put to profit in fiction. In "Tarbaby," Dan contemplates Susie Brown, a cakewalk dancer who did her number for Doctor Snell, a seller of "World's Wonder Soap and Tonic" who was passing through the small town. The incident is taken up again in the context of a subway trip in *Lawd Today*, where Jake and his friends enjoy themselves looking at the crotch of a woman passenger. In *Native Son* Bigger sees (without really looking because he is thinking of the murder) his sister Vera in the act of putting on her shoes: "Vera was sitting on the edge of a chair with her right foot hoisted upon another chair, buckling her shoe" (p. 98) and she throws a shoe at her brother whom she accuses of "looking" at her. In fact, it is Mary who really was in the situation of temptress when Bigger had brought her back home a little drunk:

> Mary slumped down in the seat and sighed. Her legs sprawled wide apart. . . . She was resting on the small of her back and her dress was pulled up so far he could see where her stockings ended on her thighs. He stood looking at her for a moment. She raised her eyes and looked at him. She laughed (pp. 69–70).

This theme is taken up many times again. In *Savage Holiday* Fowler will contemplate in the same way Mabel's nude body under a dressing-gown that often slid down when she was crying: "He wanted to reach out and cover her nakedness, hide it from his eyes, but he stood and studied her irresistible plush curves, tracing the gentle slope of her thighs, gaping as though hypnotized." (p. 121) In *The Long Dream*, Fishbelly likewise lets his gaze wander in the direction of underwear, which attracts him, whenever the occasion presents itself.

This role of voyeur, this taking possession by a stare, involves much anguish, but it is also irresistible to the male. It surpasses the spectacle, also recurrent, offered to a child or adolescent of seeing a couple in the act of fornicating: Bigger, in flight across the ghetto, little Richard in the Memphis apartment, Fishbelly penetrating the basement of the funeral parlor, or little Tony Blake surprising adults in the process of making love without feeling an intense disturbance or uneasiness (except in the case of Tony who is going to connect "making love" to "making war"); it is above all the fact that a woman client replaces his mother with Tyree, which upsets Fishbelly.

This return to the subconscious roots of literary creation would be of little interest if it only amounted to returning to a world of fantasies belonging as much to the reader as to the writer and analyzing to what extent both participate in collective imagery and a symbolic system; psychoanalysis has largely laid claim to this. Instead we are attempting to reveal how patterns of details expressing emotionally and instinctually charged or traumatic scenes are structured by language, in particular by certain key words which serve in some way to pivot connotations according to a nework specific to the writer. We hope to open up this type of analysis.

It appears that an object as neutral as a table can, each time that it represents "a long white table," take on an affective connotation which associates it with such situations as death, surgery, butchery, or rape, not to mention the black cultural references of "Saint James Infirmary." The term seems perceived by Wright in reference, more or less consciously, to his mother's paralysis (the traumatizing scene). The presence of the adjective "oblong" sometimes applies to the table; indeed it will regularly connote the idea of death by reference to a coffin. Thus the word "oblong" returns three times, referring to the table or the laidout corpse, in the passage where the prosecutor shows the corpse of Bessie at Bigger's trial. "Oblong" thus echos at the same time "an oblong strip of sky" and "the oblong Black Belt" which elsewhere designates the patch of sky that Bigger catches a glimpse of, the measure of his own tomb, and the form of the black ghetto on the map of Chicago divided into squares by the police. And above all, "oblong" refers back to the corpse of Mary which is dissolving in the furnace room: "like the oblong mound of fresh clay of a newly made grave the coals revealed the outlines of Mary's body." (*NS*, p. 100–101) In *The Long Dream*, the connection of the word with the coffin is even clearer.

The halo of connotations surrounding a term often depends on where it was drawn from, and thus it is appropriate to search Wright's readings to discover the origins of a term, perhaps in Poe's *Tales* which he liked, since Poe speaks, in "The Oblong Box," of a coffin used by a passenger to transport the body of his wife across the ocean. The theme of the woman-in-the-coffin would thus serve to complete Richard's obsessions about imagining his mother dead before his eyes. Often padded, the coffin is moreover associated with the bed or the quilt which covers Lulu lying bloodless in Mann's boat in "Down By the Riverside." In "The Man Who Lived Underground," the coffin perceived by Daniels is "the tip end of a black object lined with pink satin," (*EM*, p. 36) so much that "pink satin" is itself going to refer back to all feminine underwear and to the pink panties of Miss Houseman in "The Man Who Killed a Shadow." In "Tarbaby," Dan learns of his Aunt Lulu's death during a great storm and looks terrorized at the body exposed in an open coffin; later a nightmare will show him a dead woman who stirs and threatens to reveal that he had a child with Mary. In *Savage Holiday*, the motif becomes almost Poe-like when Erskine sees in a dream a young and beautiful dead person wrapped in fluffy muslin stretched out in a sparkling silver coffin; she is nude to the waist and is beginning to decompose under his eyes (*SH* p. 177).

In *The Long Dream*, the motif of the coffin has its place in the plot itself since the dance-hall conflagration allows the congregation to see in the church "forty-three coffins . . . lined, oblong box beside oblong box" (*LD*, p. 321). Since his father is a mortician, Fish lives in the midst of coffins and he occasionally likes to hide himself in the one in the office, sheathed in grey satin. Tracked by the sheriff after the death of Tyree, he dreams that he escapes in that manner: "He dashed out of the office in a rear room filled with coffins and he saw his mother beckoning to him and calling whisperingly: 'Fish, hide in a coffin, quick!'" (*LD*, p. 278). A place for corpses, the coffin is also, by subterfuge of satin and quilting—pink or black—a silky nest which is associated with feminine underwear, the satin-like skin of women, and the maternal womb.

In order to clarify, without in any way concluding, this exploration of systems of resonating words, let us take the case of a term equally recurrent, neutral in appearance, but which seems always to occur in a very pregnant context of sexuality, to the point that it becomes a symbol of it. It is the adjective "V-shaped." We have already encountered it in the description of Maybelle Houseman in "The Man Who Killed a Shadow" where, just as "oblong" invokes the coffin, "V-shaped" invokes the feminine sex. The V is that of spread open legs and of the gaping vagina as well as the pubic triangle. Mabel has a V-shaped neckline, thus provocative and sensual, like the girls who dance in the sensual orgy at Rose's nightclub in *Lawd Today*.

If the V is justifiable in the description of women, it is more unexpected in that of the sewer where Daniels walks up and down and whose bed is in the form of a "sloping V trough." (*EM*, p. 29) But this notation is found precisely among terms which associate the sewer with a sort of womb or uterus from which a dead baby is expelled. More surprising still is the presence of this adjective in "Down by the Riverside" when Mann is with Mrs. Heartfield. We have emphasized that his arrival as a rescuer was exactly like the intrusion into a woman's room. But, when the house collapsed, at the precise moment when, his ax raised, he was going to cut down the family in order to hide his crime, Mann again saw Mrs. Heartfield "lying face forward in a V-trough to his right where the floor joined the walls at a slant. The boy was whispering: 'Mother! mother!' Mann saw the axe but seemed not to realize that he had been about to use it" (*UTC*,p. 112). The presence of the ax-man juxtaposed to the V is significant; moreover we find the two elements associated in a dream of Erskine Fowler:

> *Whack whack whack* somebody was in the forest chopping down one of his trees and he peered cautiously and he saw a tall man swinging a high ax chopping furiously into a V-shaped hollow of a giant tree. (*SH*, p. 37)

Here the ax is clearly characterized as an instrument of penetration into the V of the tree; the sexual symbolism is all too evident. (One could bring up the use of "huge," which always seems menacing. So while the explicit adjectives designating the *Kate Adams* as "huge" and "white" in *Black Boy* are rather positive, the connotation established in "Tarbaby" by means of Dan's dream, already cited, is clearly anguishing.)

One can contrast the use of similar terms by other authors. For example, the presence of the "V" in the episode of the nude dancer in Ralph Ellison's "Battle Royal" invites comparison with the description of Miss Houseman in "The Man Who Killed a Shadow." However, even if *Invis-*

*ible Man* also treats black reactions to provocative white feminity, what a difference there is in the connotations involved:

> I wanted at one and the same time to run from the room, to sink through the floor, or go to her and cover her from my eyes and the eyes of the others with my body; to feel the soft thighs, to caress her and destroy her, to love her and murder her, to hide from her, and yet to stroke where, below the small American flag tattooed upon her belly, her thighs formed a capital V. (*Invisible Man*, p. 16).

Whereas Saul's contradictory desires render him speechless and frozen in place, the Ellisonian narrator clearly expresses his feelings, to such a point that very explicit sexuality does not seem rooted, in contrast to Wright, in fantasies. Moreover, the pubic V topped by a tricolor flag tattooed on the belly symbolizes both victory for the United States in the 1940s and the power of capitalist America ("capital" V). Thus for Ellison, the description sets up the white woman as "white bitch," symbolic of the nation—a prefiguration of the character of Lula that LeRoi Jones will create in *Dutchman*. For Wright, on the contrary, the semantic load leads back toward the fantasy. The meaning goes back to non-racial sexuality with so much force that the white librarian becomes deindividualized in order to become woman or mother. Ellison sets up his secondary character as a symbol of a system founded on power and money as much as racism, so that the reader reacts to the proposed myth with the detachment of an observer. By contrast, for Wright the incident is profoundly rooted in unconscious impulses and is used by him to arouse our fascination, provoking a reaction much more visceral since it is directed more to our fantasies than our intellect.

Study of Wright's writing and style must take into account the frequent eruption of groups of terms and images which can be brought to light more through a psychocritical approach than other stylistic decodings. Whether appearing in the order of a scene, a motif, or a simple word, these occurrences have a presence independent of their stylistic effect, whose primary function is rhetorical and literary; they create the unconscious bed-rock of the style. In order to dig deeply into the most personal aspects of writing, it is necessary to analyze the relations between fantasies and style.

*Page references are to the following editions: *Uncle Tom's Children: Five Long Stories* (Cleveland, Ohio: World Pub. Co., 1943); *Native Son* (New York: Harper, 1940); *Black Boy* (New York: Harper, 1945); *The Outsider* (New York: Harper, 1953); *Savage Holiday* (New York: Avon, 1954); *The Long Dream* (Garden City, N.Y.: Doubleday, 1958).

# Wright's Image of France

WHEN Richard Wright died in November 1960, many of the Parisian obituaries quoted Wright's statement that "this [France] is the place where I could die." Having lived in France for some sixteen years, Wright to some degree had become part of the Parisian intellectual setting and was mourned by the French as though he were a compatriot. Conversely, in the United States many saw in Wright's death-in-exile not only a comment on the racial situation in America but a reflection of the writer's personal attitudes. Some, white and black, resented his choice of living elsewhere. Some remembered the dedication of *The Outsider*—"To Rachel, my daughter who was born on alien soil"—and were offended by the dedication of *Eight Men*: "To my friends, Helene, Michel, and Thierry Maurice-Bokanowski whose kindness has made me feel at home in an alien land."

What is striking in these dedications is the recurrence of the word "alien." Though Wright could consider France a second home, something always prevented him from integrating into French life. He remained largely an outsider. This was due less to cultural differences than to the gap between the dreamed image of a country and the reality of the place. Wright's preconceived image of France as the land of freedom and the cradle of culture was somewhat shattered by his realization that postwar France was an underdeveloped country with strange ways and puzzling politics. Accordingly, he made use of France less as literary material than as a privileged vantage point from which to look back at America and forward to the Third World. France, in turn, lavished upon him all the honors reserved for the great and made him a yardstick by which to measure all black (and sometimes nonblack) literary accomplishments. French anti-American propaganda also used him as a big stick with which to beat the United States. As a result, these discrepancies between myth and reality account for the uneasiness which is to be felt when Wright, having chosen to make his home in an alien land, proved unable to reconcile that alienness and his own alienation.

Wright's early image of France was quite favorable. He shared with many black Americans the impression that it was a place where a black person could be "just another human being."[1]

The absence of racial discrimination was important in the elaboration of Wright's myth of French freedom, but probably less important than his view of France as a cultural hothouse, propitious for the blossoming of literary and artistic talent. This myth was even shared by the left-wing writers he met at the Chicago John Reed Club in the 1930s. At the time, Wright's grounding in French literature was far from negligible. He owned books by Balzac, Alexandre Dumas, Flaubert Anatole France, Theophile Gautier, Pierre Loti, Rabelais, Romain Rolland, Jules Romains, and Voltaire. And after reading Proust's *Remembrance of Things Past,* he admired "the lucid, subtle, but strong prose," was "stupefied by its dazzling magic, awed by the vast, delicate, intricate, and psychological structure of the Frenchman's epic of death and decadence."[2] Among the younger generation of writers, he admired Gide for his anticolonialist and pro-Communist stands. He saw in Malraux's *Human Condition* an outstanding example of balance between revolutionary feeling and structured art, and Aragon's *Red Front* led him to write "Transcontinental," a long piece of visionary verse. Everyone in America, black and white, seemed to agree on the cultural importance of France, and it was easy for Wright to subscribe mentally to a well-established tradition of transatlantic migration.

In 1940, when he became famous with the publication of *Native Son,* Wright thought of going to Paris, but the war prevented him from making the trip. When it actually came to taking the step, however, the example of Hemingway and Anderson proved less compelling than Gertrude Stein's enthusiastic letters to Wright—who in fact was only too ready to light out for eastern territories. The literary world of Wright's dreams was the international setting of the lost generation and their French counterparts, and he associated Gertrude Stein's verbal creativeness with the distance achieved by geographical remoteness: "She made me hear something that I'd heard all my life, that is, the speech of my grandmother who spoke a deep Negro dialect colored by the Bible. . . . Yes, she's got something, but I'd say that one could live and write like that only if one lived in Paris or in some out of the way spot where one could claim one's own soul" (Journal entry for January 28, 1945). For Wright, then, it was a question of claiming one's soul in order to write. In the United States he believed his deepest energies were dissipated by racial tensions and he mused: "All the more reason why I dream and dream of leaving my native land to escape the pressure of the superficial things I think I know. That's why I left the South, and now I want to leave the country, and some day I will, by God." While couching such thoughts in his journal for January 28, 1945, he was constructing his personal image of France, as well as his rationale for going there: he wanted to escape the pressure of a superficial way of life, in which racism was only one of the negative elements.

When Wright went to French Canada in June 1944, and again in 1945, Quebec became for him a substitute for Paris, and he had a foretaste of the more liesurely rhythm of European life at Sainte Petronille de l'Ile d'Orléans. Tired of industrialization and the straight lines of New York, Wright enjoyed the slow, mature pace of Quebec. He wrote to Gertrude Stein on October 29, 1945:

> Quebec is slow and ripe and organic and serene; there is no hurrying and no straining to attain the impossible or unique or the different. But when one returns to New York, one is struck by the hurried, the green, the vague, and the frantic. Everything is romantic, abstract. In Quebec, man has found a way of living with the earth; in New York we live against the earth.

Paris became, by association, not only a hotbed of talent but a synonym for harmony of the soul, for peace, for an adequate relationship between people and their environment.

With his growing interest in existentialism and with Sartre's visit to the United States, Wright in 1946 began to associate France less with images of an agrarian past and more with the humanistic tradition of the "Art and Action" group, reflected in the periodical *Twice a Year*. Before going to France, Wright was already convinced that the old world was in fact not as old and blasé as the United States. He imagined that he would find in Paris, if not a solution to the American problem, at least a better way of posing it, due to the rational and traditional approach of the French themselves.

How, then, did the realities of French life in 1946 balance out with what Wright imagined he would find? Freedom became for him one of the major aspects of life in Paris, compared with the atmosphere of racial tension prevailing in Greenwich Village at the time of his departure. His avowal that "I've found more freedom in one square block of Paris than there is in the entire United States" was resented in America, for Wright defined freedom, "at the risk of being branded un-American, as the right to live free of mob violence, blacklisting, character assassination, and the pressures of hysterical democracy." He remarked: "The French, amongst whom I've lived in exile for six years, do not argue about personal freedom, they just *live* it. One is not prone to speak about what one already has."[3]

Although Wright was more conversant with abstract painting and photography than with Romanesque sculpture, he enjoyed the patina and indefinable quality that age brings to Paris monuments as the expression of a tradition and a culture; he enjoyed it not as the expression of a culture he was viewing from a distance, but with a sense of immediacy and sharing. And it is no coincidence that in several instances he associated beauty with the absence of racial pressure. On May 15, 1946, a few days after his arrival, he wrote his friend Ed Aswell:

> Paris is all I ever hoped to think it was, with a clear sky, buildings so beautiful with age that one wonders how they happen to be and with people so assured and friendly and confident that one knows that it took many centuries of living to give them such poise. There is such an absence of race hate that it seems a little unreal. Above all, Paris strikes me as being a truly gentle city, with gentle manners.

Clearly, he associated Paris with culture, beauty, serenity, the absence of racial hatred, and the possibility, in a more relaxed atmosphere, of devoting oneself to more important matters.[4]

In a June 1946, letter to Mr. Scanton, Wright disclosed much about his intentions in coming to France and how he viewed the situation there:

> I came here to France to see how a nation that is not as highly industrialized as America, but a nation that is certainly highly literate will meet such problems of modernization and industrialization. The French do not really know of or understand the kind of world we have built across the Atlantic: true, they like our tall buildings, are awed by our machines, but they do not know the agony of millions who do not know where their jobs are coming from, do not know how unhappy whites and blacks can be when living amidst the world's greatest plenty. Just because France is not industrialized and because she has in the past passionately affirmed the rights of man, I'm keenly interested to see what she is going to have to say. Having no burden of a race problem, France can address herself to the burden of how the individual can have freedom with a singleness of aim that will come hard elsewhere.

In fairness, one must record a discrepancy found in one of Wright's unpublished essays. That he left the piece unfinished may evidence his dissatisfaction with it, yet the fact that he branded France guilty of the same materialism he found in America is revealing. "A Personal Report from Paris," an unpublished draft for an article, states:

> For three months in Paris I have looked for people, feelings, individuals. And I must report that this city of statues and monuments, this city of human symbols and images of man's imagination, stands today as a living monument of its opposite; for amid the symbols of past greatness with frozen history in the form of magnificent architecture staring one in the eye at every turn, men and women somehow have cut loose from the humanity that was made and saved through centuries of great effort. . . .

It is strange that Wright should have begun a piece in this vein, if we remember how enthusiastic he was about France and its freedom in his interviews and official declarations. He may have been disappointed to find that he could not write in any French newspaper without being tagged with a political label; also, he may have been influenced by Camus' gloomy views on the decline of traditional values when he wrote: "There are groups and parties in France today that stand for everything except people, except for a sense of humanity." Having found a human response only in the black market, which brought people together as individuals, albeit for economic purposes, Wright saw two sides of France: "one legal and stern, the other underground and sullen." He continued: "French society today has hardened into corals of stances, into statues of ideology, into calcifications of intellect. . . . The greatest horror in modern postwar France is a man talking of his subjective feelings." He was reacting against the desiccating influence of French intellectualism with all the force of his Anglo-Saxon empirical view of life. Yet, one cannot help thinking that he wanted to hold up to his American readers a caricature of what they had become, making it easier for them to look at America under the guise of France—both industrialized countries at different stages of their development. His final sentence applied to both: "The danger is greater now than ever; the humanity known for two thousand years is about to - vanish. . . . It is a question of man against machines, aspirations against machine-dreams, feeling against logic, freedom against regimentation, life as we know it and hope to make it against life organized like an assembly-line, packed in cans of thought, stored in ice-boxes of fear."

Of course, there was not as much fellow feeling for the oppressed as he believed the Nazi occupation would have created in France. The economic situation (food was rationed, there was little gas, the electricity was turned off several days a week) explained why cooperation against the

Germans had yielded to an egotistic struggle for survival. On the whole, however, there existed a vital interest in cultural renewal. The atmosphere, with its blend of tradition, laissez-faire, individualism, and a search for new values, was quite stimulating. Years later, after he had time to analyze the differences between the United States and France, Wright was able to explain these subtleties to the American audience in an article, "I Choose Exile," originally written for *Ebony* in 1950 (and rewritten in 1952) but which was turned down because it was too "strong." Wright declared that, after weeks of Parisian public politeness, he had discovered "the more civilized the white man, the less he feared people who differed from him." In his eyes, the French aristocracy and government officials felt so secure that they were entertained rather than bothered by everything out of the way in the domain of arts, morality, or philosophy. Paris thus was a truly international social scene:

> The friendly curiosity of the French for foreigners implies no sentimental love of the outsider; it is rather, that the French have imbibed through their education a universal scheme of cultural reference which imputes to the alien a level of humanity different from his own in outward guise but not in intrinsic substance. Eschewing the loosely democratic approach to education which is the hallmark of America, the French have imposed a rigorously competitive system of education which discourages pragmatic attitudes and exalts the sheer capacity for absorption of knowledge, thereby creating characters uninhibited in their quick absorption of alien facts, fostering humanistic emotions and forging personalities of wide availability of interest. . . .

While he was somewhat ill at ease and puzzled by French manners during his first eight-month sojourn in Paris, Wright felt himself on more familiar ground when he returned in 1947. Strangely enough, however, he seemed to get bogged down in all the difficulties involved in physically settling in Paris.

Wright often viewed the French as a strange people with irritating ways, full of recklessness, lacking order and efficiency. Whereas he responded to the French love of beauty and sense of humanity, his response to their inevitable counterparts was that of the typical American tourist. This may have resulted from his imperfect knowledge of the French language, in which he never achieved fluency.

The journal that Wright kept regularly from July 30, 1947, the day he left New York, to September 23, 1947, is a fascinating welter of conflicting impressions, many of which are negative and born of misunderstandings.

Wright is, in turn, very suspicious about a man who is to get him an apartment, but he likes the veterinarian who treats his cat for very little money. He is appalled by the traffic: "How careless the French are with their lives," he exclaims. He is furious with the new maid who fixed only string beans for a meal: "I felt like a horse," he complains. And elsewhere: "The French people really do not like children. They hate them. I've seen it in every adult Frenchman I've met."

On August 27, 1947, he jots down his pleasure: "I walked and walked the streets. It was fun. How lively and old Paris is. How like paintings the people are! What a deep serenity pervades everything here. What a pattern of living. The look of peace that shows on the faces of the people holds even in their suffering." A week later, on September 3, his mood had changed completely:

> It is so hard to get a fixed routine set in Paris these days. . . . Went to the ice house. It was closed until five o'clock! Now, I ask you, is not that the reason that France is so damned poor today? I don't understand it. I left word with the ice man to say yes or no about the ice (which he should have delivered in the morning). Imagine a man refusing money! But he did. I love the French mentality sometimes, but not always. Not when practical matters are concerned. I see that most French stores are closed not only for two hours during lunch, but for longer periods. No wonder the men do not have suits to wear, the women are shoddy. I love leisure but not the kind of leisure that leaves a nation of beggars and cheats.

The only conclusions that we can draw from such contradictory impressions are, on the one hand, that his early incursions into French life were quite superficial. Yet he soon came to consider Paris as the place where he lived, a place one no longer questions. He did not completely get over his irritation with the French lack of efficiency, but, in the long run, the inefficiency seemed to decrease and/or Wright finally got used to it. He thought less of France as an economically and materially underdeveloped country, and ceased to react like an American tourist visiting the Quartier Latin.

In many ways, it seems that Wright did not put France to good use. He did not, for instance, visit the country extensively—he spent only a few days on the Riviera, on the Côte Basque, a week or so in Corrèze, a month in Haute Savoie. He was not really concerned with life as it went on in the provinces (it was both too sluggish and too atypical for him), and he was not primarily interested in the French landscape.

Moreover, he depended little upon France as a theme or a setting for his novels. If we limit ourselves to what he wrote in exile, we find that only one novel (the unpublished "Island of Hallucinations") takes place in Paris.[5] Wright never really seemed to care enough about the French reality either to interpret it for Americans or to derive effects from it. In the notable exception, "Island of Hallucinations," France, and the reactions of American Negroes to it, are important themes: Fishbelly is brought into contact with a couple of crooks, a bevy of prostitutes, girls from the French bourgeoisie, the police, concierges, shopkeepers, and the anonymous crowds parading in protest against General Ridgeway. The "Five Episodes" published in *Soon, One Morning* (1963) are sufficient to give a fairly good idea of such local color scenes as *le chapeau américain*, or the story of the stolen hotel bed sheets.[6] Although Wright used France as a theme about as often as other black expatriate novelists, he did so rarely. Why? Wright partly answers this question in "I Choose Exile":

> Any writer who has not, at the age of twenty, stored away the fundamental basis of his so-called subject matter will never do so. I took my subject matter with me in the baggage of my memory when I left America and I'm distressingly confident that race relations will not alter to a degree that will render invalid these memories whose reality represents one of the most permanent and distinguishing features of American life.

First and foremost, Wright used France as a unique vantage point. When he first went there, he was both older and better established than James Baldwin, for instance, and he was no longer seeking his identity. In that sense, we cannot expect to find in Wright the reactions, psychological rather than political, that Baldwin records in *Notes of a Native Son*. Wright's 1946 letter to Scanton shows that he was well aware of the insights gained in exile:

> Why not come over here? Or have you already been? One gets a good look at one's country from this perspective and one learns to see one's nation with double eyes, to feel what we have got and what we have not got. I've learned more about America in one month in Paris than I could in one year in New York. Looking at this country makes all the unimportant phases of the AMERICAN problem fade somewhat and renders the true problem more vivid.

Wright did not imply that in France he was learning more about himself, as Baldwin did, but that he was learning about his country. France constituted for him not only a choice residence during the McCarthy era and a comparatively protected retreat from the tensions of racism, but it also afforded a privileged perspective into Africa and the Third World, as well as the United States. It was a place of international exchange where one could learn to define concepts and values in a non-American way.

Of course, Wright's views reflected his personal likings as much as his political choice. When he wrote "I Choose Exile," in order to explain and defend his view of the situation, he insisted upon the antimaterialistic aspects of French culture. Some of the most sensitive and humane French people he had met were poor and not ashamed of it. Some of them had actually elected to live a life of poverty:

> Born myself in a poverty that was reinforced by my color, I was naturally attracted to a hierarchy of values that did not condemn those who are poor, even by implication, to a subhuman status. In France the human ideal to be striven for is placed at the apex of a carefully graded scale of values, the prototypes of which are the priest, the soldier, the scientist, the savant, and this value scheme is taught rigidly in the schools, reflected in the church, and depicted in art and literature. I openly confess that, as an American Negro, I felt, amidst such a milieu, safe from my neighbor for the first time in my life.

He was glad to encounter in France no pretense of being a welfare state, no definition of civilization in racial terms: "Though black and of alien origin I *could* become a Frenchman, contrary to what would take place in WASP America," he remarked. "Do I think France is a paradise?" he concluded. "No. French problems are of a different genre than those at home. Whether France can survive as an island of freedom in a world seemingly bent upon stamping out freedom in the name of freedom is anybody's guess."

One of these problems was French colonialization, which had succeeded only too well. Wright remarked: "The French deal so subtly in assimilating the best minds from their African colonies that, should you denounce colonialization, the processed, educated blacks would rise to denounce you before any Frenchman would need to." His political opposition to colonialization seemed to be mixed with a kind of admiration for the French assimilationist policy, and his attitude is perhaps surprising. His resolve not to intrude into French internal politics was dictated by the fear of being expelled at a time when his return to the United States would mean facing the House Committee on Un-American Activities. That is why he never publicly spoke against the Algerian war. One of his few allusions to it, in a 1959 interview in *Folket I Bild*, shows his ability to distinguish between French racism and French nationalism.[7]

Also, Wright had apparently understood a long time in advance that

DeGaulle would ultimately betray those partisans of *Algérie française* who had placed him in power. In the foreword to the French edition of *White Man Listen* (1957), Wright wrote, after a long summary of major African developments:

> Yet the most important events affecting Africa . . . were born from France's decision, frantically bent upon discarding anything that would hinder her race towards the raw materials of the cold war: oil and minerals in the Sahara. Under Charles de Gaulle, the French government abandoned the so-long and so-proudly proclaimed objectives of its assimilationist and civilizing mission in order to transfer the burden onto the Church, educators, and the well-trained corps of black elite. . . . One should not underestimate the long-range effects of France forsaking her cherished "mission." The curtain has just been raised upon the political drama of French Africa (p. xvii).

Wright could therefore make use of France's image as a traditionally humanistic nation and as a potentially anticolonialist power in a way similar to the strategy of W. E. B. DuBois, praising France's treatment of her blacks in the 1920s in order to shame the United States. Yet, no less than DuBois, Wright was aware of, and opposed to, the subtle assimilationist policies of France. This is patent in his comparative analysis of colonial psychological rule in *Black Power* (1954). Although he opposed a certain image of France to American imperialism, he had few illusions concerning France's interest in, and knowledge of, the Third World.

However, Wright evokes the kind of cultural alliance that could occur between the humanistic forces of Europe, of which France is the symbol, and the way of life enjoyed in the so-called underdeveloped countries. His argument is simple: France is a weak country, politically and economically, but this makes for a qualitative opportunity:

> When France is equated not to England, America, or Russia, but to the one and one-half billion or so people in the world who are not yet industrialized, and when the French genius of giving voice to the hopes of mankind is realized in relation to the vast pools of industrial misery which exists within the gigantic industrial prisons of England and America, the future of France appears brighter in proportion to the degree that she senses, realizes and can articulate and harness the suffering of those trapped both in industrialized and nonindustrialized nations. Here is at once an opportunity for France to assert her traditional self and once again lead the world. Whether the French people know it or not, France seems destined to play a role which perhaps she does not want to play and the refusal of which will spell historical oblivion for her.[8]

In his last years, Wright was to become more alienated from this vision and more openly opposed to French neocolonialism; yet, Wright consistently emphasized the aspects of French life which differentiated it from racist America. This is evident in the history of the Franco-American Fellowship organization which he founded in 1950. This is also evident in his dealings with the Rassemblement Démocratique Révolutionnaire and his solidarity with the Sartre and Merleau-Ponty faction of it. Wright never believed in the racial and political innocence of France, but he displayed the image of an ideal France as a kind of ethical yardstick. During the cold war, this yardstick was seized eagerly by the opponents of the two blocs for propaganda purposes. Just as French critics made Wright into a literary yardstick for black writers, part of the French press used him to denounce racist America.

One specific example is the following anecdote, an oft-repeated "confidence," which appeared for the first time in *Combat* on December 17, 1948: "They say during the UN session, Black American writer Richard Wright was invited to lunch with Mrs. Roosevelt. 'Mr. Wright,' she said reproachfully, 'why did you choose to live in France, since you are such a great English-speaking writer?' 'Well, Madam,' Wright answered very simply, 'it was just to have the possibility of having lunch at your table.'" To anyone aware of Wright's consideration for Mrs. Roosevelt, such an anecdote is obviously made up to attack discrimination in American public facilities. As a rule, Wright's exile and his opinions of America were used by the French press to condemn the opinions of other Americans—of Faulkner, for example, when he said that he had voted for Eisenhower. Even more often, Wright's literary reputation was used to evaluate the achievements of other black American writers, like those of Ann Petry, whose novel *The Street* was translated into French in 1947. It was also used to gauge the success of white American writers like Sinclair Lewis, whose *Kingsblood Royal* (1947) was often reviewed in the same article as *The Street* and was found lacking. In addition, the achievements of French writers dealing with racial subjects were measured against Wright's. The same comparisons prevailed in reviews of works written by Africans or Indians; Joseph Zobel from Martinique was called the "French Richard Wright" when his *Rue Case Nègres* received the *Prix de la Gazette des lettres* in 1950, and in 1948 *Coolie*, by the Indian novelist Mulk Raj Anand, was likened to *Black Boy* (1945). This sort of identification continued throughout the 1950s.

Wright's work was also used to evaluate nonracial fiction and was often alluded to alongside of world classics. It was used apropos of films like, for example, Lattuada's *Senza Pieta:* "People will think of Kafka and Wright at once, faced with the odyssey of this soldier and this poor girl fighting a society and a fate which are equally relentless."⁹ Or Wright was mentioned together with Margaret Mead as an anthropological or sociological authority in order to evaluate a social analysis of American society.¹⁰ Or he was taken as an example of a committed writer. We find interviewer René Mounin thus quoting jazz critic Hughes Panassié: "I wish there always were one Reverdy to make me feel poetry, one Richard Wright to give me proof that the novel is not useless, one Léon Bloy to assure me that God exists."¹¹

Of course, Wright was not responsible for everything the newspaper reporters had him saying and doing. Many of the stories circulating, like the one about Gregory Peck's refusal to sit at the Deux Magots because Wright was there, were fictitious. This happened because Wright had indeed become a representative man, an incarnation of black American genius in exile, a living reproach to his white countrymen, but also an outstanding example of the best America could produce. His declarations were sought and regarded as definitive pronouncements whenever the racial situation became dramatic. And, largely because of him, the cases of Emmett Till and Willie McGee were well publicized in France, where public opinion was quick to condemn those instances of physical or "legal" lynching. Not without bad faith, progressive France rejoiced because Wright had elected to live in Paris. The presence of Wright (and later of Baldwin, Himes, and William Gardner Smith) greatly diminished the effect of the American propaganda services and the image they were trying to project during the McCarthy era.

As far as Wright himself was concerned, his relationship with France was both extremely complex and largely satisfactory. It was inevitable that he should react negatively to certain aspects of material life in postwar France, just as any American who was attuned to a more modern and more efficient mode of living. It is revealing that Wright frequently alluded to Paris, within his family circle, as "my sweet slum." There is a great amount of love in this, as well as some condemnation. This phrase should perhaps be taken together with that of "the alien land"—"alien" here being used as a reproach for America as well as a statement of ineradicable differences. Wright was somewhat disappointed in the high hopes he openly held for a country whose traditions could lead her to a new spiritual leadership. Yet, his real belief in that possibility was smaller than his desire to project the image of an alternative way of life, at a time when cold war politics seemingly left Europe with no choice other than the United States or the USSR. By living in France and holding it up as an example of what could be, Wright wanted to influence American opinion. To be sure, his influence on French opinion was not of his own making. Yet, the extreme importance to the French of his view of the racial and political situation is a testimony to the impact of his vigorous stands and his work in general. Because of Richard Wright, the French were a little better informed, a little more prone to understand black American culture, maybe a little more certain about what to accept and reject from America.

1. This image resulted from the experience of black soldiers in France during World War I. It was also derived from the reports of black writers, such as Langston Hughes, Countee Cullen and even Claude McKay, who had traveled in Europe in the 1920s and 1930s.

2. *American Hunger* (New York: Harper and Row, 1977), p. 24.

3. "I Chose Exile," unpublished article, 1952.

4. Wright declared on June 15, 1946, to M. Scanton: "The City is so wonderful, its intellectual life so vital that I don't think I'll return again soon. I do want to see how these people go about things. And it is good to be somewhere where your color is the least important thing about you."

5. In addition, there is a slight reference to Eva's Paris trip in *The Outsider* and a few references to Fishbelly's friends and their experiences in France in *The Long Dream*. France is also used as a setting for the second part of "Man, God Ain't Like That."

6. Had it been published, "Island of Hallucinations" would have made Wright as much of an "expatriate" novelist as James Baldwin, Chester Himes, William Gardner Smith, and Frank Yerby. For, on the whole, none of them really deals much with France. Baldwin has one novel only, *Giovanni's Room*, and one story, "This Mornng, This Evening, So Soon," over and above his essays. Himes has one novel, *A Case of Rape*, Smith one novel, *The Stone Face*, and Yerby one novel, *Speak Now*, on the relationships of blacks and whites, Americans, and French in Paris.

7. "The Algerian war," he said, "is a war which has nothing to do with the racial problem. French nationalistic feelings, because of industrial development and the incredibly quick healing of the wounds caused by the Second World War, have awakened and are now being employed to forcibly convert Muslims, who are religious fanatics and traditionalists, to French, or if you prefer, Western civilization. My feelings in such circumstances are ambiguous. Frenchmen tell the Muslims at the point of their submachine guns: 'You are French.' We, American Negroes, might wish to be forced in a similar way to consider ourselves as Americans." The interviewer, noting Wright's subtle differentiation, stressed that Wright supported liberation movements in black Africa. In answer to a question, Wright also said that "the role of socialism in the liberation of African countries seems to me highly suspicious. Wasn't it Guy Mollelt, a socialist, who launched the French attack against Suez?" In that case, Wright had been strongly pro-Nasser and anti-French.

8. Unpublished article, entitled "France Must March," probably written in the late 1940s, p. 12. He also states on p. 11: "Perhaps there is no nation in the world today less psychologically prepared to sense the needs of the people whose voice she can become than France. If there is one thing true about France, it is that she does not know the meaning of modern industrialization, the inevitable levelling of values inherent in it, the equating of man to machines . . . the race hates attendant upon such crises as men try to escape or project their sufferings upon others to find relief for their misery and excuse for action, all of which lies beyond, as yet, the boundaries of the French popular mind. Also one wonders to

what degree the French mind today knows of the sleeping millions in India, Africa, China, and the islands in the Atlantic and the Pacific."

9. "Vers un néo-réalisme," *Cahiers du Cinéma*, October, 1948, p. 56.
10. "Sur l'Amérique," *Paris*, April, 1950, p. 101.
11. "Hughes Panassié," *La Casserole*, February 1, 1950.

# Wright
# and the French Existentialists

IF Richard Wright's interest in existentialism was genrally interpreted
by American reviewers during his lifetime as a regrettable concession
to literary fashion or an incongruous "roll in the hay" with "a philosophy
little made to account for Negro life,"[1] critics and scholars have by now
recognized and seriously examined the place and nature of the existentialist world view in Wright's novels, if not in his entire body of writings. For
a time, there even existed a tendency to overemphasize the influence of
the French school of existentialism, as opposed to the German school or
preexistentialist writers like Dostoevsky and Nietzsche. Partly with the
aim of restoring a proper balance, I have already attempted to document
the actual contacts and collaboration—mostly political—between Wright
and such leading French existentialist thinkers and writers as Sartre,
Camus, and de Beauvoir, while providing a more precise, if more sober-
ing, view of possible literary influences.[2] In this article, I will reconsider
this relationship, focusing upon the convergence of philosophical views
and their possible impact on the shaping of Wright's only existentialist
novel. I will touch as well upon the emotional and ideological coloring
that the discovery of French existentialism imparted to Wright's "metaphysical decade," as we might call the years of meditation, pessimism,
questioning, and self-examination that resulted in the writing and publication of *The Outsider*.

Wright's encounter with French existentialism took place in the mid-
1940s at a crucial time in his career, when, having rejected Communism,
if not Marxist perspectives and explanatory principles, he was for the first
time without the sustenance and burden of an ideology. Also, in contemplating the possibilities left open for human values in the industrialized
West at the close of World War II, he had become utterly disillusioned.
His correspondence with Gertrude Stein, among others, documents his
rejection of the consumerism and materialistic goals of American life—

what Henry Miller described at the time as *The Air Conditioned Nightmare.* As Wright turned to Europe as a repository of humanistic concerns in the tradition of the Enlightenment, the pronouncements of the leading French intellectuals—existentialists like Sartre, Camus, and de Beauvoir (each of whom visited the United States on lecture tours and made public their reactions to the American and the European situation)—undoubtedly played a part in reinforcing Wright's own pessimistic leanings.

Wright's existentialism, however, should by no means be limited to his contacts with the French existentialist group from the mid-'40s to the mid-'50s. His interest in an existential world view both predates and postdates those contacts. On the one hand, works like *Native Son* and *Black Boy* already express an existential vision of life, couched in Dostoevskyan terms, which is closely linked with the oppressed, traumatic, and precarious aspects of the Afro-American experience. On the other hand, Wright's genuine interest in and knowledge of Kierkegaard and Heidegger, among the German school of existentialists, lasted throughout his later life and became just as integral a part of his *Weltanschauung* as Marxism. This paper does not deal, therefore, with all the dimensions of Wright's existential philosophy. It concentrates, rather, upon the period (roughly from 1946 to 1953) that saw the genesis of *The Outsider* in order to emphasize possible convergences between Wright's outlook and that of the French existentialists, when it does not prove possible to speak of outright influences.

Wright had three major general preoccupations at the time: how to inject a personal philosophy into Marxist theory; how to restore morality to political action; and how to save mankind from atomic destruction through the reactivation of humanistic values.

The publication of *Native Son* and its reception by the American left-wing and Communist intelligentsia had raised for Wright the problem of how far a Marxist writer could go in presenting a humanist, or personalized, version of his ideology. Aside from all the misunderstandings, the problem arose: did the writer who accepted Marxism enjoy the liberty of expounding a personalized philosophy? In 1937 Wright had outlined his literary program in "Blueprint for Negro Writing" in the CP-sponsored *New Challenge,* but he had not renounced ideas expressed in earlier pieces, often unpublished, like "Personalism," and he remained very much a humanist. A close analysis of Max's speech in *Native Son* reveals he is attempting to state certain ideas and concepts that are implicit in

Marxist philosophy but that, since Marx and Lenin were more interested in politics and economics than in literature, were not previously stated in humanistic terms. Wright had perceived the important failure of Marxism to treat the human personality. In attempting to remedy that, revolutionary novelists like Gorki and Malraux were compelled to use a sort of mysticism for which they were faulted by Communist critics.

On another level, Wright's autobiographical essay "I Tried to Be a Communist" (1944) concerned, among other things, the morality of politics (i.e., the morality of American Communism) and how it was shaped by the nature of race relations in American society. Wright's exposure of its faults, which pointed to what was vital to the theory of (Marxist) action, was in fact an example of that morality in action. After the explosion of the atomic bomb in 1945, he felt more than ever that mankind must move to a humane, intelligent path of action or be removed from the planet. International unity was becoming, more than ever, a political necessity and a matter of life and death.

Ralph Ellison and Wright were close friends at that time, and they often discussed existentialism, especially that of Kierkegaard and Heidegger. In the summer of 1945, Ellison sent Wright, who was thinking of going to Paris, a copy of *Horizon*, the avant-garde British magazine, with an article about new literary developments in France. By this time, Ellison had become as disillusioned and disgusted by American Communist politicians, especially black ones, as Wright had and hoped American complacency could be jostled by "speaking from a station that gets its power from the mature ideological dynamo of France and the Continent."[3] Therefore, when Ellison called his friend's attention to the achievements of the French existentialists, he did so, significantly, out of an interest in writing and commitment, not from a philosophical world view:

> I've been reading some fascinating stuff out of France concerning plays written and produced there during the Occupation. Kierkegaard has been utilized and given a social direction by a group who have organized what is called "Existential Theater," and, from what I read, their psychological probing has produced a powerful art. France is in ferment. Their discussion of the artist's responsibility surpasses anything I've ever seen. . . . They view the role of the individual in relation to society so sharply that the leftwing boys, with the possible exception of Malraux, seem to have looked at it through the reverse end of a telescope. I am sure that over there the war has made the writer more self-confident and aware of the dignity of his craft. Sartre, one of the younger writers, would have no difficulty understanding your position in regard to the Left. He writes:

"Every epoch discovers one aspect of . . . the condition of humanity, in every epoch man chooses for himself with regard to others, to love, to death, to the world (Kierkegaardian categories, aren't they?), and when a controversy arises on the subject of the disarmament of the FFI, or of the aid to be given to the Spanish Republicans, it is that metaphysical choice, that personal and absolute decision, which is in question. Thus by becoming a part of the uniqueness of our time, we finally merge with the eternal, and it is our task as writers to cast light on the eternal values which are involved in these social and political disputes. Yet we are not concerned with seeking these values in an intelligible paradise, for they are only interesting in their immediate form. Far from being relativists, we assert emphatically that man is absolute. But he is absolute in his own time, in his own environment, on his own earth. The absolute which a thousand years of history cannot destroy is *this* irreplaceable, incomparable decision, which he makes at *this* moment, in these circumstances. The absolute is Descartes, the man who escapes us because he is dead . . . and the relative is Cartesianism, that coster's barrow philosophy which is trotted out century after century, in which everyone finds whatever he has put in it. It is not by chasing after immortality that we will make ourselves eternal: we will not make ourselves absolute by reflecting in our works desiccated principles which are sufficiently empty and negative to pass from one century to another, but by fighting passionately in our time, by loving passionately, and by consenting to perish entirely with it."[4]

This letter is revealing of Ellison's own reasons for becoming interested in Sartre, whose philosophy confirmed his opinion that "man is absolute in his own time, in his own environment," i.e., that the black writer will achieve universality by concentrating on the specific, by dealing with his own experience. This restored his self-confidence and belief in the worth of his craft in the face of the political dictates clamoring for "commitment" under the banner of the CPUSA that he was forcefully rejecting.

Wright was similarly concerned with the responsibility of the artist, as evidenced by his moving answer to the South American artist Antonio Frasconi:

There is . . . beyond the boundaries of imperious politics, a common ground upon which we can stand and see the truth of the problem. . . . Out of what vision must an artist create? The question seems vague, but when it is conceived in terms of political pressure from Left or Right, it has vital meaning. . . . I hold that, on the last analysis, the artist must bow to the monitor of his own imagination, must be led by the sovereignty of his own impressions and perceptions.[5]

So much for the vindication of independent thinking and personal outlook. But Wright also emphasized responsibility and commitment to truth:

We must beware of those who seek, in words no matter how urgent or crisis-charged, to interpose an alien and dubious curtain of reality between our eyes and the crying claims of a world which it is our lot to see only too poignantly and too briefly.[6]

In many ways, the French existentialists were addressing similar problems: the responsibility of the intellectual, the defense of humanistic values, the importance of solidarity, the relationship between truth and freedom. These are clearly the concerns and qualities that Wright so much admired in Sartre. He had found him rather reserved when he first met him at a gathering at the home of his friend Dorothy Norman, the editor of *Twice a Year* and a liberal columnist for the *New York Post*. But later, in 1946 and in 1947, when Wright lived in Paris, he often spoke and wrote of Sartre with the utmost enthusiasm and reverence: "Sartre is the only Frenchman I've met who had voluntarily made the identification of the French experience with that of mankind." "How rare a man is this Sartre," he noted in his journal after a conversation during which the French philosopher compared the plight of the colonized world to that of the French under Nazi occupation.[7] Again, after another conversation on the role of the intellectual regarding the political and human situation, Wright noted, not without a touch of delighted awe:

Sartre is quite of my opinion regarding the possibility of human action today, that it is up to the individual to do what he can to uphold the concept of what it means to be human. The great danger, I told him, in the world today is the very feeling and conception of what is a human might well be lost. He agreed. I feel very close to Sartre and Simone de Beauvoir.[8]

Wright reiterated—somewhat naively—his respect for Sartre's intelligence and perspicacity in his "Introduction to the *Respectful Prostitute*," which presented the play to the American reader:

Jean-Paul Sartre, principal exponent of French Existentialism, has brought his keen and philsophical temperament to bear upon the problem of race relations in America. . . . The French mind—especially French minds of the Sartre level—is rigorously logical. . . . The dismally lowered tone of personality expression in America seems ludicrous to the mind of a man who, above all modern writers, is seeking and preaching the integrity of action. . . . It took a foreign mind to see that the spirit of virgins could exist in the personalities of whores. Let us then be thankful for the eyes and mind of Jean-Paul Sartre who, in *La Putain Respectueuse*, is helping us to see ourselves. . . . Finaly remember that the artist is, in the last analysis, a judge and it is the business of a judge to render judgments.[9]

Wright could not but be impressed at this time. He had hardly begun to discover French existentialist philosophy with the help of Dorothy Norman and was only relatively more conversant with the work of the German school, even though, as Ellison's letter suggests, his knowledge of Kierkegaardian categories was more thorough and anterior. This is not to say that Wright did not attempt to study French existentialism. He acquired several introductory treatises, like G. de Ruggiero's *Existentialism* (1946) and Jean Wahl's *Short History of Existentialism* (1949), as well as several books by Sartre in English translation, especially *Existentialism* and *The Psychology of Imagination,* before 1950. Yet *Being and Nothingness* was not translated until 1957, and Wright did not master French well enough to read it in the original. Sartre's metaphysics were, therefore, somewhat unclear to him and less important to his own concerns than such political and social essays as "Anti-Semite and Jew" and "What Is Literature?" and, possibly, than literary works like *Age of Reason, The Reprieve, The Diary of Antoine Roquentin,* and the short stories "Intimacy" and "Men Without Shadows," not to mention Sartre's plays, of which he knew at least *The Respectful Prostitute, Huis-Clos, The Chips Are Down,* and *Les Mains Sales.*

I have dealt elsewhere at some length with Wright's participation in the political ventures of the French existentialists under the banner of the Rassemblement Démocratique Révolutionnaire from 1949 to 1952. I have also explained how the *Temps Modernes* group perceived Wright as a "representative man" and cast him in that role for a time.[10] It remains to be seen, however, to what extent Wright's reverence for Sartre's stance as a committed intellectual and his experiments as a *romancier à thèse* may have inspired Wright's own efforts in *The Outsider.*

Although the early pencil drafts of the novel no longer exist, the half-dozen successive versions of the manuscript are sufficient evidence that, even though it was planned and begun before Wright's first trip to Paris and his acquaintance with French existentialism, the novel was, in some limited manner, influenced by that way of thinking as well as by that style. It must be remembered that Wright apparently started to write a sort of political thriller much in the vein of his earlier naturalistic novels. Drawing on episodes of the then-unpublished *Lawd Today,* he based the experience of his new protagonist, Cross Damon, on the day-to-day, routine, oppressed, and confined existence of Jake, a Chicago postal worker. Admittedly, the sense of confinement and entrapment in a web of circumstances of such a routine recalls Antoine Roquentin's *"engluement"* and subsequent "nausea." Even more Sartrean, if one turns to the plot, is the underground railway accident that allows Cross to start again from scratch with a new yet-to-be-defined identity. This is the "second chance" given by Sartre to one of the protagonists of *The Chips Are Down*. Yet such occurrences that allow man to "create himself out of nothing" do happen in everyday life, and Wright may have thought of the accident episode before leaving the United States. More probably, his reading the trilogy *Les Chemins de la Liberté* (at least the first volume of it) confirmed Wright in his choice of inserting long philosophical exchanges and considerations in the midst of a well-filled, detective-like plot. Perhaps the example of Sartre should not, in this case, have been followed, since his *romans à thèse* do not make very lively reading. It might have been preferable for Wright to rewrite his own novel as a first-person narrative (as he nearly decided to do after reading Camus' novel *The Stranger*).

Does this mean that the influence of Camus prevailed? It would be quite hazardous to make such a statement.

If one considers the way Wright discovered Camus' writings before he met the man, chronological considerations compel us to state, first of all, that in spite of the many resemblances between *Native Son* and *The Stranger*, there never did exist any kind of contact between the two men that could account for possible influences in either direction. Resemblances are coincidental, more a result of convergence.

Wright first heard of Camus in the spring of 1946, around the time he first met Sartre. The first works by Camus that he read deserve closer scrutiny than I have granted them previously because they set the tone for Wright's perception of the Algerian-born novelist. At the end of 1946, *Twice a Year* printed a lecture Camus had given in the spring of that year in New York under the title "The Human Crisis." Strangely enough, when one considers the bulk of Camus' writings and his general outlook, the views he expressed then were exceedingly despondent and pessimistic, notwithstanding a last-minute appeal to "the best in mankind." Such views must have reinforced Wright's contemporary pessimism regarding the morality of politics and the direction of human history in postwar America, where consumerism and the cult of material success were again rampant. Camus spotted what he called "the clearest symptoms" of the human crisis. He denounced "the rise of terror following upon such a perversion of values that a man or a historical force is judged today not in terms of human dignity but in terms of success."[11] Somewhat unexpectedly, Camus was not indicting man's inhumanity to man in wartime—although he later did so—but the overshadowing of human-oriented goals by the quest for material wealth and "happiness." French intellectuals had, as a rule, leveled accusations of crass materialism against the United States in the 1920s and 1930s: the idea was far from new. Yet Camus made American materialism sound ominous and pervasive. He perceived it as the condition of modern man, as a plague coming to Europe:

> If that unhappy man, the Job of modern times, is not to die of his hurts on his dunghill, then must the mortgage of fear and anguish first be lifted, so that he may again find that liberty of mind without which none of the problems set for our modern consciousness can be solved.[12]

Wright's own categories of fear and anguish were probably more "metaphysical" (more Kierkegaardian) than "intellectual," which is the dimension Camus stresses here, but he could not disagree with Camus' second "symptom," namely, loss of "the possibility of persuasion," of appealing to an individual's feelings of humanity to get a human reaction. "For SS," Camus wrote, "were no longer men, representing men but like an instinct elevated to the height of an idea or a theory."[13] This is precisely what Wright tried to prove in *The Outsider* of Communist leaders like Blount or Blimin; and this is what he had opposed in his analysis of the Trotskyite trials in "I Tried to Be a Communist." A corollary of the lack of human response of "commissars" was indeed mentioned by Camus, who conceptualized it as "the replacement of the natural object by printed matter"—the overwhelming rise of bureaucracy—so that, in short, "we no longer die, love, or kill, except by proxy."[14] Camus ended with a discussion of the substitution of the political man for the living man: "No longer are individual passions possible, but only collective, that is to say abstract, passions"[15] in the new cult of efficiency and abstraction.

Although Damon's opponents and targets in *The Outsider* are precisely the cosmic "blocks" of fascism and political totalitarianism—both based upon an essential repudiation of individual needs and feelings—the protagonist's quest is more specifically oriented toward the creation, if not the discovery, of individual norms, which in his utterly nihilistic criticism of existing social values, he hardly manages to claim at the very end. "Man is nothing in particular": Cross's statement to Houston, which in many ways recalls Sartre's definition of man as "a vacant passion," may thus have been, in deeper ways, supported and corroborated by Wright's reading of "The Human Crisis." Indeed, Camus wrote that the cult of efficiency and abstraction explained why man in Europe today experienced only solitude and silence: he could not "communicate with his fellows in terms of values common to them all." Hence, "since he is no longer protected by a respect for man based on the values of man, the only alternative henceforth open to him is to be the victim or the executioner."[16]

Admittedly, the reasons for Cross's outright "metaphysical egotism" could be found more at the personal than at the societal level, as evidenced by his treatment of his women or comrades at the beginning. One should also consider the racial dimension that prevented him from respecting the nonvalues of so-called American ideals. Yet he might have adhered to the ideals of Communism had he not discovered the ruthless authoritarianism of leaders cultivating what Camus calls "abstraction" when not seeking a sensuous enjoyment of power. It followed that Cross's espousal of Nietzschean theories of a godless, amoral universe can also be explained in the terms used by Camus: no longer protected by human norms, man believes in nothing but himself. Camus concludes:

> If we believe in nothing and nothing makes sense and we are unable to find values in anything, then anything is permitted and nothing is important. Then there is neither good nor evil and Hitler was neither right nor wrong. . . . And since we thought that nothing makes sense we had to conclude that he who is right is he who succeeds.[17]

As a result, Wright's definition of "man as nothing in particular," which might be construed in the positive, optimistic Sartrean perspective of man as a potentiality to be actualized through existential choice, seems to come closer to Camus' more despondent view of man as neither good nor evil, and deprived of values. This is the path Cross explores as a murderer, although in his heart of hearts he wishes he were neither victim nor executioner. This reading of Camus thus sheds some added light on his final exclamation about being innocent and having experienced the utmost horror. He is innocent because he is not responsible for the human condition, which is "nothing in particular." He is crushed not only by the horror inherent in this metaphysical predicament, but by the realization that, in Camus' terms, "we knew deep in our hearts that even the distinction was illusory, that at bottom we were all victims, and that assassins and assassinated would in the end be reunited in the same defeat."[18]

Camus and Wright parted ways, however, in their unequal emphasis on politics. In spite of his condemnation of fascism and Communism, or at least of the means used by the latter, Wright, like Sartre and de Beauvoir, believed that political commitment still represented a means for action, and he eagerly joined in the efforts of the Rassemblement Démocratique Révolutionnaire to reject both the United States and the USSR in the name of Europe's freedom of choice. As for Camus, he not only declared that politics must whenever possible be kept in its proper place, which is a secondary one, but also stated emphatically:

> The great misfortune of our time is precisely that politics pretend to furnish us at once with a catechism, a complete philosophy, and at times even a way of loving. But the role of politics is to set our house in order, not to deal with our inner problems. I do not know for myself whether there is or not an absolute. But I do know that this is not a political concern. The absolute is not the concern of all, it is the concern of each. . . . Doubtless our life belongs to others and it is proper that we give it to others when it is necessary, but our death belongs to ourselves alone. Such is my definition of freedom.[19]

Only much later, and only halfheartedly, did Wright thus limit the role of politics in "The Voiceless Ones," a review of Michel del Castillo's *The Disinherited.*[20]

It is evident that Wright's ideology converged with that of the French existentialists, if it was not directly influenced by it at the time. The tone of their respective articles for the "Art and Action" commemorative issue of *Twice a Year* in 1948 is strikingly similar. Wright's "Letter to Dorothy Norman" ends with the declaration that politics and consumerism curtail the definition of man:

> The Right and Left, in different ways, have decided that man is an animal whose needs can be met by making more and more articles for him to consume. . . . A world will be built in which everybody will get enough to eat and full stomachs will be equated with contentment and freedom, and those who will say that they are not happy under such a regime will be guilty of treason. How sad that is. We are all accomplices in this crime. . . . Is it too late to say something to halt it, modify it?[21]

On the following page, Camus' article, entitled "We Too Are Murderers," begins:

> Yes, it is a fact that we have no future, and the present-day world bodes nothing save death and silence, war and terror. But it is also a fact that we ought not tolerate this, for we know that man is long in the making and everything worth living for, love, intelligence, beauty, requires time and ripening.[22]

One could believe that Wright is simply pursuing his argument. As a matter of fact, Wright's letter, sent to Dorothy Norman on March 9, 1948, was not intended for publication; and Camus' article, originally published in *Franchise* in 1946, largely developed the concepts of his lecture "The Human Crisis." At the time, such positions and ideas were in the air in existentialist circles, and it is difficult to attribute the authorship of any of them to any one intellectual. Even Stephen Spender, in "The Spiritual Failure of Europe," expressed similar views in his criticism of the Soviet Union and the United States. He found that the problems of our time were more real in Europe than elsewhere and thus more likely to be stated and solved there:

> Wherever nations and great interests are powerful, they become victims of illusions even if these illusions are euphemistically called political realism. The fundamental illusion of power politics is that freedom begins with the protection of the powerful group.[23]

To return to the similarity of Wright's and Camus' views in the late 1940s, it is likely that Wright's composition of his existentialist novel was influenced in subtle ways by his reading of *The Stranger* in August, 1947. He read the book in the American edition at a very slow pace, "weighing each sentence," admiring "its damn good narrative prose," and remarked:

> It is a neat job but devoid of passion. He makes his point with dispatch and his prose is solid and good. In America a book like this would not attract much attention for it would be said that he lacks feeling. He does however draw his character very well. What is of course really interesting in this book is the use of fiction to express a philosophical point of view. That he does with ease. I now want to read his other stuff.[24]

Wright's remarks are somewhat surprising. On the one hand, he already knew of the use of fiction to express a philosophical point of view through the novels and theories of Sartre and de Beauvoir. Thus, when he calls Camus' use "very interesting" and "done with ease," he refers to the actual blending of message and narrative—something he himself proved little capable of doing in *The Outsider*, where long political and metaphysical speeches stand out like didactic asides. On the other hand, when Wright finds a lack of passion and feeling in *The Stranger*, he refers to a lack of warmth in the style and the pace of the narration, not in the protagonist, since Meursault's indifference is precisely one of the motives for his acts. In *The Outsider* Wright's hero is never "devoid of passion" and acts more upon the compulsion of his egotistical desires than from the utter existential indifference that characterizes Meursault.

Moreover, Wright's narration is never cold or detached, not because the novelist wants to please an American audience who, he supposed, likes "feeling," but because he simply cannot write in Camus's precise but detached fashion. He needs passion and feeling to carry his narrative along. Wright noted nine days after reading *The Stranger* that he felt he ought to write his novel in the first person because "there was a certain note of poignancy missing which a first-person note would supply,"[25] but he made no real attempt to do so. Either *The Outsider* had reached too definitive a stage, or Wright felt incapable of changing his own style; *The Stranger's* influence was not enough to modify significantly the tenor of his own novel. Moreover, had Camus been a determining influence, it is likely that the scenes dealing with Damon's reactions to his mother would have been modified in light of Meursault's reactions to his own. Yet it appears that Wright's motivations for his picture of the mother and son's reciprocal rejection are to be found in idiosyncratic, personal attitudes, rather than in a detached attempt to illustrate metaphysical estrangement.

Leaving later political opinions and racial choices aside, it appears that although Wright and Camus shared a common conception of the role and responsibility of the artist and intellectual in the modern world, as well as a deep-seated pessimism, their artistic temperaments differed far more than those of Wright and Sartre. Another remark that Wright jotted down in his journal on August 7, 1947, is revealing: "There is still something about this Camus that bothers me. Maybe it is because he is the artist and Sartre and de Beauvoir are not primarily." Wright accurately perceived himself, Sartre, and de Beauvoir as less preoccupied with art and less able to achieve the perfect aesthetic adequacy to be found in Camus. He may have felt some regret but could not and would not change his own style of writing.

Simone de Beauvoir was both more congenial and less impressive than Sartre or Camus in Wright's eyes. Not that her thinking was less vigorous than theirs, but her manners were more open and her metaphysical interest always focused upon everyday implications and applications. As a result, Wright found more in common with her than with the two men, insofar as he tended to define Sartre as the metaphysician and Camus as the aesthete.

Since de Beauvoir spoke some English and understood it fairly well, their exchanges were more frequent, too, and Wright knew more about her work and opinions than he did about any other French existentialist. Before reading *The Ethics of Ambiguity* and *The Second Sex*, in 1949 and 1953 respectively, he had been able to ponder de Beauvoir's long and important essays included in the 1948 *Art and Action.* Under the title "Literature and Metaphysics," the first essay provided a theoretical framework for precisely the problems Wright was grappling with when writing *The Outsider,* i.e., the conditions of writing a successful "metaphysical novel." De Beauvoir was convinced:

> There is no doubt that the novel cannot be successful if the writer limits himself to disguising in a more or less alluring fictional cloak a previously constructed ideological framework. . . . It is impossible to see how an imaginary story can serve ideas which have already found their proper mode of expression.[26]

She emphasized the analogous relations between novel writing and metaphysics, the role and value of subjectivity as expressing the temporal form of metaphysical experience, and the aspect of spiritual adventure to be encountered in a novel, which she saw as "an effort to conciliate the objective and the subjective, the absolute and the relative, the intemporal and the historical." Her goal was no less than an attempt to "grasp the meaning at the heart of existence; and if the description of essence belongs to the sphere of philosophy proper, the novel alone makes it possible to evoke the original outpouring of existence in its complete, singular, temporal truth."[27]

Such language was not very different from Wright's definition of a novel's aims and of what it should arouse in its readers, even though he failed to give enough concreteness to his demonstrations in *The Outsider.*

More interesting to him must have been the essay on "Freedom and Liberation," which opposed one of the main objections raised against existentialism, namely, that the precept "seek freedom" proposed no concrete plan of action. De Beauvoir reexamined the concept of freedom to restore its concrete meaning and show that it could be realized only by man's committing himself to the world and embodying his ideal in definite rules of conduct.

Positive freedom was defined as a movement to "unveil being" and turn it into existence: a movement that was constantly being transcended, since man had to "pursue the expansion of his existence and take this effort in itself as an absolute."[28] This expansion was, in many ways, what Wright claimed for Cross Damon. Yet de Beauvoir approved of a personal movement of expansion only insofar as she grounded it in ethics, so as to condemn, in the name of theology, a sort of "happiness" that artifically expanded man's existence through consumerism but really prevented him from transcending it. She analyzed the process of freeing oneself from oppression: there are two ways of transcending the given, to escape (to go on a journey) or to free oneself (from imprisonment), which are very different things, since the present is accepted in the one case, rejected in the other. This led her to criticize Hegel's concept of *Aufhebung*, which is the foundation of his optimism and brings him to regard the future as harmonious development, in the name of realism. She argued that revolt did not integrate itself into harmonious development but constituted a violent disruption, which led Marx to define the proletariat in terms of a negation. Wright actually discussed the concepts and implications of alienation and freedom with Sartre and de Beauvoir. He may have been led to some of his own conclusions about man's responsibility to others and about the limits of individual freedom as incarnate in Damon's end by such assertions as this:

> Freedom need be respected only when it is directed towards freedom and not when it evades itself and falls off from its own principles. . . . And it is not true that the recognition of other people's freedom limits my own. To be free does not mean to have the power to do anything whatsoever; it consists in being able to transcend the given towards an open future; the existence of others as free defines my situation and is even the condition of my own freedom. I am oppressed if I am thrown into prison, not if I am prevented from throwing my neighbor into prison.[29]

One can easily see just how de Beauvoir's conception of other people's freedom meets Sartre's definition of *"l'enfer, c'est les autres,"* or in terms of Wright's fiction, how Damon's nihilism can be reconciled with Fred Daniels's belief that he must share his underground vision with others. De Beauvoir writes, "To be free consists in being able to transcend the given towards an open future." Damon discovers this at his own expense, when he realizes that his disregard of others blocks his capacity for change, for establishing a love relationship with Eva especially, i.e., for transcending his personal problems, even though he was miraculously able to recreate his social relationships out of nothing after the train wreck. Damon has no "open future," not because he is chased and killed, but because his egotism without norms negates the notion of openness, which is the bedrock of freedom.

It would be easy to multiply examples of interface between the theories of French existentialism and their application to literature, and Wright's own use of certain metaphysical concepts in *The Outsider*, but it may be more revealing to stress some differences.

One can regret that Wright did not pattern *The Outsider* more consistently after the simple plot, classical structure, and terse style of *The*

*Stranger,* but his idiosyncrasies oriented him more toward a mixture of melodrama and rhetorical exposition. Edward Margolies aptly points out in his comparison of Damon and Meursault that "both men kill without passion, both men appear unmoved by the death of their mothers; both men apparently are intended to represent the moral and emotional failure of the age."[30] When writing a notice for the jacket of *The Outsider,* Wright himself specified that "the hero could be of any race." He claimed, "I have tried to depict my sense of our contemporary living as I see it and feel it." He also saw the novel as his first literary effort "projected out of a heart preoccupied with no ideological burden save that of rendering an account of reality" as it struck his sensibilities and imagination. It seems, however, that the motivation and behavior of Meursault are more emblematic of modern man than those of Damon. This may be because the earlier section of the novel is patterned after the naturalistic depiction of black ghetto life in *Lawd Today* and also because Damon's resentment is rooted in racial offense, economic oppression, and a familial atmosphere in which the male is spiritually crushed by women. Damon's "metaphysical resentment" would only come second, or even third, after his hatred for political manipulation and totalitarianism.

Many American critics have found that *The Outsider* was plagued by a problem of motivation. Yet, the gratuitousness of Damon's half-dozen murders poses no problem when it is seen as a prevalent feature of French existentialist fiction and when one recalls that Sartre and Camus refrain precisely from exploring the ambiguous relationship between the condition of freedom and the desire to kill.[31] In the case of Wright's hero, his search for unlimited freedom makes him his own victim when his hatred of others turns into self-hatred. And the root of his compulsive violence must be traced back to the behavior of much earlier Wrightian protagonists like Big Boy and Bigger Thomas, those oppressed and temporarily impotent youngsters who are seized by a compulsion to "blot out" their fellow creatures as they would some insect.

This behavior must be related to the condition of social and racial oppression under which the presence of the "other" (the white man, the capitalist boss) is equivalent to torture and hell, where "*l'enfer, c'est les autres.*" But Wright quickly leaves this trend of thinking whereby he might have rejoined the Sartrean perspectives of *Huis-Clos. The Outsider* set out to prove another existentialist theme: "*l'enfer, c'est soi-même,*" which Wright developed most completely in *The Man Who Lived Underground* before he was aware of it as an existentialist concept. In spite of its rhetoric, *The Outsider* rather aptly reveals the gloomy abysses of man's mind when he is totally outside life. Again, the problem is less the satisfaction of the desires and compulsions of the individual than it is man's need for purification. Trapped in his *mauvaise foi* (although his inauthenticity at the beginning of the novel is rather different from Roquentin's or Meursault's), Damon does not really feel the type of nausea experienced by Sartre's hero—his *engluement* is more the condition of being unable to escape from the social trap—and, in spite of a recurrent use of phrases that may have been borrowed from the French existentialists, the reader is reluctant to believe that Cross can simply decide to be his "own little God" and follow his unrestrained desires. Even the five sections of the novel do not really correspond to Kierkegaardian categories beyond the concept of dread. The final titles, "Despair" and "Decision," are interesting insofar as they recall the mood, if not always the concepts, emphasized both in the gloomy forebodings of Camus' essay on the crisis of man and in de Beauvoir's more spirited analysis of freedom and commitment. Wright's outlook, however, is more unremittingly bleak and somber, and also more narrowly individual than even Camus'. On the whole, the French existentialists were preoccupied with societal survival through the restoration of human values and morality, whereas Damon's trajectory is a negation of all social norms; and this final decision, at the end of his metaphysical journey to the end of night, is more the result of intrinsic dread than the outcome of clearly defined, freely made choice. In the course of Wright's narrative, a world grounded upon the freedom of existentialist choice does not seem possible. Although he symbolically slays the totalitarian and authoritarian monsters of fascism and Communism (presumably for, among other reasons, the greater freedom of mankind), and although he finds in Houston a kindred spirit and an emblematic opposite, Damon never really bridges the gap between himself and others, as is made clear by Eva's suicide when she knows the "horrible truth" about her lover. If Camus' saying "Our life belongs to others but our death belongs to us alone" is true, then Damon is unable to do anything with his death, except to utter a desperate cry of horror that is just as ambiguous as that of Kurtz at the close of *Heart of Darkness*. The "horrible innocence" of Damon—a victim of inhuman society and metaphysical fate as much as of totalitarian ruthlessness—is compounded by his being one of the Nietzschean "new men," one of the godless race who suffer no obligations, since they recognize no values. At this stage, therefore, Wright seems to part ways with the French existentialists. Again, his definition of man as "nothing in particular" does not correspond to Sartre's conception of man as "anything," i.e., as a potentiality to be fulfilled and actualized through choice and action. Wright's view is far more nihilistic than Sartre's; even though Damon's final claim is for human solidarity and compassion, his murderous past and the general atmosphere of *The Outsider* leave us with the impression that this change of heart *in articulo mortis* does not suit the protagonist's previous behavior, that this is a last-minute choice inflicted upon by the novelist.

One may wonder about the reasons for these differences in mood between Wright and the French existentialists, mostly Sartre and de Beauvoir, with whom Wright had so much in common and with whom he worked for years along common political lines. Was it that, for the French intellectuals, existentialism remained less visceral, more conceptual, more "intellectual," in a word, than for the man who had painfully emerged from the deprivations and insecurity described in *Black Boy*? Was it due to Wright's "American" situation—the plight of a modern man in a country of extremes, a country more urbanized than France, which could not fall back on the comfortable traditions of lay humanism to explain theoretically and vindicate what was happening to it? When they expressed their horror at a "valueless universe," the French existentialists often did so in order to excite others to a redefinition of the essential moral and human qualities of social life. When, under the brunt of political disillusionment, Wright explored the implications of a normless existence, he did so with characteristic thoroughness and impetus, with the result that he outdid even Camus' gloomiest forebodings. The results of his attempt are undoubtedly clumsier and psychologically less convincing than the novels of Sartre or Camus; yet for all its aesthetic faults and not too subtle conceptualization, *The Outsider* remains a fascinating piece of writing, and one that still speaks to our present needs. By comparison, *Les Chemins de la liberté* is best regarded as a historical testimony about the mistakes and hopes of the war generation.

1. See, among others, J. Saunders Redding, "Home Is Where the Heart Is," *New Leader*, December 11, 1961, pp. 24–25: "The one thing French that caught him was Existentialism, and this held him only long enough for him to write his unqualifiedly bad novel." At a 1964 symposium, transcribed in Herbert Hill's *Anger and Beyond* (New York: Harper, p. 209), Redding was of the opinion that "Existentialism is no philosophy to accommodate the reality of Negro life, especially Southern Negro life," and he agreed with Arna Bontemps, who dismissed Wright's metaphysical attempts as "a roll in the hay with the French existentialists."

2. See my article, "Richard Wright and the French Existentialists," *MELUS*, 5 (Summer, 1978), pp. 39–51; also the relevant chapter of *The Unfinished Quest of Richard Wright* (New York: William Morrow, 1973), especially pp. 320–22.

3. Ralph Ellison, Letter to Wright, August 18, 1945.

4. Ellison, Letter to Wright, July 22, 1945.

5. Richard Wright, "Richard Wright to Antonio Frasconi—An Exchange of Letters," *Twice a Year*, 12–13 (Fall–Winter, 1945), p. 258.

6. "Wright to Frasconi," p. 251.

7. Wright, Unpublished journal, August 7, 1947.

8. Unpublished journal, September 7, 1947.

9. Wright, "Art and Action," *Twice A Year* (1948), p. 14–15.

10. See Fabre, "Wright and the French Existentialists."

11. Albert Camus, "The Human Crisis," *Twice a Year*, 14–15 (Fall–Winter, 1946–47), p. 22.

12. Camus, p. 22.

13. Camus, p. 23.

14. Camus, p. 23.

15. Camus, p. 24.

16. Camus, p. 24.

17. Camus, p. 24.

18. Camus, p. 26.

19. Camus, p. 29.

20. Wright wrote: "May it not develop that man's sense of being disinherited is not mainly political at all, that politics serve it as a temporary vessel, that Marxist ideology in particular is but a transitory mankeshift pending a more accurate diagnosis, that Communism may be a painful compromise containing a definition of man by sheer default?" See "The Voiceless Ones," *Saturday Review*, 43 (April 16, 1960), p. 54.

21. Wright, "Two Letters to Dorothy Norman," "Art and Action," *Twice a Year* (1948), 73.

22. "Two Letters to Dorothy Norman," p. 73.

23. "Two Letters to Dorothy Norman," p. 79.

24. Wright, Unpublished journal, August 7, 1947.

25. Unpublished journal, August 7, 1947.

26. "Art and Action," p. 89.

27. "Art and Action," p. 92.

28. "Art and Action," p. 97.

29. "Art and Action," p. 100.

30. Edward Margolies, *The Art of Richard Wright* (Carbondale: Southern Illinois University Press, 1969), p. 135.

31. See Kingsley Widmer, "The Existential Darkness: *The Outsider*," *Wisconsin Studies in Contemporary Literature*, 1 (Fall, 1960), pp. 13–21. This essay very competently addresses itself to the comparison of some of the conceptual components of the novel with those emphasized by Kierkegaard and other German existentialists on the one hand, and by Sartre on the other.

# Wright's Exile

SINCE Richard Wright's death, much has been written about his self-exiled life in Paris and his relationship to America, white or black. During his life, he was frequently attacked in the columns of the American establishment press, and very little was written which aimed to defend him or to explain the near-necessity and the true meaning of his exile. Any attempt to summarize the reactions of the American press to Wright's books from 1946 to the present, or to trace the effect of Wright's supposed "anti-Americanism" or American critical attitudes, would amount to a full study in itself. Therefore, I shall only briefly allude to it. Similarly, the attitude of the white American colony and the government services in Paris toward Wright deserves a long analysis of its own. My lecture is thus bound to be somewhat sketchy, and many of the subtleties and intricacies of political attitudes, personal antagonisms, and literary jealousies can only be hinted at. In order to present what I consider the most important facet of Wright's relationship with America while in exile, I shall limit myself to examining Wright's own point of view. This point of view, deeply logical though sometimes changing, informed his public declarations, his political stands, and even his writing during the late 1940s and the '50s. This period was of course one of the most tense in American history, witnessing not only the birth of the cold war but also the frantic rise of McCarthyism—a period during which the prewar investigations of the Dies Committee seemed innocuous in comparison with the probings of the Senate Subcommittee on Un-American Activities, a period during which Wright certainly would have suffered, had he remained in America, both from his former membership in the Communist Party, and from his vigorous fight against racism. The younger people among you should bear in mind that, a few decades ago, the spoken criticism of one's country was considered dangerous enough to be regarded as sufficient reason for silencing someone—dangerous enough for a writer of the stature of Richard Wright to represent a threat to the image that America was then bent upon disseminating abroad. Hence the historical importance of Wright's own attitude and pronouncements as a critic of America.

It goes without saying that Richard Wright had been deeply dissatisfied with the black man's place in the American system for a long time, even a long time before he joined the Communist Party (perhaps more as a way of getting out of the cultural ghetto than out of a sense of outrage). It is impossible to find in the whole of his works a single sentence of unreserved praise for his mother country. Nor does one ever encounter in his journal or private correspondence the spontaneous ejaculations of wonder or ease that abound when he thinks about France, though this praise of France is usually quickly followed by criticism. The only glorification of America in his works that I can recall is in a 1936 poem entitled "Transcontinental," but this is a glorification of what America *could be* under a Soviet regime. And his review, written in 1945, of *Struggling Upwards and Other Works* by Horatio Alger, which he had read so avidly in his youth, shows how completely he had eschewed the myth of the American dream.

His removal to France did not appreciably change his attitude towards the United States, and his exile was more the result of the attitude of white Americans towards him and his image of America than it was the result of his discovering in France a more humane style of life and a freer cultural atmosphere. When he wrote "I Choose Exile" (which *Ebony Magazine* had requested in 1950 but refused to print and which other American magazines prudently discarded), Wright was already trying to explain, if not justify, his choice which was already described as un-American in 1951. He was on the defensive; thus, he was picking his words cautiously and weighing them when he wrote:

> I'll define my idea of freedom, though I'm certain I run the risk of being branded as Un-American. If I am, then I readily plead guilty; but I insist I am *not* Anti-American, which, to me, is the important thing.
>
> My Un-Americanism, then, consists of the fact that I want the right to hold, without fear of punitive measures, an opinion with which my neighbor does not agree; the right to travel wherever and whenever I please even though my ideas might not coincide with those of whatever Federal Administration might be in power in Washington; the right to express publicly my distrust of the "collective wisdom" of the people; the right to exercise my conscience and

intelligence to the extent of refusing to "inform" and "spy" on my neighbor because he holds political convictions differing from mine; the right to express, without fear of reprisal, my rejection of religion.

These un-American sentiments add up to a fundamental right which I insist upon, the right to live free of mob violence, whether that violence assumes the guise of an anonymous blacklisting or of pressure exerted through character assassination. ("I Choose Exile," unpublished ms., pp. 1–2.)

At that time, Wright was forced to define his attitude toward America in relationship to what was taking place in the United States, where the tensions due to the cold war had turned the administration into a kind of super-surveillance bureau. A few years earlier, his attitude had been very different: he did not take a political stand in favor of individual rights and democracy so much as he criticized American mass culture. In a 1946 letter to Gertrude Stein, he alluded to Phillip Wylie's *Generation of Vipers* and Henry Miller's *The Air-Conditioned Nightmare*, preferring Wylie's book as the stronger of the two, because, in his opinion, Wylie fought America as an American, and Miller fought America as an American who went to Europe. He concluded:

I'm very interested in this matter how one regards one's country. It is very easy to damn America by rejecting America and it is very hard to damn American while accepting America. Most of the new generation of writers have no illusions about America, yet they feel themselves above all as Americans. I criticize America as an American and you do too, which I think is the only real way to do the job. Miller's rejection of America seems to me the act of a weak man. (Wright to Gertrude Stein, April 12, 1946.)

This distinction between criticizing America as an American and rejecting America as an expatriate is an important one because, to the end of his life in exile, Wright did not yield to the temptation, which would have been amply justified by the reactions of official America to him, to reject America. He hoped America would be transformed and that his criticism could be of help in the process. Such is clearly his attitude in 1952, when he had had plenty of opportunities to see his country from afar and to gauge foreign reactions to it. "I Choose Exile" ends with these words:

Yet, exile though I am, I remain unalterably and simply American and, as such, I've often asked myself, if, armed with these gloomy insights garnered from an exiled life, I could somehow aid my country in its clumsy grappling with alien realities; if I could somehow warn Americans against a too self-righteous display of wealth in the face of a naked and shivering world; if I could in some way inject into the American consciousness a consciousness of *their* consciousness. . . . Daily press dispatches and tourist word of mouth descriptions of what is transpiring back home make me doubtful. Would not such advice sound suspiciously like Communist propaganda? Would it not seem to place a morally objectionable question mark after our fondest convictions of the invulnerability of material might? Any offer of help of that sort might well merit a militant attack on the part of those determined, in their shortsightedness, to defend at any cost their American purity. . . . So I watch my country from afar, but with no sense of glee, no smug self-satisfaction; rather it is with a strange perturbation of heart. ("I Choose Exile," pp. 16–17.)

As the years passed and the hostility against him grew, however, Wright's attitude began to change. Let us now examine the forms this hostility took and how it affected the writer in exile.

One of the first incidents Wright had encountered apropos of his going to France had been, after the "friendly" advice offered by several New York acquaintances to dissuade him from going, a disguised refusal of the State Department to grant him a passport. Finally, thanks to the intervention of Gertrude Stein's friends, like Chagall's son-in-law, French cultural attaché Claude Levi-Strauss offered Wright an official invitation, making it impossible for the government to withhold a passport without an official explanation to the French diplomats. Thus, the State Department completely reversed its attitude: officially, Wright was to be in charge of some American paintings loaned to the French government for an exhibition. After having been prohibited from going, he was reluctantly made a kind of ambassador in the hope that he would moderate his remarks on American race relations. The American Embassy in Paris tried to woo Wright at first. He relates the following anecdote in "I Choose Exile": "At a cocktail party a strange white American took me discretely aside and whispered in my ear: 'Listen, for God's sake, don't let these foreigners make you into a brick to hurl at our windows!' I realized that a bare recital, when uttered in an alien atmosphere, of the facts of Negro life in American constituted a kind of anti-American propaganda" (p. 8).

Wright always refused to play the game. He answered the questions of the French journalists frankly, he told it "like it was," and naturally the gap between him and the people at the American Embassy quickly widened.

I would like to digress here a moment to distinguish between the reactions of the Embassy people to Wright's presence and his statements, and the attitude of white Americans in Paris toward him. Because of his race, Wright was kept at a distance by most WASP members of the American colony. Of course, he never tried to win their acceptance, since he hated their company and the kind of shallow social life they were leading. Apart from a few personal friends and acquaintances among the American whites, Wright received a friendly welcome from the Reverend Clayton Williams, at that time pastor of the American Church in Paris, the directors and staff of the American Library in Paris, especially Harry Goldberg, several other government employees at the American Cultural Center, and most of the staff of the American Center for Students and Artists and the Benjamin Franklin library. On the whole, there was far less racial prejudice among government officials and employees than among the rich WASP set, American firms in general, and even the American Hospital in Neuilly. But, because the employees of the Embassy represented the policy of the government, Wright encountered among them an understandably larger opposition on political grounds, especially when Senator McCarthy sent Roy Cohn on a European trip to put pressure on U.S. libraries to ban so-called un-American books.

At that time, Wright was notorious for opposing the Marshall Plan, for siding with the coalition of left-wing groups called Rassemblement Démocratique Révolutionnaire both against the United States and the Soviet Union, and for his interviews in French newspapers denouncing racism on American soil. He then went even further: he tried to fight racism in the American colony in Paris itself. This was, along with his hope of creating a rapprochement between progressive and liberal French intellectuals and their American counterparts, one of the major aims of the short-lived but by no means negligible French-American Fellowship Association, which he founded in 1949. I personally think that James Baldwin is unfair to the association in his "Alas, Poor Richard" article. He describes it as "one of the most improbable and old-fashioned of English melodrama" (*Nobody Knows My Name*. New York: Dial Press, 1961, p. 208) and pretends not to have taken it seriously, but the record shows that he took it seriously enough at the time to attend more than one meeting and to assume the responsibility of investigating the employment opportunities for black Americans and the racist policy of white American firms in Paris. After a flagrant instance of racial discrimination in the hiring of a nurse at the American hospital, the Franco-American Fellowship held a press conference, and Wright gave a long interview to *France Observateur* (later published in *Crisis,* June, 1950, under the title "American Negroes in France"). The incident was greatly publicized by the French press, and, although Wright received several indignant letters from white Americans, none of them could disprove his statements. During the first half of 1950, Wright and other members of the association were busy asking the Supreme Court to intervene in the case of the seven black boys at Martinsville, Virginia, who had been found guilty of rape and sentenced to death. Above all, they helped M.R.A.P., the major French organization against racism, to build up a wide campaign in favor of Willie McGee, and later raised funds for his widow and children.

Wright never lost a chance to denounce American rasicm in all its aspects. Thanks to him, the image of the United States that the French public held was a little removed from the image broadcast by official propaganda. Hence the inimical reactions from the Embassy. During the period in which McCarthyism was most virulent, the situation became critical for Wright: had he been expelled from France under any pretext, he would have had to face the Committee on Un-American Activities at home. Besides, it was not uncommon for American citizens abroad trying to renew their passports to have them confiscated when these citizens were too openly critical of their government. Wright lived in constant fear of this and thus he had to reinforce his friendships with the few people he knew in the French government, even at the cost of maintaining a public silence about the Algerian war in the following years. An instance of this concern can be found in a letter he wrote to the editor of the *Yale Law Journal* on May 5, 1952, in response to its article "Passport Refusals for Political Reasons":

> As an American living abroad . . . What struck me was that the article dealt with so few cases of the State Department's refusing to grant passports . . . Would the writer be interested in gaining contact with other people who had their passports taken from them? If so, I can put him in touch with at least three others.
>
> The purpose of this letter is to beg a world of information from the writer. If the State Department notifies an American citizen living abroad that his passport has been cancelled, and if the passport remains in possession of the owner and is not stamped cancelled, and if the American citizen refuses to surrender said passport, what law is he violating? The passport in question, let us suppose, has just been renewed for a period of two years . . . In asking this question I'm assuming of course that the American citizen in question is not attempting to avoid legal sanctions, that he is living in a country where the United States government does not have to protect him.

It is clear that Wright had no theoretical case in mind; rather, he was preoccupied with his own status and what he would have to do, were his passport actually cancelled.

But Wright was allowed to remain in Paris. America dealt with him in other ways, sometimes far more subtly. During the 1950s, and especially after the publication of *The Outsider*, the reaction of American critics and the American press in general toward Wright's books was one of dissatisfaction at his remaining away or at his being critical of American policy in the Third World. A more or less disguised attempt was made to dismiss Wright's criticism of America as politically and culturally irrelevant, under the pretense that he had been away too long or that he had been blinded by Communism (although he had repudiated it) and by existentialism. Most of the adverse criticism boiled down to the unformulated accusation of "un-Americanness," of dealing in foreign ideologies, or alien philosophies, of having forsaken the good old American truths. I must stress, however, that there was comparatively little criticism of that sort in the form of reviews of the books Wright published while in exile. We must not imagine that there was a vast conspiracy of silence towards him and that it worked; rather McCarthyism and the changing times had apparently made the American audience unmindful of what Wright had to say. Some critics still maintain that, indeed, Wright's work had then become irrelevant to the American scene, but let me avoid that point of controversy for now.

The most striking instances of unfavorable criticism of Wright's attitudes are, in my opinion, to be found in an invidious article written for *The Reporter* by Negro journalist Ben Burns in 1956 and in the slanderous way *Time* magazine reproached Wright with "Living Amid the Alien Corn" in 1957.

Ben Burns, whom Wright knew personally, had been one of the *Ebony Magazine* editors who had refused "I Choose Exile" in 1952. At the time, Wright had courteously replied: "Frankly I have come to feel . . . that the sentiments I expressed in that article were a little too strong for your magazine. I don't quarrel with you for this. You are on the home scene and you know better than I do what kind of an impression you want *Ebony* to make." (Wright to the Editors of *Ebony Magazine*, January 23, 1953.) After a while, Wright had finally managed to have his piece returned in order to send it to the *Atlantic Monthly*. When that magazine also refused it, he declared to Paul Reynolds: "It simply means that fear has reached even to Boston. Being far away from America gives me a kind of insight into the country which, perhaps, even those there do not have. It just means that one can't praise even the culture of an ally, and France is our official ally" (Wright to Reynolds, January 30, 1953). He even went so far as to promise Reynolds that he would talk only about the effects of industrialization, and in a noncommitted, "non-national" way, to the *New York Times* reporters who were supposed to interview him. He was therefore surprised and angered when he read Burns's attack in *The Reporter*. Among criticism in general of the black circle in Paris, which he called "Café society," Burns wrote that:

> Wright's venom, retailed constantly by expatriates at sidewalk carés plus years of headlines about Dixie lynching, has succeeded in poisoning European thinking about racial problems in America. No amount of documents on the change of status of the U.S. Negro, no statistics . . . avail to revise these European opinions. Richard Wright enjoys a good audience on the Left Bank for his hate school of literature. ("They're Not Uncle Tom's Children," *The Reporter*, March 8, 1956, p. 22.)

Burns went on to prove, quite rightly, that there was racism in France, that Wright did not dare talk about the Algerian war for fear of being expelled, and that the average American Negro was better off financially than many Frenchmen. But in shamelessly resorting to these arguments, he was only repeating the old tricks used by any country to turn away criticism of its racial policies. Wright's reactions to the matter are contained in a letter to Reynolds: "It is simply foolish to say that I poisoned the mind of Europe; if that is true, I am more powerful than either Moscow or Peking. . . .Ben Burns saw me only in one café where he asked to be taken. . . . To my mind, subversion is a legal business and I felt that Burns was taking the role of the Attorney General when he said that I bordered on the subversive," he wrote on April 13, 1956. Afterward, Wright staunchly refused to have anything to do with "that individual."

The other important episode consisted in *Time* magazine's attributing to Wright a sentence he had never spoken in an interview he had never granted. In a November 17, 1958, article entitled "Amid the Alien Corn," attacking black expatriates in Paris, Wright was said to have declared, among other things, that "the Negro problem in America has not changed in three hundred years." Now, on another occasion Wright could have said that the mind and mood of white America had not changed much in three centuries, but such a phrasing of his thought was inaccurate, and besides, he had not said that to a *Time* reporter, since he had refused to grant an interview. *Time* had used Gisele Freund to photograph him and then afterward concocted a false interview.

Wright tried to fight *Time*. Gisele Freund wrote a declaration for him, dated November 22, 1958, in which she said: "Contrary to the report and the impression created by *Time* magazine, I state emphatically that I did not interview you for *Time* magazine," and she noted that at the time she did not know who had commissioned the photographs. On November 25, 1958, *Time* magazine wrote to Wright's lawyers in New York: "The photographer immediately reported the quotations to *Time*'s Paris Bureau. . . . Moreover the quotations seem to be Mr. Wright's sentiment concerning this country. . . . Furthermore I do not believe that the quotations attributed to Mr. Wright are in any way actionable according to our libel laws or the laws of France. In the circumstances, the editors of *Time* will not consider publishing any retraction settling your client's claim."

Wright did not sue, since he could not have gotten more than the symbolic dollar for damages, but he achieved a kind of victory nevertheless. The Paris bureau of the magazine refrained in the future from attacking other expatriates: "They claimed," Wright wrote Paul Reynolds, "that they were inspired by another article appearing in a British periodical . . . planted by an American to start an international fuss about American Negroes living in France (Wright to Reynolds, November 19, 1958), adding in another letter, "The local *Time* let it leak out that they had gathered a whole batch of letters hostile to me from their *Time* readers and they were going to run them. I think we stopped that." (Wright to Reynolds, December 8, 1958).

I shall not go into details, but this attack and the tactics used by *Time* magazine certainly were part of a wider effort to discredit black expatriates and to make their expulsion easier if they could not be silenced. These were the typical cold war methods of dealing with embarrassing people. Wright provided an excellent analysis of such tactics long before radical magazines like *Ramparts* revealed the many connections and fronts of the CIA. He expounded on these tactics in his last lecture, given at the American Church in Paris in early November, 1960. He denounced, for example, the system used by America to control American Negroes:

> It is a deadly fight in which brother is set against brother, in which threats of physical violence are hurled by one black to another, where vows to cut or kill are voiced . . . Having lived on the fringes of that system, I feel free to speak of it; I think I've grasped its outlines with a certain degree of objectivity. . . . My speaking of it has this aim: perhaps I can make you aware of the tragic tensions and frustrations which such a system of control inflicts upon Negro artists and intellectuals" ("The Position of the Negro Artist and Intellectual in American Society," unpublished lecture, p. 11).

Wright proceeded to depict the black American's struggle against economic reality and psychological conditioning. He felt that politically, the Communist stance was often inimical to the Negro, but that the United States government was afraid of his Communism. He believed that the statement Paul Robeson had made in 1949, that the Negroes in America would not fight against Russia, was foolish and irresponsible, yet the U.S. government had apparently taken that threat seriously. Robeson had been blacklisted and ousted, perhaps not so much because the government was afraid of him but because he represented alien ideas circulating among Negroes. Communism was merely a pretense, for any other doctrine would have served as well, Wright added. He then analyzed the methods through which ideological control was achieved, through spying, through infiltrating potentially revolutionary organizations with black undercover agents of the FBI or CIA:

> Obviously we are entering a period where complete control over the ideology seeping into the Black belts cannot be completely maintained. Books, mass means of communication, the developing tourist habits of the Negro, have broken down the walls . . . Negroes who harbored revolutionary ideas were not talking, they were wary. They had to be found and identified . . . Hence Negroes who could talk Communism were sent into the Black Belts. Indeed I'd say that there is more Communism being talked among Negroes today than ever but it is a false Communism; the language of the informer, the spy. . . . I'd go so far as to say that most Communism in the Black Belts today is sponsored by the American government. I'll go further, I'll say that most revolutionary movements in the Western world are government-sponsored; they are launched by agents provocateurs to organize the discontented so that the government can keep an eye on them. ("The Position of the Negro Artist and Intellectual in American Society," unpublished lecture, p. 23–24.)

Wright had spotted several black spies operating in Paris, and he said half-jokingly: "Sometimes I have patriotic moods and I have dreamed of setting up in Paris a bureau to invent identities for stray Negro spies." ("The Position of the Negro Artist and Intellectual in American Society," unpublished lecture, p. 24 b.) Wright resolutely tried to confront that situation for the sake of fighting political and moral corruption: "I think that mental health urges us to bring all of these hidden things into the open where they can be publicly dealt with. What have I been describing to you? I've been describing various forms of moral corruption—corruption which has its roots in fear and greed" ("The Position of the Negro Artist and Intellectual in American Society," unpublished lecture, p. 34).

Before we continue with Wright's delineation of the governmental methods of control over the black man, I would like to answer a few questions that have undoubtedly crept into your minds: For example, if Wright knew that the CIA sponsored many so-called progressive organizations, why did he himself deal with these organizations, and even accept money from them?

First of all, Wright was unaware at the beginning that the Congress for Cultural Freedom, which had been set up in 1951, I believe, was indirectly controlled by the CIA. He gave several lectures for their Paris bureau and wrote articles for *Preuves* and *Encounter* magazines. In fact, he went to Bandung on their money, but I must add that he insisted on the conditions that he would not represent anybody other than himself, that he would not accept any kind of censorship and that he would speak freely of whatever he would see. I must also add, in all fairness, that the people in charge agreed to all this and kept their promise. Afterwards, in the late '50s, they wanted Wright to go to India and give lectures there, hoping that this would serve their propaganda, but he refused and things remained at that point, all contact between them ceasing.

When, shortly after the 1956 Congress of Black Writers and Artists, the American Section of the Society of African Culture (AMSAC) was founded, Wright knew that several of its members had tacitly agreed to play the game of the U.S. government as regards negritude, pan-Africanism, and African politics. He collaborated with them as long as he thought that what they were doing could, in one way or another, serve the aims of African nationalism and decolonization. But when he found out that help from them came only with strings attached, he refused it. In 1959, he applied for a grant of several thousand dollars in order to go to West Africa again and to do a story on former French colonies. John A. Davis, then AMSAC president, apparently feared that what Wright would say might harm the position of AMSAC and, in that case, AMSAC would not want to sponsor Wright's book, thus getting nothing for their money (John A. Davis to Wright, May 2, 1959). "After due reflection," Wright answered, "I have come to the conclusion that the prospect of doing 'harm' would psychologically cripple me in trying to gather material on French Africa. . . . I'd not like to go there with the feeling that I'd have to inhibit myself in whatever I'd write. I think that the wiser course for me would be to seek more disinterested sponsorship. By doing so I'm personally responsible for what I'd write and the public reaction" (Wright to John A. Davis, June 3, 1959). The tone of this letter is friendly, but it clearly indicates where Wright drew the line in any compromise.

Now let us return to Wright's exposure of the American government's handling of American Negro protest organizations and nationalist movements in Africa and his description of the effect of McCarthyism on black expatriates in Paris. It should be kept in mind that these remarks of his were prompted more by a desire to open people's eyes than by a desire to strike back at the personal attacks he himself had undergone. During his last lecture, Wright repeatedly used personal examples and mentioned names of black writers who had been involved in such disputes, but only to make his disclosures believable. He was much more interested in dealing with general policies and principles. Speaking of black writers, he said at the beginning of his talk:

> Their words can be disputed, and this disputation does not apply to figures or facts but to attitudes. For example, the white writers and critics of America find it morally correct to hurl criticisms at a Negro writer if he lectures about the race problem, say, in Sweden. He is told that it is better to 'wash dirty clothes at home' rather than in public or where Communists can hear him. There are times when the white American press, periodicals such as *Time* or *Life*, will castigate a Negro novelist not for what he says but for the geographical position which he has taken up on earth. Hence a Negro American writer living in Paris will be sneered at in the white press of America for having chosen to live there. Naturally a white writer does not come in for such critical blastings. ("The Position of the Negro Artist and Intellectual," p. 1.)

Wright was clearly trying to vindicate the black American writer's right to speak out, for himself, for the black community, for the world. He felt the duty of the Afro-American writer lay in defending not only the rights of the Negro but the rights of man, and he could do so in a more efficient and more objective way when criticizing his own country from a distance:

> At home I had spent half of my lfie advocating the rights of the Negro and I knew that if my fight was not right, then nothing was right. Yet I always felt a sneaking sense of futility because I knew there was something basically wrong in a nation that could so cynically violate its own Constitution and democratic pretensions by meting out physical and psychological cruelties to a defenseless minority. From the distance of a freer culture, my feelings somewhat changed. Anger turned into a sort of amazed pity, for I felt that America's barbaric treatment of the Negro was not one-half so bad as the destructive war which she waged, in striking at the Negro, against the Rights of Man, and against herself! ("The Position of the Negro Artist and Intellectual," p. 11.)

It was clearly not a question of personal reactions, whether to racism or to the pressures of the State Department, so much as a matter of principles, of acting in the way Wright believed a true American should act. For we must not be mistaken. In spite of a strong temptation to resign his citizenship near the very end of his life, Wright never ceased to be a loyal American citizen, loyal to his country, not as it was at the time but as he imagined it could be one day: a country whose nationality would be defined through all the components and races which form it, and not purely through the dominant groups or classes which claimed to represent 100 percent America. Seen in these terms, the question of Wright's Americanness or un-Americanness becomes nearly irrelevant.

This question of Wright's Americanness was nowhere better defined than in a piece he wrote, probably in the late '50s for delivery to a French audience. To the question "Am I an American?" Wright gave not one, but some eighty-six answers, each one beginning with "I am an American but . . ." and the "but," of course, is the important point. (The order of the eighty-six answers in the unfinished and often illegible draft is arbitrary and Wright would probably have reorganized the sequence; I have therefore taken the liberty of grouping related answers in order to stress the main lines of his thinking. In the following quotation from this piece, the numbers appearing at the end of the quotation are those of each answer.)

Briefly, Wright appears to be proud of his country's past and some of its present achievements, but not at the expense of any other nation; he does not feel that the U.S. is the end-product of all history, holding the only truth. He is ashamed of her racial and imperialistic policies at home and abroad, her religious and political intolerance, her way of buying off leaders of the Third World, of labeling Africa as primitive and despicable. He regrets that the United States was not first in declaring war on Nazi Germany and that it supported the fascist regimes of Franco, Batista, and Syngman Rhee. He feels that the so-called melting pot has never melted anything and that the WASPs are still apeing the cultural standards of Europe to the detriment of indigenous creation.

In opposition to what he has always deplored in American civilization— even by 1942 he was describing Americans as "lovers of trash"—Wright gradually forms a definition of what he means by "American," in a style strongly reminiscent of Gertrude Stein's roundabout way of staying with a theme or an idea. We can find in it a vindication of Wright's exile:

> I am an American but tomorrow I could surrender my citizenship and still be an American (49).

I am an American but I can live without America and still be an American, which ought to—I feel—prove what an American is or ought to be (64).

I am an American but I would rather surrender being an American so that the American in me can be believed (66).

I am an American but I feel most American when I no longer know that I am an American, for I feel that being an American ought to mean freedom from the psychological cruelty of being solely identified as one (36).

I am an American but I insist upon talking about the meaning of being an American because I know that being an American means more to the world and mankind than what is defined as being an American today (58).

I am an American but I am persuaded that America means infinitely more than she thinks she means to the world today (65).

So far we see that Wright insists upon two points: first, today's America contrasted with what it was yesterday, and second, America is more than she thinks she is, opposing therefore, the international idea to the national one.

Rather surprisingly, Wright also insists on the value of tradition: "I am an American, but I realize and sense the meaning of my revolt that made me an American can be sensed and felt at its deepest only in relation to that rich and fecund Europe against which America once rebelled" (17). Elsewhere he alludes to 1776 and to Emerson's self-reliance as a universal concept. And he adds, Whitman-like: "I am an American but perhaps of the kind you have forgotten, self-reliant, irritated with authority, full of praise for those who can stand alone, respecting the sacredness that I feel resides in the human personality" (46). He extolls individualism and personal responsibility, which sets him apart, in his eyes, from the "flock" of mass society. He appeals to a sense of the past: "I am an American but not of today's America, tense, frightened, too self-conscious to be confident and humane in its leadership of the world for which it seeks to speak" (5). "I am an American but not afraid of Communism, feeling that the revolution launched by my nation is as powerful (if we Americans would ever believe it!) as any launched anywhere" (47). "I am an American, but chosen migrations, a multiplicity of social adjustments in many lands and many climes have made me feel that I could, as an American, live here among you without feeling that I am among moral inferiors; indeed, I am that sort of American—an amalgam of many races and many continents and cultures, that I feel that the real end and aim of being an American is to be able to live as a man anywhere" (12).

I am not an American myself but I feel moved by this beautiful definition Wright gave of his nation as something international. Other statements make this intellectual definition the more moving because we realize the suffering he underwent in order to cling to his definition of what an American should be. To his French audience, he could proudly declare:

> I am an American but for the twenty-four years that I have been a professional writer I have never used my pen to extoll American humanity at the expense of other people, nor have I sought to degrade other peoples' mores or national habits to the advantage of my country. (2) . . . I would die for my country rather than lie for my country (43).

He was bound to deplore and condemn modern America's too-exclusive concern for comfort, wealth, and material values:

> I am an American but I can live without air-conditioning, without hot and cold running water, and without tranquilizers (19).

> I am an American but I need not use the ideals of my country as an excuse to ask you to give me access to the minerals or the strategic positions of your country (38).

> I am an American but I could not dream of insulting or corrupting the human spirit by offering dollars as inducements for others following my way of life (9).

> I am an American but I refuse to take part in the secret moral swindle that would make me feel that because Mr. Krushchev is a white man, I'd rather deal with him and swallow communism—which I probably claim I hate—and fight a so-called Red China because it is yellow (72).

All of Wright's choices are, again, summed up in the declaration: "I am an American but I dream of being able to live in a world where race, dollars and status are not the final definition of human life" (20). "I think that 'why' is as important as 'how'" (41). This is a philosopher's phrase, demonstrating an ultimate concern for metaphysics or eschatology, a capsule of Wright's thinking about the meaning of human life. He is an individualist and a humanist who fights any restrictive definition of man, even if cast in the form of a great American ideal. In that sense he embodies some of the best qualities America has ever produced, and, no doubt, many of you have probably noticed how modern his attitude is and how relevant to our present concerns with freedom, the cultural revolution, and the making of a world civilization. It is all the more heartbreaking to hear him say:

I am an American but had I not fled my native land, I would have perished in the atmosphere of political hysteria of McCarthyism and I would not have been able to stand here before you (82).

I am an American but I try to keep my heart from freezing in a cold war I never made (70).

# Wright, Negritude,
# and African Writing

ALTHOUGH from *Native Son* (1940) to *The Long Dream* (1957) many black protagonists in Richard Wright's fiction cling to the prevalent stereotype of Africa as the "dark continent," these negative views held by the teenage friends of Bigger or Fishbelly by no means reflect the position of the author. As early as 1940, in his biting answer to David L. Cohn's criticism of *Native Son*, Wright declared that although African culture had been torn from the Negro in the New World, he "possessed a rich and complex culture when he was brought to these alien shores. He resisted oppression."[1] Even though Wright did not believe in the practicality or desirability of Marcus Garvey's movement, he had shown an interest in African culture, which he also expressed during his 1946 visit to France, long before he could contrast his expectations and African reality during his 1953 stay in the Gold Coast. He was not, however, a believer in "negritude." In opposition to the theses developed in Melville Herskovits's *Myth of the Negro Past*, Wright's conceptual approach to Afro-American culture through the perspective of the Chicago School of Social Research led him to emphasize, along with E. Franklin Frazier, the relative lack of "African survivals" in the United States. From the start, he thus tended to stress differences, rather than similarities, between Afro-American and African cultures. For personal reasons, especially because of the oppressive role of religion in his childhood, he also tended to consider religious beliefs shackles to individual freedom. However, in the literary field much of his writing reflected his opposition to the stereotypes of the "noble savage," extolled during the Harlem Renaissance, which emphasized a somewhat mythical bond with African origins. As a result, Wright's initial outlook on African culture was that of a Western-educated, Marxist-oriented agnostic, quite conscious of the differences between Afro-American and African social, political and cultural conditions.

Before going to France, Wright had never read anything by an African writer, and he did not know of "negritude" as a literary movement. It was Leopold Senghor who sought him out by invitation on June 24, 1946, and introduced him to Césaire shortly thereafter. At that time Wright could not feel close to either man. As an agnostic opposed to institutionalized religion, he could not share Senghor's Catholic views; an as ex-Communist, he did not trust Césaire who belonged to the French Communist Party, then vehemently attacking Wright and the Existentialists with whom he associated. Wright's first major contact with French-speaking African intellectuals came through Jean-Paul Sartre in 1947. Alioune Diop, then launching the magazine *Présence Africaine,* wrote Wright on October 2, 1947: "Sartre assured me that you'd agree to be counted among our sponsors." Including Senghor, Paul Hazoumé, and Césaire, shortly afterwards asked to withdraw by the French Communist Party, the sponsoring committee already numbered half a dozen progressive French intellectuals. Wright accepted at once and sent his novella, "Bright and Morning Star," for publication in the first issue. He recommended Gwendolyn Brooks's "Ballad of Pearl May Lee," also printed in the same issue in mid-November. From the start, then, Wright played a part at *Présence Africaine,* not only in the exchange of views that preceded the writing of the editorial arguing for cultural orientation and ideological freedom, but also as a sort of representative of the English-speaking members of the black diaspora.

In February 1948 upon the suggestion of Camus, Wright, and Leiris, an association, the Friends of *Présence Africaine,* was launched in France partly modeled on the one existing in Dakar, open to all "that had faith in the future of the Black man and were ready to work for the evolution of Africa by setting forth examples to its youth." As a sponsor of the magazine, Wright participated less in its lecture series than in its funding campaign, calling on such potential patrons as Baroness Rothschild. The magazine, which had financial difficulties after Senghor's withdrawal on July 8, 1948, had cut funds received indirectly from the French government. Senghor disagreed "on moral grounds." As he saw it, the magazine no longer worked for the cultural restoration of Africa which, he believed, should be its aim.

The magazine continued as a quarterly and Wright advised the publication of pieces by Horace Cayton, Samuel W. Allen, E. Franklin Frazier, and others, although he apparently preferred to have his own articles appear in *Les Temps Modernes.*[2] He saw *Présence Africaine* as primarily serving the needs of French-speaking Africans, and he did not find in the aims and principles of negritude, as he understood them, an echo of his own. Interestingly enough, Wright did not, at the time, have any contacts with Aimé Césaire or Senghor, for the reasons already mentioned. It was Alioune Diop who, in an effort to befriend him, sought him out with the aim of deepeing their mutal understading. In 1949 Diop sent Wright a long letter, indicating how much he looked up to Wright who was, at the time, hailed in Paris as one of the most important new American writers. Diop began: "Before sharing some reflections and problems the Negro question evokes in me with the authority and competence of a man who lived, and is still living, the intensely specific drama of the American Negro with such manly passion for human freedom, I should like to say that these reflections of mine can only have meaning concerning the African world, since I am too ignorant of the Negro American universe to be able to speak of it. On the contrary, I expect that you will shed light upon that world across the Atlantic which fascinates my imagination as much as it surprizes and puzzles my mind" (p. 1). Diop recounted his intellectual growth and arrival in France in search of answers. Concerning colonization, he had found no other explanation than "the conflict of two types of genius." Although he did not underestimate Communist action in favor of blacks, Marxism offered in his eyes no sufficient explanation. Starting from the ideas recently outlined by the Reverend Placide Tempels in his *Bantu Philosophy,* Diop developed an African worldview that insisted on vital forces and the cult of ancestors. Such ontology accounted for the African's cult of authority and Diop believed that "neither revolution nor progress have real meaning for us" (p. 9). The European considered freedom an end, not a means, while the African valued happiness more; he had been colonized "because he prefer[red] the succulence of life to freedom" (p. 12). Diop considered history as a fate bound to happen unless some general catastrophe intervened. He believed, however, that "the Black man must acquire intellectual, manual, social, and spiritual reflexes that would be just as quick and efficient as those of Europeans, which means that he should become alienated like the workers drugged by work on the assembly-line" (p. 13). The black man would have to test his faith in the abstract idea, whether explicative or constructive, seemingly "necessary to acquisition of such reflexes as aimed at production only" (p. 13).

Diop sounded quite ready to learn, and he asked Wright to enlighten him and to correct his errors; he especially wanted the "Negro American problem" explained to him and hinted at a community of views between him and Wright, declaring himself ready to express his true feelings about Sartre's "Black Orpheus," which "[he] could not express publicly because [they] need[ed] Sartre" (p. 15).

It is important that Wright's first real contacts with "negritude" should have taken place through Diop because Diop, although he shared a number of beliefs and perspectives with Senghor, was somewhat distrustful of the dichotomy between the rational and the intuitive that Sartre, following Senghor, tended to emphasize. Wright's secular, Marxist views did not make him see history as fate nor explain colonialism primarily in cultural terms, but Diop's belief that blacks should also use the concepts of the West was one of Wright's favorite themes. In his July 1946 letter to *Les Nouvelle Epitres* he even saw Afro-American adaptation from feudalism to industrialization as a symbol of the social and personality changes that could light the path of Africa and Asia: "Negro life in the U.S. dramatically symbolizes the struggle of a people whose forefathers lived in a warm, simple culture and who are now trying to live the new way of life that dominates our time. . . . What happens between Blacks and Whites in America foreshadows what will happen between the colored billions of Asia and Africa and the industrial Whites of the West."[3]

Diop's influence on Wright's approach to African reality remained slight, however; Wright became acquainted with the problems and evolution of Africa through personal contacts with English-speaking blacks. Very early after his arrival in Europe, he felt more inclined to get information from, and exchange views with, South African Peter Abrahams and Caribbean George Padmore.

Wright had met Abrahams in Paris in 1946. The young South African was then "poor as hell, literally starving and freezing in London."[4] He had asked Wright to read some of his work, and the latter helped him get published in the United States. Wright sent the manuscript of *The Path of Thunder* to his friend Ed Aswell, an editor at Harper's, who submitted it for the Harper prize it won for 1947. Wright's correspondence with Abrahams continued until the latter's divorce in mid-1948, and it is worthwhile noting the literary, more than political, interchange that took place between them.

Wright's achievement was, of course, used as a yardstick to measure that of Abrahams. The *Birmingham Post* wrote of *Mine Boy:* "Books written by Negroes often have peculiar clarity and strength. Richard Wright's *Black Boy* was a case in point, and now Peter Abrahams gives a warm, vital picture." Abrahams commented: "I felt very flattered at the association."[5] Because Wright had set an example with *Black Boy,* Abrahams was prompted to some extent to write *Tell Freedom* in the way that he did. In October 1946, he wrote Wright that he had been working on it intermittently, retracing "the making of me which is intimately tied up also with the making of my generation of black men in South Africa, and also with my definition of freedom which, if well done, should at once be the definition of a group." Both Wright and Abrahams were the products of resistance to white oppression; both had somehow cut loose, as Abrahams exclaimed: "I feel like you, uprooted, with nothing to go back to."[6]

Like Wright, Abrahams faced a series of conflicts having to do with the meaning and decline of civilization. First came the struggle of man against nature in order to survive, in which he felt more personally involved since it was the struggle of his people. Then came the class struggle, and finally the problem of the intellectual, especially "the struggle to retain his individualism in a society which frowns upon it. . . . Moral and philosophical values are important to him because he is a thinking man."[7] The two men differed, however, in their estimate of their original group cultures. Although Wright sometimes looked back with some nostalgia upon the organic worldview of southern black life, he generally deplored its subservience, deprivation and stagnation. For him, reading and learning had been a way out of a stifling network of religion and custom. Not so for Abrahams, who, as an African, questioned the meaning of "Western civilization":

> The only places where I have found that simple human dignity, that respect for the other man, and the gracious feel of tolerance and humanity have not been either among the heroes of the class-struggle or the "thinking men" but among my simple "backward" people. My contact with the West has convinced me that there is something much more vital, much more dynamic and creative among the Africans I have grown up with than in all the thought processes that I have passed through in the West. . . . What will happen to this with the advance of "civilization"? Must simplicity and humanity go under in the interest of progress? What is the most important component of civilization, is it human or mechanical? Must thought processes become involved and insincere? Must the class-struggle warp those who are involved in it?[8]

Not that Wright had not by the mid-forties questioned the pseudo-spiritual values of the United States whose materialism and consumerism he characterized in much the same way as did Henry Miller in *The Air-Conditioned Nightmare.* But Abrahams went further than Wright in questioning the very value of "education." In a discussion of his new novel, Abrahams declared that Lanny, his protagonist and spokesman, suspected that education would not solve everything: "Old Woman Fieta tells him to go away because education would only bring unhappiness to his people, would raise new desires that cannot be satisfied and thus bring unhappiness and trouble. . . . Since all he can give them is education, he wants to do so. But most certainly he is not aware of the implication of education either for himself as an individual or for his people."⁹ And Abrahams posed the problem of education in relationship to social awareness: "Positive social awareness among the South African educated half-caste is zero. Teaching is a mechanical job. The best way of earning a living."¹⁰

Surprisingly *Mine Boy* had been chosen by the South African press as one of the three best books for 1946, possibly because it illustrated the wonder of a "colored" boy able to write. In a way, Abrahams therefore represented in Wright's eyes the sort of man he himself had been (or could have been) in segregated Mississippi, and this led him to see South African developments as paralleling recent Afro-American history. However, Abrahams's sense of African identity and his faith in the organic worldview of common folks somewhat challenged Wright's conviction that the future of Africa lay in confronting the West on equal terms. This conviction of Wright's grew out of his own experience but even more out of his increasingly close relationship with George Padmore, by then the foremost proponent of pan-Africanism. At that stage, where Africa was concerned, politics certainly became for Wright more important than literature or culture.

Padmore was in London when Wright stopped there on his way to the United States in early 1947, and it was he who initiated Wright into the complexities and intrigues of the tactics of decolonization. Padmore's pan-Africanism, which inspired Nkrumah's tactics for the liberation of the British Gold Coast, roughly amounted to steering a course close to that of Socialism, keeping clear of the Communists while using them against the colonial powers. As former Communist Party members who had remained Marxists, the Caribbean activist and the Afro-American novelist had much in common.

Padmore apparently influenced Wright toward a distrust of lyrical African literature and the primarily moral-cultural approach then advocated by Senghor, as well as intensifying suspicion of French-educated black intellectuals who, Padmore claimed, always turned out finally to be more French than black. This partly explains why Wright became more interested in African life than in the theories surrounding it. With Padmore's help, he undertook a six-week trip to the Gold Coast where he collected material for *Black Power: A Record of Reactions in a Land of Pathos.* It is not our purpose here to analyze Wright's reactions to Africa as a Western black. He was able to understand much, yet unable to recognize certain spiritual realities or to sympathize with them, and the sincere expression of his astonishment was more illuminating than superficial professions of kinship and "togetherness."

In spite of his own reservations concerning the usable past, Wright expressed some distrust about the possible consequences of "developing" Africa along the lines of modern, technological societies. He had called the land pathetic in its brooding atmosphere of superstitious fear and dark poverty, but would not the pathos be greater if such an organic universe were suddenly replaced by the fragmented one of the city?

> What would be the gain if these benighted fetish-worshippers were snatched from their mud-huts and their ancestor idolatry and catapulted into the vast steel and stone jungles of cities, tied to monotonous jobs, condemned to cheap movies, made dependent upon alcohol? Would an African, a hundred years from now after he had been trapped into the labyrinths of industrialization, be able to say when he is dying, when he is on the verge of going to meet his long-dead ancestors, those traditional mysterious words:
>
> 'I'm dying
> I'm dying
> Something big is happening to me'?[11]

Wright did not avoid the question of the cultural choices of soon-to-be independent African countries; yet, in the light of Nkrumah's experiments with democracy as Gold Coast Prime Minister, he concluded *Black Power* with the strong note that African effort should become militant, that the fight against colonialism should be first and foremost economic and political, with the result that any element in traditional culture furthering European domination should be eradicated.

In April 1955 the free nations of the Third World held an international conference in Bandung, Indonesia. Although prior to Bandung, Wright seemed little interested in the cultural policy of *Présence Africaine*, which gradually became more politically committed,[12] and although he resorted to the Congress for Cultural Freedom to pay his fare to the conference,[13] the impact of Bandung undoubtedly prompted him to help bring about on the cultural level what had been accomplished there in the political field.

On July 12, 1955, the initial committee, set up to organize the First Congress of Negro Artists and Writers which would be the cultural counterpart to Bandung, consisted of Diop, Maran, Césaire, Senghor, and Wright. Paul Hazoumé joined them a week later. Early themes suggested for the conference included black contributions to culture, the styles of thought characteristic to black people, and black relationships with white intellectuals. Wright participated in the meetings enthusiastically. He helped prepare the final version of an appeal calling on all black writers and artists to assert, without any ideological discimination, a non-Western cultural consciousness. Aware of the urgency of knowing each other before revealing themselves to the world, Negro men of culture would examine their situation and responsibilities, while describing and defining the genius of their peoples.

On November 22, 1955, Wright was requested to give a paper "dealing with one of the major cultural problems of [his] country, in order to establish a link between the French-speaking and English-speaking African public."[14] During the March meetings of the committee, he helped reduce to ten the fourteen major topics considered, taking into account the advice of George Padmore. His friend was ready to cooperate "but with a long spoon," finding the proposals for the conference confused and "typical of these French boys who are great talkers." Voiced by Wright, Padmore's suggestions, also taken up by Dorothy Brooks, the British Societé Africaine de Culture representative, were finally adopted. A short manifesto stated the appeal simply without alluding specifically to politics; a statement of the main topics to be discussed was organized around three points; reports were invited on all the topics, thus opening the way for a general floor discussion from delegates; chairmen for each session would be selected.[15] As a result, an exploration of the cultural situation in French-speaking African countries would be the responsibility of Senghor, in English-speaking ones of Dr. Busia, and in the Americas of Eric Williams. The second point, a denunciation of Western cultural imperialism, would be undertaken by Césaire representing nonautonomous countries and a denunciation of racial discrimination by E. Franklin Frazier. The third point, "perspectives," with Wright as a coordinator, would deal with industrialization and nationalism. Diop would provide a synthesis. Throughout the conference, workshops would be held on religion, history, literature, and the arts.

At that time Wright committed himself as a participant and suggested, as possible American delegates, the names of Dean Dixon, E. Franklin Frazier, Ralph Ellison, Langston Hughes, Chester Himes, Joel A. Rogers, and Melvin Tolson. He would also contact the NAACP for suggestions of nonwriters. Dean Dixon was sick and could not come; executive secretary of the NAACP Roy Wilkins suggested asking John A. Davis, the director of the American Information Committee on Race and Caste, which could provide funds for four additional delegates. The committee planned that, among the seventy-odd papers, Josephine Baker would speak on the international audience of the black artist, Paul Robeson on song in black folk culture, Langston Hughes on poetry and racism, William E. B. DuBois on the cultural experience of Afro-Americans, and Wright on modern institutions and the reality of nationalism. Papers would be circulated in advance to allow questions from other participants. Wright decided to base his paper on "Traditions and Industrialization," the topic on which he was to prepare a synthesis for the third section of the conference.

Only by mid-September 1956 did Wright learn that the Afro-American delegation would comprise John A. Davis; president of Lincoln University Horace M. Bond; *Crisis* editor James W. Ivy; William T. Fontaine of the University of Pennsylvania; Mercer Cook, professor of Romance Languages at Howard University; and "perhaps Ralph Ellison."[16] From the initial list, many, like Josephine Baker, were already engaged or, like E. Franklin Frazier, could not come for personal reasons.[17] George Padmore, too sick to travel, sent a message stressing his hope that the conference would "take into account the political aspirations and demands of Africans and peoples of African descent."[18] W. E. DuBois's message was more disturbing. As a Communist, he had been refused a passport and he stated that "any Negro-American who travels abroad today must either not discuss race relations in the United States or say the sort of things which our State Department wishes the world to believe."[19] The Afro-American delegates and Wright felt compelled to state their independence from any official American view.

During the conference, Wright became somewhat acquainted with the latest African writing in English when Davidson Nichol spoke at length about Amos Tutuola's *Palm Wine Drinkard*, Ekwensi's *People in the City*, and Mbonu Ojike's *My Africa*, which Nichol compared to Camara Laye's *L'Enfant Noir* and contrasted with Wright's and Abrahams' "sombre, violent and corrosive" autobiographies.[20] Wright also listened to Frantz Fanon's contribution on "Racism and Culture," which summed up research largely prompted by and based upon Wright's own writings.[21] He only responded specifically, however, to Senghor's paper, "The Laws of Black African Culture." During the evening debate on September 19, he posed the question of cultural kinship between members of the black diaspora; both he and Senghor were black, yet one was American and the other French: "There is a schism in our relationship, not political, but profoundly human. . . . Where are the instincts that enable me to understand and latch onto this culture? . . . I cannot accept Africa because of mere blackness or on trust." And he questioned the role of African traditions during colonization:

> Might not the vivid and beautiful culture that Senghor has described . . . have been a fifth column, a corps of saboteurs and spies of Europe? . . . The ancestor cult religion with all of its manifold, poetic richness that created a sense of self-sufficiency—did not that religion, when the European guns came in act as sort of aid to those guns? Did that religion help the people to resist fiercely and hardly and hurl the Europeans out? I question the value of that culture in relationship to our future; I do not condemn it, but how can we use it?
> Must we leave it intact, with all the manifold political implications involved in that, or must this culture suffer the fate of all cultures of a poetic and indigenous kind and "go by the board"? . . . I want to be free and I question this culture, not in its humane scope but in relationship to the Western world as it meets the Western world.[22]

A partial answer was given to Wright's first question. Senghor spoke of an African cultural heritage which Afro-Americans should rediscover and study especially in their folk culture because it was a component of their temperament; classics for black Americans should be sought in Africa, not in the Greek tradition of the West. Then, Jacques Stephen Alexis, from Haiti, rephrased Wright's question as if the latter's problem had been one of belonging to American culture or to black African culture first; and the second of Wright's questions remained unanswered.

In "Culture and Colonization," however, Césaire himself had partly answered it when, at the end of his paper, he stated that the problem was too easily summed up as a necessary choice between indigenous tradition and European civilization. One could no more reject indigenous civilization as childish and inadequate than one could refuse European civilization to preserve one's indigenous cultural heritage. Yet new African culture could not shun tradition completely in the name of rationalism since the destruction of taboos had also turned out to be a form of cultural subversion facilitating colonization through missionary effort.

Wright's contribution, "Tradition and Industrialization," has been well-known since its inclusion in *White Man, Listen*. Seen from the distance of three decades, it reflects Wright's hopes and preferences more than it is an objective analysis of the situation. Wright started by defining himself as a black Westerner, detached from the West because of racial conditions, yet with Western reactions when confronting those regions of the colored world where religion dominated. He equated Westernness with a secular outlook on life and a belief that human personality is an end in and for itself. Placing his own situation in the context of intellectual post-Reformation Europe, he saw as a central historical fact the destruction of the irrational ties of religion and custom in Asia and Africa by an irrational West. As a result, the elites of the Third World were the freest men in the world, and the best thing the West could do was to help these Western-educated leaders to modernize their countries without questioning their methods. In the light of Padmore's *Pan-africanism or Communism,* Wright's plea was for enlightened pan-African political orientations. He remarked that, day after day at the conference, however, he had witnessed the ever-living importance of the religious and traditional view and, when he spoke, he interjected into his paper such remarks as: "I was hoping and dreaming for black freedom but . . . I wonder now if I can say that the African elite is more secular-minded than the West."[23]

In social and intellectual terms, Wright's position on the changes brought about by colonization came close to that of E. Franklin Frazier, as expressed in his message to the conference. Emotionally, it was more akin to Padmore's, who had written him after the publication of *Black Power:* "It needed saying and it is best that you said it. It will find popular endorsement among the younger Africans who haven't got a vested interest in all this mumbo-jumbo. The ju-ju won't work on people like us— detribalized blacks."[24]

Needless to say, Wright's views opposed, for political reasons more than literary ones, "negritude" which was being made into a kind of ideology or mystique. He was not far from espousing the strategies expounded by Padmore: "Only Stalinism can smash this mess [tribalism] and liberate these people. After that it will be time for de-Stalinism and democracy. Kwame [Nkrumah] feels the same way but has to pay lip services to Western clap-trap."[25] At the same time, Wright shared with Padmore and the Afro-American delegation a distrust of the French educated Africans' love of brilliant talk and an apparent lack of pragmatism.[26]

The final resolution passed at the conference must have seemed militant and political enough to Wright. It concluded that "the growth of culture is dependent upon the termination of such shameful practices in the twentieth century as colonialism, the oppression of weaker peoples and racialism." Among other things it urged intellectuals to create "the practical conditions for the revival and growth of Negro cultures." Wright himself corrected a draft of the English translation for final publication in *Présence Africaine.*

His own reactions to the problems raised by the conference best appear in a list of some twenty-five points he jotted down, possibly for a letter to John A. Davis. In his eyes, in spite of the absence of Moslems which indicated African conflict, the level of the conference had been higher than that of Bandung, with a real, though hidden, political aim, and Europe met a defeat as a result of it. The view of European academic world had been challenged, and this should mean an immediate broadening of its outlook on Africa. Besides, white participation should be shorn of all psychological projection, for the European and the African were only too prone to lean on each other for emotional support and dependence.

He noted that, following Senghor's analysis, his own questions concerning African culture had been evaded throughout the entire meeting. He believed a corps of experts should survey Africa to learn what was left of tribal cultures, what was usable in them, and what shortcuts to modernization would be valid. Remarking upon the state of mind of the French Africans, their preoccupation with the past, and his own sense of blood and kin, Wright thought that the Western world's past relationship with Africa was basically responsible for the differences between them and himself. In vying with the Communists for the loyalty of Africa, non-Communist pan-Africanists or Westernized elites (with whom he sided) were handicapped by racial feelings and psychological projections, but Africa was close and there was a religious tie, Christianity, although this was being reexamined as tainted with racism and should perhaps be de-Europeanized. The Communists would be more free in overhauling their concepts, but black nationalism was draining off pro-Red sentiment as shown by the case of Césaire who had just left the French Communist Party to protest Stalinism.

Wright expressed his concern about the attitude of American Negroes. The reaction of the United States delegation to DuBois' message and Aime Césaire's speech indicated that it was afraid of Communism. The delegation's attempts to establish rapport with Africa, Wright believed, should be most carefully made for it generally had a complex about its relationship with Africa. Criticism levelled against the Africans must be levelled from within or defiance would result on their part; this is why he had slightly changed his paper when reading it at the conference. He wanted, however, continued Afro-American participation inside the organization in order to temper it, but participation in terms of identification and sympathy. This is why he had inserted a "racial" note at the end.

This interesting document reveals Wright's choices and sheds light on the role he played at the time as a sort of intermediary and mediator between Africans and Afro-Americans.

At the conference, the American delegates had been upset by the political undertone of the papers, especially Césaire's "Culture and Colonization," in which the Afro-Americans were described as a semicolonized people. During the September 21 evening debate, Mercer Cook had wondered what he was doing in this political boat when Diop had initially spoken of a "purely cultural" conference, and he had regretted that he felt less and less solidarity with his African brothers. John A. Davis, too, had asked: "What [Césaire] means when he says the situation of the Negro in America is best understood in terms of colonialism? If he means in terms of races, I could understand that. . . ." But Davis continued: "What American Negroes want—I should make this very clear—and have been fighting very hard for, is complete equal status as citizens. . . . We do not look forward to any self-determination in the belt if this is what Mr. Césaire had in mind."[27]

Césaire had asserted at length that the situation of black Americans was a sequel to slavery, i.e., a form of colonial regime, and emphasized that with the sincere aim of exploring black culture one was inevitably led to examine it in the context of colonialism, hence in political terms. Yet the situation was far from clear between the two groups.

In a warm letter of thanks to Wright on October 1, 1956, Mercer Cook remarked:

> I've heard that the United States delegates impressed some as being "too Western, too American, too conservative." Perhaps our long experience in fighting prejudice has taught us there are methods more effective than wild eyes and empty words . . . Is it true that several of the Haitian papers are published in the current issue of *Les Lettres Françaises?* If so, does that mean that the Communists have really taken over *Présence Africaine* or does it merely reflect the political views of the Haitians concerned?

Wright could reassure Cook that the papers were those of René Depestre and Jacques Alexis, known for their Communist leanings. And John A. Davis, sharing Wright's rational bias, could commend him specifically for doing an important job in "preventing our friends from returning to the irrationalism of primitivism and then turning to xenophobia."[28]

In mid-December 1956 the Société Africaine de Culture was created to further the aims of the conference, with Jean Price-Mars as president and Alioune Diop as executive secretary. The aims of the society were to affirm, defend, and enrich national African cultures and to issue pronouncements on the meaning of international events affecting their destiny: "One can understand what risks are run by peoples whose cultures are unprotected, or are dominated by a foreign culture, when set in front of Western powers." The Paris group nominated Josephine Baker and James W. Ivy among the ten vice-presidents, and Wright, Cook, Davis, Fontaine, E. Franklin Frazier, Langston Hughes, W. E. B. DuBois, and Paul Robeson among the sixty members of the executive council.

While Diop sought financial aid in order to spend some time in the United States, Davis was frantically cabling Wright in January 1957: "P. A. suggests DuBois, Baker and Robeson. Cannot go along. Welcome your intercession. Please inform me."

The Afro-American delegates' position was clear, as John Davis expressed it:

> We feel very strongly that the American members of the executive council should be chosen by the American delegation and not by *Présence Africaine* in Paris. . . . None of us feels he could serve if Dr. W. E. B. DuBois and Paul Robeson are to be members of the executive council because we feel that their presence on the Council will destroy the influence of the Society of African Culture in America . . . None of us agrees with Dr. DuBois' present political line and he is at present persona non grata in his own organization, the NAACP . . . Beyond all this, Dr. DuBois and Paul Robeson, by their words and acts, are now dedicated completely to a political doctrine. While we believe that members of the organization should be both deeply aware of and outspoken on political developments in the world, we believe that they must do this as independent thinkers. As you so rightly say in your introduction to "Lettre à Maurice Thorez," Aimé Césaire has denounced "une forme d'imperialisme culturel." Neither Robeson nor DuBois has denounced it: in fact, there is every reason to believe they serve it with all their strength. Can such men contribute to "la libération de l'initiative spirituelle, culturelle et, partant, politique des peuples noirs?"[29]

Davis's allusion to Césaire's break with the French Communist Party, which had taken place shortly after the conference to the great relief of the American delegates, did not affect Diop. The Paris members were all against political discrimination of any sort. The American delegates, however, had a strong argument, more fundamental than specific: If they were to be responsible for the development of the Society of African Culture in the United States, they must at least nominate all American members to the Executive Council.

The matter was taken up in a meeting after Diop's return from Africa and it was decided that national chapters alone would be empowered to nominate members for the Society or its Council. Diop answered Davis on April 19, 1957:

> We were understandably ignorant of the degree of concern which the names of these two cultural leaders we admire could raise among other American Negroes. However, if it is our duty to respect the initiative of national delegations . . . it is also our duty to reassert the principles of our action, among which [is] the fundamental principle of *non-discrimination on ideological* grounds between men of culture . . . If we rejoice that Aimé Césaire has "denounced a form of cultural imperialism," this is because his move makes him independent from Moscow or Paris. I would never condemn him, or have him condemned, as a Marxist or Communist. The principle of non-discrimination I allude to precedes the Conference. And Césaire would have remained with us even without his Letter to Maurice Thorez. Our attitude is common in Europe and Africa. The Société Européenne de Culture which includes nearly all important European writers is based upon a dialogue between Communists and non-Communists. Our aim is different. We want to free ourselves from the cultural imperialism of the West and to make our own originality emerge. But the case of the Society of European Culture shows that, outside the United States and the Soviet Union, people are not willing to accept the exclusion of other writers on account of their ideological choice. I would have been surprized, last September, to learn that Dr. DuBois' participation would have deprived us of your valuable collaboration. It is therefore more imperative than ever that frequent exchanges should take place between black men of culture of all nations.[30]

Wright's role became less indispensable when, to comply with Diop's wish that national delegations should become associations and enjoy more leeway within the international S. A. C., the United States delegates to the first conference established the American Society of African Culture (AMSAC). They kept all important offices, and elected Duke Ellington and Thurgood Marshall, then director of the legal defense and education fund of the NAACP, to the executive council to replace Dr. DuBois and Paul Robeson. Among its aims the constitution of AMSAC stated that it would seek to promote the "highest values inherent in American political and cultural life." Wright's carbon copy of this constitution bears in his handwriting the assertion "*highest human, democratic, non-racial values inherent in American cultural and political life.*" Although he was absent from the July 15, 1957, meeting which Césaire, Senghor, Edouard Glissant and David Diop attended, their reaction was the same as his; they considered AMSAC's decision to "promote the highest values inherent in American political and cultural life" as proof of American nationalism. They accordingly proposed a modification of the S. A. C. constitution to make more explicit their own aims and nondiscriminatory principles and they also set up a French society, distinct from the International S. A. C., open to all black men of culture residing in France, with an executive committee of ten members to which Wright was nominated.

In November 1957 Wright again served as an intermediary when Diop, acting for S. A. C., requested a $5000 three-month loan from the Council on Race and Caste in World Affairs, which John Davis codirected. Wright also supported AMSAC's desire to have an American, competent in French and in editing, on the staff of *Présence Africaine* to improve communication between French-speaking and English-speaking Africans and to allow greater use of materials in English. However, Diop would have none of it, and misunderstandings cropped up again. In an effort to reach more black intellectuals, Diop had requested from Davis information regarding American Negro men of culture and thus aroused suspicion of new interference in AMSAC's affairs. On December 5, 1957, Davis complained: "We have very strong feelings in this country about the S. A. C.'s random solicitation of members here. The confusion that would result would destroy our organizational efforts. Indeed, two organizations of African Culture in the United States would result." Diop, who visited the United States in late 1957, was disappointed with his trip and with the Afro-American drive toward integration, which he thought was no different from assimilation. This time, Wright advised James T. Harris, John Davis's assistant, that the inculcation of the concept of black nationalism would more easily enable the establishment of the intellectual framework within which Africans and Afro-Americans might achieve their mutual tasks. He considered black cultural and political nationalism as the only possible coming together of the two groups on a "racial" basis, because, although the experience of shared oppression was what they really had in common, he had often experienced the distrust which Western ideas raised in African circles. He knew that "nationalism" was the only stance capable of dispelling the Africans' often-justified suspicion that Afro-Americans only wanted to become integrated into American society and did not care about preserving their ethnic and cultural identity. The AMSAC, however, did not share Wright's opinion.[31]

In late 1957, the theme for the Second Conference of Black Artists and Writers was defined as "Unity and Responsibility of African Negro Culture." Concordant data drawn from the past, from colonial oppression, and from the present need to bring peoples together, would be gathered and the responsibility of black men of culture in establishing a unifying cultural policy would be examined. The emphasis would be placed on the common bond created by colonial oppression, and on nationalism as a national consciousness. The appeal sounded militant enough: "In 1956 we diagnosed the disease; in 1958, we propose a remedy: that our people should work and strive in concert." To the unification of Europe against the United States, "of which Europe was but an economic vassal" and against the Soviet Union, the Bandung powers had responded as constituting the proletariat of the modern world. The black intelligentsia was . thus asked to act in direct response to the colonial situation.

Wright, however, did not attend the July planning session in London where the appeal was drawn up although Diop cabled him that Wright's remaining with the writers from English-speaking Africa urgently required his presence. The conference would take place in Rome in September and Wright interpreted the choice as a move of the Catholic faction in *Présence Africaine* to symbolically bring the whole proceedings under the aegis of the Vatican. Urgent work, the need to fulfill contracts, was his excuse when he was repeatedly invited; AMSAC even offered to cover all his expenses. His real reason, however, was the suspicion he had often discussed with George Padmore that black Frenchmen were not really striving to decolonize Africa because their religious outlook prevented their resorting to the radical tactics needed. The conference had to be postponed until Easter 1959 due to the French general election in which many delegates were involved. This enabled Diop to invite Wright to a meeting with friends in October [32] and, in late November, to request a lecture on "The Black World and the Bandung Peoples" but Wright did not accept. He also refused an invitation to attend an AMSAC conference of writers in New York. [33]

In fact, the second conference proved far more political in character than the first. France was in crisis over Algeria and Fanon's contribution, "On the Reciprocal Support of the Fight for Liberation and National Cultures" could serve as a program. Speaking about the responsibilities of the intellectual, Césaire urged the participants to hasten the process of decolonization by hastening the rise of popular consciousness. As for

Senghor, he could not attend and sent a telegram. The United States delegation was composed of James W. Ivy, Robert L. Carter, St. Clair Drake, Samuel Allen, Jay Saunders Redding, all of whom delivered papers, and also Mercer Cook, Horace Mann Bond, Elton Fax, Adelaide Cromwell Hill, and Pearl Primus. Wright did not send a message. However, he accepted the position in mid-June 1959 after he had been elected in his absence to the Executive Council of the International S. A. C.

According to Alioune Diop, Wright did not attend the Rome conference because he wanted to preserve his freedom to speak out. Yet he made efforts not to cut himself off from the Présence Africaine group and when Wright died, Thomas Diop, who had often served as an interpreter for them all, was invited to pronounce his funeral eulogy.[34]Amadou Hampaté Ba, the Mali delegate to UNESCO, similarly wrote a moving, if somewhat high-sounding piece, "Richard Wright, My Brother", expressing widely-felt dismay: "The death of my friend and brother Richard Wright is a heart-rending experience for Alioune Diop and Aime Césaire, to mention only two among so many Blacks."[35]

To the end, Wright showed interest in African culture, although his approach remained far more political than literary. True, he sponsored the African Popular Theatre group in 1958, but he apparently bought no African literary work other than Tutuola's *Palm Wine Drinkard.* Meanwhile in 1959 he desperately tried to obtain funds from cultural organizations and foundations to carry out in French-speaking Africa the kind of inspired reportorial job he had done on Ghana in *Black Power.* His efforts were in vain. The Congress for Cultural Freedom appeared to be linked with the CIA; the Ford Foundation would not help; AMSAC feared that, once the book was written, they might not want to associate themselves with it.[36] Senghor was the only one to offer governmental help on behalf of the Federation of Mali but he understood that Wright's desire to be independent from any government was a basic condition.

Senghor, who greatly admired Wright, apparently never despaired of persuading him to see African realities with a perspective closer to his own. On receiving *White Man Listen,* he congratulated Wright for having written a body of salutary truths, but he expressed a reservation:

> You cannot conceal your distrust of Christianity in general, of Roman Catholicism specifically. I can explain your distrust by your situation as an Afro-American, as a man of Anglo-Saxon, Protestant culture. I do not believe, however, that such distrust is founded. The facts are proof that the Catholic

church has maintained, since the Liberation of France, a large effort to decolonize, to such a degree that a colonialist was able to use *The Vatican Against
France* as a title for one of his books.[37]

Again, when responding to Wright's desire to visit French-speaking
Africa, Senghor expressed his hope that he could meet him there: "This
would enable me to make you feel certain realities."[38] And Senghor's final
impression of Wright, reflecting as it does his own outlook, is not wide of
the mark:

> He was a rather secretive man, considering he had an intense inner life. His
> whole life and work tend to be proof that he was a torn man, very much like me,
> all things considered. A man torn between the past and the future of his race,
> between the values of Negritude and those of European civilization. It is
> significant that he would have preferred to live in Europe, in France. I believe
> he was literally obsessed with the racist atmosphere of American civilization
> and that he wanted to escape from it as from some ghetto. It is significant, also,
> that he misunderstood the Movement for African liberation. He tended to
> consider it too much as an antiracist racism, not as a de-alienation phenome-
> non. . . . At any rate, I always had the highest admiration for him as a writer and
> as a man because, at heart, he was the very expression of black "passion," which
> may well be the most meaningful fact of the second half of the twentieth
> century.[39]

A number of African writers have expressed over the years corresponding views of the appeal that Wright's writings, especially *Black Boy,* had
exerted upon them as a significant example of the universality of black
themes and as an example of ethnic self-expression to be emulated. This
was the case for Peter Abrahams and Ezekiel Mphahlele, among others,
not to mention West Indian writers like George Lamming or Joseph
Zobel. Probably better than any other, Camara Laye expresses the exemplary quality of Wright's attempt when he declares that: "Wright gave the
American public an example of the life led by millions of black children in
America" and that his own *L'Enfant Noir* translated the life common to
African children just as *Black Boy* related what is collective in the black
American experience." Laye adds, speaking of *Black Power:*

> There were certain uniquely African problems that escaped Wright, not be-
> cause of any failure of perception but because coming from America, he had not
> lived the African experience despite the fact that he was a black man. Within
> this context I talked about Wright's concept of the African revolution, if you
> want to call it that. He believed that Africa and the black man throughout the
> world should form a philosophical unity, and we were in agreement on this. But
> he did not fully understand the African experience and African civilization. . . .

In Africa, the problem is not our achieving equality or civil rights: we are not concerned with any sort of integration with a white society. Although we aspire to modernity we do not want to become Europeanized, or white, and risk losing what is typically African.[40]

Whereas prointegrationist Afro-Americans, like the AMSAC delegates, considered Wright's support of black nationalism as a meeting ground between Africans and the black diaspora as premature and ill-advised in 1959, it appears that Wright's proposal that traditions be abolished when they caused stagnation was often interpreted by Africans as a danger of their being Europeanized at the risk of losing what was typically African. Wright stood, at best, halfway between integration and negritude, attempting at times to mediate between the aspirations of two different and often diverging groups, but African writers generally saw him as the American he never ceased to be. It is significant that his deepest influence on a non-American black writer should have been on Frantz Fanon, whose West Indian heritage made him, more than any African, aware of the complexities of the black Western intellectual caught between white masks and black skin.

---

1. "I Bit the Hand That Feeds Me," *Atlantic Monthly* 155 (June 1940); 827. The best study of the image of Africa in Wright's fiction is Jack B. Moore's "Richard Wright's Dream of Africa," *Journal of African Studies* 2 (Summer 1975): 231–45. *In The New World of Negro Americans* (New York: Viking, 1964), Harold J. Isaacs contrasts Wright's reactions to Africa with those of other writers such as Langston Hughes. See pp. 247–60 especially.

2. On September 3, 1949, Diop wrote Wright, congratulating him for "I Tried to Be a Communist": "What you said opened my eyes. And it will be a still deeper revelation for young Africans. You should educate them. I'll tell you how." Diop's long, undated letter also quoted was probably written in December 1948 or January 1949.

3. This appeared in English in "A World View of the American Negro," *Twice Year*, nos. 14–15 (Fall 1946–Winter 1947): p. 348.

4. Peter Abrahams to Wright, September 28, 1947.

5. Abrahams to Wright, July 22, 1947. Wright was then ready to leave the United States again for self-exile in France.

6. Abrahams to Wright, March 17, 1947.

7. Ibid.

8. Ibid.

9. Abrahams to Wright, April 14, 1947.

10. Ibid.

11. *Black Power*, p. 227.

12. "When the magazine was reorganized in the early 1950s, the sponsoring committee, of which Wright was a member, disappeared and Afro-Americans were represented on the editorial committee by Césaire and René Depestre. Partly due to the initiative of African students who had voiced their grievances against French colonialism in a special issue, the Spring 1955 editorial for the new series sounded a new militant note: "All articles will be published provided . . . they concern Africa and do not betray our anti-racist, anti-colonialist aims, nor the solidarity of colonized peoples."

13. As a result, the magazines of the Congress for Cultural Freedom had exclusive rights to publish Wright's impressions of Bandung; this may explain why he did not meet a July 1, 1955 request by *Présence Africaine* to state his feeling on the significance and possible consequences of Bandung generally and, particularly, how it could benefit African liberation.

14. Mrs. Diop to Wright, November 22, 1955.

15. Padmore to Wright, March 13, 1956. Padmore was wary of possible French official reactions and he added: "Don't announce the names of our delegates for fear the French stop them at the border. . . . Beware and don't have your name officially identified with the conference. These French can go "Dutch" and plan with the crackers to get you out."

16. Ellison did not attend. Since *Présence Africaine* could pay only 8.430 francs to delegates who delivered a paper, plus 10 shillings per printed page, virtually no delegate could come from abroad without additional subsidy. All Afro-Americans presented papers: Bond on West African nationalist movements, Fontaine on segregation and desegregation in the United States. James Ivy on the NAACP. The articles by Cook and Davis were printed in the June 1957 issue of *Présence Africaine*.

17. He sent a message, stressing views quite close to Wright's outlook: ". . . A world revolution is in progress . . . the culmination of the changes which were set in motion by the scientific discoveries which led to the industrial revolution and the economic and political expansion of Europe. . . . As a result of two World Wars there has been a shift in the power structure of the world and Asia and Africa are beginning to shape the future of mankind. In Asia and in Africa, where the impact of European civilization uprooted the people from their established way of life, new societies are coming into existence." *Présence Africaine* 8–10. (June–November 1956): 380.

18. Ibid., p. 384.

19. Ibid., p. 383.

20. "The Soft Pink Palms," *Présence Africaine* 8–10 (June–November 1956): 115. Wright's interest in the literature of English-speaking West Africa remained very slight, however; he acquired *The Palm Wine Drinkard* in 1953, but no other book of the kind.

21. On January 6, 1953, Fanon had written Wright a fan letter: he had all of Wright's books in French and even *Twelve Million Black Voices* in English. He had tried to show the systematic reciprocal ignorance between whites and blacks in *Black Skins, White Masks* and was working on a study of "the human scope of [Wright's] works." What attracted Fanon so much in Wright's depiction of Negro masses was his exploration of their revolutionary potentialities. Besides, Wright had used the concept of the Afro-American group as an internal colony in his July 1946 letter to *Les Nouvelles Epitres*. In *Black Power*, he had caught "the challenge of the barefoot masses against the black aristocracy and middle class," Padmore assured DuBois on December 10, 1954, thus antedating and possibly inspiring some of Fanon's theories on Third World revolution.

22. *Présence Africaine* 8–10 (June–November 1956): 68.

23. Ibid., p. 356. These extempore remarks do not appear in the version of "Tradition and Industrialization," printed in *White Man Listen*.

24. G. Padmore to Wright, May 1954.

25. G. Padmore to Wright, January 29, 1957.

26. Padmore wrote, for instance: "I want this book *Pan Africanism or Communism* in the hands of black Frenchmen. They need this ideology to help them break away from Thorez [Communist] influence. I can see them striving but Senghor and these boys can't help because they're too confused. . . . We've already entered the 21st century and these boys are still in the Middle Ages, with their damn culture-drums and skulls" (To Wright, January 29, 1957); "Senghor . . . is a typical black Frenchman playing national Assembly party politics. We can expect nothing from these café intellectuals with their corrupt politics" (To Wright, October 19, 1955).

27. *Présence Africaine* 8–10 (June–November 1956): 213–125.

28. He added: "I hope that you can guide them along the road to national emergence, to a healthy evaluation of that which is best and rational in Western culture" (Davis to Wright, November 17, 1956).

29. Ibid.

30. A. Diop to John A. Davis, April 19, 1957.

31. In a letter to Wright (of which the first page is missing), James T. Harris commented upon this argument and concluded, "However we need give a good deal more thought and discussion to this."

32. Diop insisted: "I do not want to convince you [Wright] of the value of the thesis in favor of a conference in Rome. (I would personally have liked to be agreeable to you but hardly anyone would have taken your side), but simply to tell you that, in the matter, we have only feelings of esteem and brotherly consideration for the writer and the man of color in you" (Diop to Wright, October 30, 1958).

33. Wright wrote: "I must be practical. The novel upon which I am now working is contractually owed by the first of March and I must have it finished by then. And a trip before then would throw my schedule off kilter" (Wright to Harris, January 21, 1959). A year before, Wright had refused to write "a description of the process of the social, economic and political life of Africans studying and living away from home—with special emphasis on the intellectual and psychological development" which Harris had requested, on January 28, 1958, for inclusion in a special issue of *Présence Africaine* for which he had the responsibility.

34. Interview by M. Fabre, March 1971. In an October 17, 1959 letter to the ambassador of Ghana, Wright stated, however: "I consider the ideas of this magazine and the gentlemen who run it to be highly dangerous. They are strongly hostile to the idea of Black nationalism. And there is a strong but hidden Jesuit influence in the group of men about this magazine."

35. *Démocratie 60* 59 (8 December 1960): 26.

36. John Davis to Richard Wright, May 23, 1959 and Wright to Davis, June 3, 1959. See my *The Unfinished Quest of Richard Wright* (New York: William & Morrow, 1973): pp. 490–91.

37. Senghor to Wright, July 28, 1959.

38. Senghor to Wright, July 21, 1959.

39. Senghor to M. Fabre, February 28, 1964.

40. "The Writer and His World," interview with Camara Laye by Steven Rubin, *Africa Report*, May 1972, p. 24.

# *Appendixes*

A. "Superstition" by Richard Wright

B. Poetry by Richard Wright

C. An Interview with Simone de Beauvoir

D. A Letter from Dorothy Padmore

# *"Superstition"*

Three friends, having done justice, in leisurely fashion, to a savory, well cooked dinner, and overcome by a delightful lassitude, were enjoying, somewhat languidly, their black coffee and cigars in the sitting room of the apartment. An atmosphere of contentment pervaded the room, while outside the December snow fell silently and softly, as though fearful to disrupt the peaceful solitude of the scene.

The conversation having turned to subjects of a weird and mysterious nature, each of the friends, Matt Brocson, Fently Burrow, and Bert Meadows, had a story to tell—a true story of some baffling incident that defied explanation.

Brocson and Meadows finished their narratives, amid a deep, penetrating silence, as though the room and its occupants were temporarily in a state of suspended animation.

At last Fently Burrow spoke as follows: "I also know of a strange incident—so strange indeed, that the horror of it has never left my mind, and will, I am sure, remain with me till my dying day."

"Tell it, then!" Meadows said eagerly, having fallen under the influence of Burrow's persuasive voice.

The two men lit their cigars and settled back into their chairs to listen to Burrow's tale.

Burrow continued:

"Winter before last, a few weeks before Christmas, the rental firm for which I am now working sent me South to look over some property and renew a few leases. The journey was long and arduous, and when I arrived in Koogan, for that was the name of the place, I was fearfully depressed and my nerves were jaded. I sought a hotel, but, alas, every one was filled. A merchant's association and a secret order were holding conventions. It was cold and raining—it had been raining, I was told, for a solid week—and I can assure you it was not the sort of weather to tramp muddy and unpaved streets looking for lodging.

"Finally, I inquired of a hotel clerk if he knew of any private home where I might find shelter.

"'Yes; I know of a Mrs. Lancaster who lives in the suburbs; she would be glad to take you in. That's the only one I know. All the public places are filled with convention guests,' he told me.

"I had to accept, though I dreaded the inconvenience. I thanked the clerk, procured a taxi, and was off to Mrs. Lancaster's address.

"Koogan is a small town with a population of about two thousand. Trees line all its streets, and its wooden houses, which are badly in need of paint, stand out like gaunt sores against the bleak sky. The impression I gained was one of forlornness; in so far as progress was concerned it seemed as if Time had forgotten the place. The incessant rain, the cold and penetrating damp, the overhanging gloom overwhelmed me and made me wish for Chicago—

"An hour's ride through rain and mud brought me to the suburbs, and the driver finally drew up to a white-washed picket fence, beyond which, about thirty yards from the road and accessible by a gravel walk, stood, stark and lonely against the sky, an unpainted two-story house. The whole scene depressed me, or was it simply my frayed nerves? On each side and to the rear of what was called a lawn for the want of an adequate name, stood several elm trees, their branches denuded by the winter winds. No other houses were visible; the whole landscape was amazingly bleak and bare. In the far distance the mournful whistle of a departing train, the faint and musical tinkle of a cowbell, a solitary dog bark, the monotonous beat of the rain—I revolted; my firm is paying my expenses and I would much rather have had a hotel room, but necessity is necessity.

"I left the taxi, paid the driver, and lugged my baggage up the gravel walk. I was about to knock when the door was opened by an aged woman in black.

"'You're looking for a room?' she asked in a querulous and expectant tone, scrutinizing me through a pair of thick lens spectacles. She held the door barely open, as if afraid.

"'Yes. Is this Mrs. Lancaster?' I asked as I put my baggage upon the wet veranda.

"'Yes, come right in.'

"When inside I began to tell her of how I came to her house.

"'That was Mr. Beattle who gave you the information,' she explained when I told her of the obliging hotel clerk. 'He promised to send me someone. Are you a convention guest?'

"Briefly, I stated my business in Koogan. As I talked she turned on a light, revealing her tanned and lined face. She was exceptionally frail, so frail that she seemed to cling to life by bare effort. She looked between sixty and seventy years of age. When she spoke her whole body swayed with her words, as if it cost her a tremendous effort. Her hands, gnarled and worn, were kept constantly clasped to her thin waist. Her hair, snow white and well kept, was piled high upon her head, and her eyes seemed entirely lifeless, so sunken were they.

"After divesting myself of my hat and coat she invited me into a large room with an abnormally high ceiling across which flitted fantastic shadows from a blazing log fire. As I entered the room a bent and aged man, somewhat older than she, dressed in a loose fitting black suit, and whose head was wrapped in a black silk skull cap, looked at me quizzically from his seat at the far end of the fireplace. His skin was ebony.

"'Burrow is my name,' I informed her.

"'Mr. Burrow meet my husband, Mr. Lancaster,' Mrs. Lancaster introduced us.

"I acknowledged Mr. Lancaster's presence by a hearty handshake and seated myself before the fire.

"The room was decorated for Christmas; bright strips of tinsel dangled from the pictures along the walls. A huge wreath of bright green holly was suspended above the mantle on which rested, in conspicuous display, the portrait of a smiling young girl. Red and green ropes of friezed paper criss-crossed the ceiling. A matting of intricate design adorned the floor. The sizzling sound of green burning logs filled the room, giving off a queer, pungent odor. From all appearances the room was cozy, but for some reason, perhaps it was the influence of the nearness of old age, the room seemed heir to a blanket of decay and melancholy.

" 'Just make yourself at home,' the old lady coaxed me. 'There's no one here but my two daughters who are paying me a visit. They will stay thru the holidays.'

"I thanked her and assured her that I would. We began to talk. The conversation drifted to local topics: The conventions being held; a recent bank failure; the rising prevalence of crime. I told them about the habits of large cities to which they listened eagerly. I gathered from their talk that Mr. Lancaster was an ex-school teacher who was now enjoying a pension; he had taught school for fifty years. The conversation was soon interrupted by the sound of descending footsteps upon the stairs, and, directly, two women, one slender and one matronly, entered the room dressed in cosmopolitan clothes. I rose as they entered and Mrs. Lancaster introduced us.

" 'Mr. Burrow, Mrs. Woodson, my oldest daughter.'

"Mrs. Woodson acknowledged me by a slight nod of her sleek head and a faint smile. She was, I learned later, a widow and had spent most of her life in an Eastern city. She was of medium height, large limbed, with black hair and black eyes. Her skin was dark-brown and her lips were rouged scarlet. The low cut collar of her simple frock showed a thick neck; her face was fleshy, slightly sensual.

"Mrs. Woodson, in turn, presented me to her sister, Lillian Lancaster, whom I instantly recognized as the likeness of the portrait upon the mantle. Lillian was a small and frail woman who markedly resembled her mother. She appeared to be in her early twenties. Her narrow face, pale and emaciated, attracted me. Her hair was brushed backwards and revealed a broad, bulging forehead below which, shining in contrast to her pallid features, were a pair of dark sunken eyes. They seemed lit with a strange light. She seemed feverish and nervous, as if preyed upon by a secret illness. The most unusual thing about her was a timid and perpetual smile, a smile that seemed melancholy and slightly cynical. A peculiar air of resignation pervaded her whole being.

"We seated ourselves before the fire.

" 'Looks like a family re-union,' I said by way of opening up a conversation.

" 'Not quite,' Mrs. Woodson volunteered with a smile. 'We have three brothers who are not here. They live about a hundred miles south of us.'

" 'Did you ever hear of an old superstitious saying,' Lillian Lancaster asked, turning to me, 'that when a family has a re-union some one is going to die?'

" 'No, I have not heard it. I'—I stammered, looking at her sharply. Her question seemed appropriate of her pale face and visionary eyes.

" 'Oh! Lillian, how can you think of such?' Mrs. Lancaster exclaimed. 'This is Christmas, let's don't talk of death! And who, in God's name, believes such?'

" 'It has happened often,' said Lillian Lancaster defensively, addressing me. 'I well remember when Mrs. Green, who was a next door neighbor of ours, had a family re-union her daughter died. The next year they held another re-union and another daughter died. They became afraid of re-unions and did not hold one for several years. Finally, they had another re-union and Mrs. Green died. There must be something to it after all.

"'Phooh! Nonsense!' Mrs. Lancaster admonished; but she was interrupted by Lillian who was seized by a violent cough. She seemed as if in a spasm. It racked her whole being. It was as if some invisible hand had grasped her shoulders and sought to wrench the life out of her delicate body. She was an object of pity. The coughing slowly subsided and she dabbed at her mouth and eyes with a small handkerchief. We gazed at her with apprehension.

"The conversation changed; but it could be plainly discerned that the effect of her words, or was it her violent cough, had registered on every face. Mr. and Mrs. Lancaster looked at their daughter with something akin to wounded pride. Mrs. Woodson, for no reason at all, avoided my eyes, and for some cause I became a trifle uneasy. At that moment an indescribable atmosphere filled the room. At that moment the coming tragedy cast its shadow, and that shadow, like all the shadows that attend human events, was unseen by human eyes. The causes in our lives that later develop into glaring effects are so minute, originate in such commonplace incidents, that we pass them casually, unthinking, only to look back and marvel.

"An impatient rap upon the front door sent Mrs. Woodson out of the room and left us in silence. Sounds of raised and gruff masculine voices mingled with exclamations of feminine surprise and joy reached us. Presently, through the doorway walked three masculine forms dressed in dark clothes. Glistening drops of rain were upon their faces and hands. They paused in the center of the room, while Mrs. Woodson ran forward, exclaiming:

"'Oh! Mother, here are my brothers—'

"'My sons!' Mrs. Lancaster screamed with joy, embracing each.

"I stood in the background and looked on, amused at the efflorescence of kisses, embraces and salutations.

"'We didn't know you were coming,' Mr. Lancaster said, his voice charged with fervent paternal joy.

"'And you didn't write,' admonished Mrs. Lancaster in a motherly tone as she gazed fondly into the features of her oldest son, a clean-shaven man with a beaming smile. 'You should have notified me that you were coming.'

"'We decided all at once. We thought we'd surprise you,' the younger son explained. 'You see, we're really here on business, the convention, you know. Oh! but I'm glad to see my little sister Lillian!'

"He placed his arm brotherly and affectionately around the frail shoulders of Lillian, who, when about to express her pleasure and gratitude, was seized with a fit of violent coughing. It was so sudden and acute and racked her frail body to such an extent that she was forced to kneel upon the floor, exhausted and gasping for breath, with tears streaming from her eyes.

"'My Lord! What's the trouble?'

"'Mercy, Sister, you must be ill.'

"'Do you cough like that often?'

"The brothers, astonished at her condition, fired sympathetic questions at her.

"'Oh, it's just a cold,' Lillian replied apologetically, dabbing her eyes and nostrils with a small handkerchief that showed faint traces of blood. Her cheeks were flushed pale and her lips seemed white. Her brothers and parents, overly anxious and solicitous, almost lifted her into her chair.

"There followed a period of awkward silence in which all seemed tongue-tied. Mrs. Woodson saved the situation by introducing me to her brothers: Robert, Ross, and Ellis who pumped my hand rather absentmindedly and wished me a 'Merry Christmas.'

"Again we were seated before the fire; but all seemed constrained and reserved. Lillian's eyes were cast downwards, her slender hands tightly gripping the damp handkerchief. She seemed ashamed of something. Her attitude was touching. I felt an unrecognizable sensation and started to quit the room, but Ross Lancaster's words made me sit still.

"'What do you know about this? A regular family re-union! The first one we've ever had!' Ross boomed forth, rubbing his hands together as a merchant does who has just completed a successful business deal.

"His words brought back Lillian's prediction so vividly that I positively jumped. A family re-union! How unexpected! My eyes were drawn to Lillian's pale face and again I experienced that unrecognizable sensation that I had felt a few moments before. Mr. Lancaster, who was leaning forward stirring the fire, let the tongs fall upon the hearth with a startling clang, and jerked himself sharply erect. Lillian looked around wildly, like a trapped deer. Mrs. Lancaster involuntarily raised her hand to her mouth and stared quite horrifiedly into the fire, the dancing shadows of which gave one the illusion that their features were appearing and disappearing out of nothing. A family re-union! Its implications of predicted death! I studied with frank curiosity this exhibition of terror of the unknown.

"The brothers were quick to notice this transformation.

"'What's the matter?' asked Ellis Lancaster.

"No one answered. Mrs. Woodson shot a quick glance at me which I failed to interpret. The purposeful silence that greeted Ellis' question served to augment the brothers' curiosity the more. They insisted:

"'What's the matter?'

"'What's wrong?'

"'Say, why don't someone speak?'

"Mr. and Mrs. Lancaster looked at me, I don't know why. Perhaps they were afraid of unmasking their superstitious natures before a stranger; they simply assumed a timid and guilty air, saying nothing. Finally, the silence became so distressing that Lillian forced herself to speak, reluctantly to be sure.

"'We were discussing family re-unions just before you came in'; she spoke in a deprecatory tone as if she sought to minimize the salient danger that lurked in her words. 'It is believed that when a family has a re-union someone is going to die.'

"Silence followed her words. The brothers dropped their heads, as if they had been chastised school boys, and looked stupidly into the fire. Their faces were ludicrous and pathetic. I felt decidedly uncomfortable, not to say unwelcome and was on the point of asking to be shown my room when Mrs. Woodson, perhaps for the sake of pride, or perhaps to save her parents from embarrassment, rose and said in an unnecessarily loud voice:

" 'Mr. Burrow, dinner will be at eight; allow me to show you your room.'

"That broke the spell.

"I was shown to a cold, almost bare room on the second floor where I refreshed my appearance for dinner. When I came downstairs the family was already seated at the table, awaiting my arrival. The table was lit with candles of various colors that illuminated an array of steaming food.

" 'A large convention you're having,' I remarked as I seated myself between the two sisters.

" 'Yes,' the younger brother replied affably. 'Quite a crowd of us here.'

"All became silent as Mrs. Lancaster blessed the food. My effort at conversation had failed and the dinner proceeded in silence save for the spasmodic outbreaks of coughing that seized Lillian. Finally her cough became so acute that she was forced to leave the table. I can see her now, her eyes gleaming with a feverish light, her small white handkerchief, showing traces of blood, dabbing incessantly at her eyes and mouth. I did not know that when she quitted the table, asking us in a timid voice to excuse her, that it was to be the last time I was to see her alive in this world. . . .

"I returned to my room directly after the completion of the meal. The room was cold and damp; it was still raining outside. I turned down the corner of my bed, and lit the fire that had been laid in the grate. I was not sleepy and my thoughts drifted to the eccentric family downstairs. I had never before seen such a frank exhibition of superstition. Why had they been so wrought up? It all seemed so absurd, yet it was fascinating. At last I went to bed with the image of the frail Lillian hovering before my eyes; I could not forget her vicious cough and her melancholy smile.

"I had not been asleep long, however, when I was awakened by noise of a slamming door and the stride of masculine footsteps across the hallway. I caught the sound of subdued and excited voices, and heard the word 'doctor' repeated several times. As the voices gradually died out I drifted back to sleep, my mind filled with visions of Lillian and her glittering eyes.

"When I awoke the next morning Mr. Lancaster was lighting a fire in my room. He informed me, in his halting way, that Lillian was very ill. The doctor had attended her that night. Pneumonia. Acute pneumonia, the doctor had said. Her case was grave. I breakfasted alone with Mr. Lancaster; the rest of the family was attending Lillian. I expressed my regrets and the hope of a speedy recovery, which he seemed not to hear.

"Later that day I procured a taxi and went to the business section to transact my firm's affairs. When I arrived back at the Lancasters' home I had my dinner with Mr. Lancaster who informed me that his daughter was very 'low.' She was in a coma. The doctor was expecting the crisis that night or early tomorrow. I again expressed my sympathy and hope and returned to my room. I had hardly seated myself when I heard a low knock.

" 'Come in,' I called, expectantly.

"Ross Lancaster, the youngest brother, stepped into the room.

"'How are you?' I asked and pushed a chair forward.

"'Very well,' he mumbled preoccupiedly as he seated himself.

"He immediately began to discuss his sister's illness.

"'You know,' Ross asserted, 'I believe that conversation about family re-unions has something to do with my sister's illness.'

"'Oh, nonsense,' I admonished; though I had been thinking the same thing.

"'I don't mean that it was the cause of her illness, but it is, I believe, the cause of her lack of confidence to recover. Mother, Father and all seem to have fallen under a sort of spell. They seem hypnotized, enchanted by something evil. It is as if they were waiting for her to die; as if they knew that she was going to die. They act and think as if her death is a foregone conclusion.'

"I stared at him, speechless with wonder. He rose and paced the length of the room nervously. Finally he paused before me with a puzzled look upon his face. It seemed as if he was about to speak. I waited in suspense.

"'Oh, I know this sounds like foolishness to you,' he muttered confusedly, and rushed out of the room before I could reply.

"It continued to rain and I remained indoors all that forenoon. I lunched with the three brothers, who barely said a word during the entire meal. So uncomfortable did I become that if there had been any possible way to have secured a room elsewhere I certainly would have done so. On my way to my room I glimpsed Mrs. Lancaster and Mrs. Woodson, who acknowledged my presence by a slight nod. Their faces seemed anxious and harried, and, perhaps it was my morbid fancy, both of them seemed rather ashamed and resentful at my presence.

"Late that evening Lillian died.

"The news of her death was conveyed to me by the sound of sobs, wild and unrestrained. Mrs. Lancaster wandered from room to room distractedly, dabbing a small handkerchief to her convulsed face, muttering mournfully: 'I knew it; I knew it; I knew it.' She would pause at times as if to bear her grief stoically; then, flinging herself upon the divan, give vent to sobs, prolonged and dry. The brothers wept too, but in private. Mr. Lancaster sat mutely before the fire, stupefied in his sorrow, gazing vacantly and saying nothing. Their grief seemed queerly accentuated by the background of Christmas decorations. I offered my services, but Ross Lancaster informed me, gratefully and humbly, that all necessities were being carried out.

"They planned, I learned from Mrs. Woodson, a hasty funeral; the brothers had to return immediately to their businesses. No one mentioned 'family re-unions,' but it seemed that sometimes a look of shame would for a moment obliterate the look of grief upon their faces.

"I was forced to leave before the burial took place. So saturated were they in their grief that none save Mr. Lancaster took any notice of my departure. As I paid him the price of my stay he looked at me rather queerly; that look made me feel as if I were an intruder.

"'Give my regrets to your family,' I told him as I stood in the hallway whose Christmas decorations seemed to cast a pall of irony over the grief-stricken home.

"'What do you think of it, Mr. Burrow?' Mr. Lancaster asked me, looking me straight in the face.

"I paused, glanced at him and then at the black shining coffin, dimly visible in the gloom of the front room.

"'What do *you* think?' I asked, avoiding his question.

"He hung his head and mumbled in a thick whisper:

"'It's queer, as God knows.'

"He left me standing in the hall, puzzled and bewildered. I stepped into the front room where Lillian's coffin stood. There was a deep silence and the smell of flowers. I bent forward and looked upon the dead features of Lillian. She seemed unbelievably small. Her face, strangely pale in death, seemed to hold a look of puzzled anxiety. Upon her lips (it might have been my morbid imagination) I seemed to see that same peculiar smile. . . . As I stood there in the deep shadows and silence of death the words of Ross Lancaster came back to me with a surging forcefulness:

"'They act and think as if her death is a foregone conclusion.'

"A sensation of terror and dread gripped me and I turned hurriedly away."

Fently Burrow paused and gazed at his listeners. He had, beyond a doubt, created an impression. The impression did not last long, however, for Matt Brocson smiled ironically, and said:

"That was simply a natural death. I don't see anything superstitious about it."

"Primitive people always look upon death in such a light. Simply because they thought it was caused by a family reunion certainly does not make it true," said Bert Meadows as he began to lace his shoes that did not need lacing.

"But I'm not through yet," Burrow interposed. "there's some more to this story."

Bert Meadows and Matt Brocson, with a skeptical air, relit their cigars and Burrow resumed his story.

"As luck would have it, my firm sent me back to Koogan last Christmas. When I arrived it was steadily raining. You must remember that it was raining when I arrived the year before. It gave me the impression that it had rained steadily ever since. No conventions were being held this time; the 'Forward Lookers' had chosen another town in which to conclave. There were plenty of rooms to be had in hotels, but I did not go to any of them. That bleak Lancaster landscape haunted my mind and I was irresistibly drawn there.

"Perhaps you will say that I was motivated by a morbid curiosity or that I am devoid of any sense of decency, but I was determined to go back to the Lancaster home and hear with my own ears what those decrepit and superstitious people actually thought of Lillian's death.

"I felt a sense of shame and rudeness when I procured a taxi and started for the suburbs. As I rode I noticed that Koogan was the same as I had left it the year before, only it appeared muddier and gloomier. The same downcast sky, the same unpainted wooden houses, the boggy and slushy streets and the same spacious bleakness filled me with a sense of depression. This sense of depression was mingled with something akin to eagerness; eagerness to fathom the truth of that eccentric family and, if possible, the meaning of Lillian's death.

"Finally the taxi halted before the same white-washed picket fence, now sagging and almost down, which separated the Lancaster estate from the rest of the world. I stood upon the gravel walk, hesitating. The Lancaster home loomed forbiddingly, barely visible in the midst of the driving rain. The windows were dark, dark as the enigmatic souls of men. A spasm of uneasiness seized me as I knocked timidly at the door. When the door opened I had a fantastic notion that I was experiencing a dream, so similar were the sensations of that moment and the year before. There stood Mrs. Lancaster! The same snow-white hair piled high, the same black dress, the same frail and aged form! She gazed at me for a moment through her thick lens spectacles in stupefaction, and then a look of sudden and frightened recognition crossed her wrinkled features.

"'Mr. Burrow!' she exclaimed in a tremulous whisper, her whole body swaying as she spoke.

"'How are you, Mrs. Lancaster?' I asked, struggling with a feeling of guilt. 'I thought you might have a room—'

"My voice trailed off. She looked at me for a while in complete silence. What passed through her mind at that moment? No one will ever know. What made her lower her head in confusion? Did my sudden appearance revive in her the memory of the events of the past year?

"'Oh, yes,' she spoke with a start. 'Come in.'

"As I stepped into the hallway the oppressive atmosphere of the whole house seemed to smite me. The same hall, the same Christmas decorations! Nothing changed! As I pulled off my hat and coat I trembled, I don't know why. I placed my bags in a corner, and, at her command, followed her into the front room. I felt as if I ought to apologize. The room was as it was the year before. At the far end of the fireplace sat Mr. Lancaster, gazing at me questioningly, with a black silk skull cap upon his snow-white head. He had aged greatly. It was in his shriveled figure, like a weed gone to seed, that I discerned the passage of time.

"'How are you, Mr. Lancaster?' I greeted him. He got up with some difficulty and shook my hand. His handshake was not as firm as it had been the year before.

"'Very well, thank you. We're still plodding on. Nothing to complain of,' he replied. 'And how are you?'

"We all three seated ourselves and began an inconsequential conversation about the weather, the growth of Koogan, the coming presidential election. An atmosphere of comfort pervaded the room.

"'Yes, the world is changing; time is passing—' Mr. Lancaster's voice drawled. I nodded my head in approval.

"CRASH!"

"All of us jumped. Mr. Lancaster sat forward in his seat as if petrified, a look of horror frozen upon his aged face. Mrs. Lancaster uttered a short scream and stared into the blazing fire, biting the knuckles of her bony hand.

"Upon the stone hearth lay a framed picture, its glass shattered into a thousand fragments. It was some moments before I could find out fully what had happened. The portrait of Lillian, the portrait that had interested me so much the year before, had, for no apparent reason, fallen to the hearth.

"The fall of that picture was momentous! It seemed as if another presence had walked into the room; it was as if the ghost of Lillian—for what is a ghost but the images of our own minds—had come into our midst. The superstitious atmosphere of the year before descended upon all of us. For five minutes we sat silent, not daring to move. The monotonous ticking of the clock, the sizzling sound of the green burning logs, intensified the pregnant silence.

"Suddenly the sound of footsteps was heard, the door opened, and Mrs. Woodson walked into the room. My presence caused her a gasp of surprise, but she quickly recovered herself.

"'My God!' she exclaimed as she noticed our blanched faces. 'What has happened?'

"No one answered. I was too confused to speak. (Mr. and Mrs. Lancaster had not told me that Mrs. Woodson was in the house. Her sudden appearance was a distinct surprise for me. I learned afterwards that she had decided to remain with her parents, owing to their advancing age.) Mrs. Woodson quickly found the cause of our speechlessness. She came forward, mumbling apologetically, and proceeded to remove the bits of glass.

"That shattered picture of Lillian seemed to give that superstition-ridden house a definite atmosphere. No one mentioned Lillian, but her presence, owing to that fallen picture, was as manifest as if her very coffin had been in our midst.

"An awkward silence prevailed. Conversation was impossible. Finally, at my request, Mrs. Woodson showed me to my room. She lit my fire as I placed my baggage in a corner. When about to leave she looked at me as if imploring aid.

"'Mr. Burrow,' she began rather shame-facedly, 'I don't know what you think of this. Did you see how they acted? I don't know what to do sometimes. My mother has forbidden my brothers to come home while I am here. She fears family reunions. She thinks it means sure death!'

"'But, Mrs. Woodson,' I said, 'they're old and must be humored.'

"'Yes. That's right,' she assented weakly and fell silent.

"'Are your brothers coming home this Christmas?' I asked and was immediately sorry, for my question caused her such agitation.

"'I don't know. They do not know that I'm home. They may come,' she said and added quickly, as if to change the conversation, 'Dinner will be at eight o'clock.'

"It was evident that she did not wish to talk upon that subject. I said no more, feeling that further conversation would be painful to her. When she had gone I stood in the center of the room, stunned with what I had seen. I heartily upbraided myself for having come. I felt despicable and mean; I likened myself to a spiritual ghoul ravaging the superstition-ridden souls of these pathetic people. I had an urgent desire to leave at once, but my sordid curiosity dominated my sense of fastidiousness and I decided to remain.

"At eight o'clock I made my way down to the dining-room. All were seated, awaiting my arrival.

"'Come right in,' Mrs. Woodson exclaimed cheerfully. It was obvious that she was trying to cheer up the old couple. She seemed ashamed to let a stranger see her parents so nervous and fearsome over so trivial a cause. Despite her attempt at sociability the situation remained awkward and dinner was eaten in silence.

"The rain beat persistently down upon the house-top as if it sought to isolate the Lancaster home from the rest of the world; as if it sought to sever it from the protecting powers of civilization. A vague sense of dread, caused by the lashing fury of the wind and rain, permeated the room. For an instant I became giddy and my head swam; it seemed as if that room containing Mrs. Woodson and those two old people were lost—lost hopelessly and irretrievably into a wild, superstitious and mythical past. The whole room seemed bathed in a cloak of mental darkness, a darkness governed by unknown and malevolent powers—powers loosed and unrestrained. It was the footsteps of a dead and unfathomable past marching triumphantly over the living present. It was the essence of a negation of life; the quintessence of a triumph of death!

"Suddenly the sound of masculine footsteps was heard upon the veranda, and then an impatient knock. Mrs. Woodson looked at me wildly. The knock was repeated. Mrs. Woodson went to the door and it took only a minute to ascertain that it was the three Lancaster brothers.

"At that moment the room became so oppressive that I wanted to scream. It was like a nightmare!

"'Oh, brothers!'

"'Sister!'

"'Mother!'

"The brothers came into the room just as they had the year before, bringing the smell of fresh and cold dampness from the outside. Raindrops glittered upon their clothes, faces and hands.

"Mrs. Lancaster leaped to her feet.

"'Sons! Sons! Oh, my God! My God! why did you come! Oh, why did you come?' the old woman screamed in a tense whisper. 'Something awful will surely happen!'

"The brothers paused, stricken dumb by the sound of their mother's passionate voice. A silence—deep and awful—a silence fraught with the meaning of something dreadful seemed to freeze the entire room. I shall never, as long as I breathe, forget that silence. In that silence there was revealed, hideously and repellently, the stark nakedness of the fearful hearts of a primitive folk—fearful hearts bowing abjectly to the terror of an unknown created by their own imaginations. The outside world had fallen away, leaving only that room and its superstitious implications present. It was as if a long skeleton-like hand had reached upwards through an unknown past and claimed the hearts of these primitive folk. It was awful! I felt as if I was floating out upon cold and naked space! The very contents of their inmost hearts were laid bare in that one moment: the unreasoning fear of death. Their pathetic fears and hopes seemed transformed into something concrete. Worst of all, it displayed the worthlessness and nothingness of what they called life. It was amazing by its very bleakness!

"They stood there, staring into blank space.

"THUD!

"The silence was broken. Mrs. Lancaster's frail body had fallen limply to the floor. It was the thud of her falling body that brought us back to the concreteness of the present. My body was bathed in a cold sweat, and it was only by grasping the back of a chair that I saved myself from falling. Mr. Lancaster crumpled into a chair and Mrs. Woodson let out a terrified scream as she bent over the prostrate body of her mother. The three brothers stood open-mouthed, as if turned to stone.

"I aided Mrs. Woodson in lifting her mother's body onto a divan, and, rousing the three brothers, sent them for the doctor. Mrs. Woodson used every restorative possible, but to no avail. I felt a profound sense of futility as I watched Mrs. Woodson work over her mother and my sense of futility was made concrete when the doctor arrived and pronounced Mrs. Lancaster dead. A heart attack!

"The shock of a family re-union and its superstitious implications had been too much for her.

"I did not remain for the funeral. My curiosity, my confoundedly morbid curiosity had been satisfied, yes, more than satisfied!"

Fently Burrow brought his tale to an end. Bert Meadows and Matt Brocson simply gazed at him in silence. Burrow's story allowed no comment; it carried the air of finality and conviction in every word. His two skeptical listeners sat still and silent, touched to the depths of their beings by wonder and awe, by something profound and greater than themselves.

# *Poetry*

### Rest for the Weary

You panic stricken guardians of gold
are wise to tremble
and snatch of yourselves hurried counsel
with white faces of grave concern.
For the claws of history
have stripped from your tawdry lives
the tinselled pretence
leaving nothing but vulgarity
of your studied pride
and the naked uselessness
of your existence.
But O weary laden tyrants
do not despair!
Even these encumberances
will not long weigh you down
for soon our brawny hands shall
relieve you of all your burdens!

### A Red Love Note

My dear lovely bloated one:
when we send you our final love-notice of foreclosure
to vacate this civilization which you have inhabited
long beyond the rightful term of your tenure,
there won't be any postponements, honey;
no court delays,
no five-day notices, darling;
no continuations, sugar-pie;
it'll all be over before you know it! . . .
And the immortal kiss that we will plant upon you and your kind
will make you think that the world is going up in smoke.
It'll be nice and sudden, dumling,
It'll be like love,
It'll be a red clap of thunder rising from the very depths of hell!

---

All the poems published here are in the order in which they appeared.

### Child of the Dead and Forgotten Gods

O you innocent liberal!
O you naive darling!
O you poor lost child of the dead and forgotten gods!
What a prize find you are!

Do tell us what ilk or brand of sweetened milk you sip!
Do tell us how you can plead for mercy at the bargain-counters of justice!
Do show us the magic talisman you use in dispelling the blood and stench of
      history!
Do tell us of the enchanted oil you would spread upon the bitter and
      irreconcilable waters of the class struggle!

What did you say?
Louder! I can't hear you!
Louder, please! There's so much noise!
Speak louder, for the pounding of police clubs on the skulls of strikers
and the scream of the riot-siren to disperse the unemployed
And the noise and clamor of slaughter and rapine and greed
drown out your soft talk of peace and brotherhood!


### Strength

The life of a lone comrade
when pitted alone in action
against the legions of tyranny
is a gentle breeze, ineffectually tearing
at granite crags. But when
united with millions and millions
of other lives, steeped in the sense
of an historic mission, the magnitude
of a task to be done, steeled
by the inevitable victory to be—
it becomes a raging hurricane vast and powerful,
wrenching and dredging by the roots the rottening husks of the trees of greed.


### Everywhere Burning Waters Rise

     Everywhere,
on tall and smokeless stackpipes,
on the empty silos of deserted farms,
on the rusty blade of the logger's axe,
on the sooty girders of unfinished skyscrapers,

the cold dense clammy fog
of discontent is settling. . . .

Everywhere,

on tenemented mountains of hunger,
in ghetto swamps of suffering,
in breadlined forests of despair,
on peonized plains of hopelessness

the red moisture of revolt
is condensing on the cold stones of human need. . . .

Everywhere,

men are gathering in groups talking, talking, tiny red pools are forming;
hundreds are joining protest parades marching, marching, small red rills are
  trickling;
thousands are surrounding food-stores storming, storming, rising red rivers are
  flowing
till on the lowlands of starvation meeting
and swelling to a roaring torrential tide
and becoming strangely transformed into waters of fire
and blazing their way to the foaming sea of revolution. . . .

Sweep on, O red stream of molten anger!
Surge and seethe like liquid lava
into every nook and cranny of this greed-reared temple
and blister the rottening walls with your hot cleansing breath!
Lick and lap with your tongues of flame
at its golden pillars of oppressive privilege,
lick and lap until they melt,
melt from the fury of your heat!
Shower and sprinkle the foul air with sparks of white hate
and sterilize this hellishly infected floor
until the last germ of decadence is dead!
Eat with your fiery teeth
at the beams and rafters of exploitation,
eat, eat until they crumble to powdered black ashes!
Burn and burn and burn quickly!
Burn,
for a chafing multitude is waiting,
is waiting to build on the cleared and conquered grounds!

### I Have Seen Black Hands

I am black and I have seen black hands, millions and millions of them—
Out of millions of bundles of wool and flannel tiny black fingers have reached
    restlessly and hungrily for life.
Reached out for the black nipples at the black breasts of black mothers,
And they've held red, green, blue, yellow, orange, white, and purple toys in
    the childish grips of possession,
And chocolate drops, peppermint sticks, lollypops, wineballs, ice cream cones,
    and sugared cookies in fingers sticky and gummy,
And they've held balls and bats and gloves and marbles and jack-knives and
    sling-shots and spinning tops in the thrill of sport and play
And pennies and nickels and dimes and quarters and sometimes on New Year's,
    Easter, Lincoln's Birthday, May Day, a brand new green dollar bill.
They've held pens and rulers and maps and tablets and books in palms spotted
    and smeared with ink,
And they've held dice and cards and half-pint flasks and cue sticks and cigars
    and cigarettes in the pride of new maturity . . .

II

I am black and I have seen black hands, millions and millions of them—
They were tired and awkward and calloused and grimy and covered with hang-
    nails,
And they were caught in the fast-moving belts of machines and snagged and
    smashed and crushed,
And they jerked up and down at the throbbing machines massing taller and
    taller the heaps of gold in the banks of bosses,
And they piled higher and higher the steel, iron, the lumber, wheat, rye, the
    oats, corn, the cotton, the wool, the oil, the coal, the meat, the fruit, the
    glass, and the stone until there was too much to be used,
And they grabbed guns and slung them on their shoulders and marched and
    groped in trenches and fought and killed and conquered nations who
    were customers for the goods black hands had made.
And again black hands stacked goods higher and higher until there was too
    much to be used,
And then the black hands held trembling at the factory gates the dreaded lay-off
    slip,
And the black hands hung idle and swung empty and grew soft and got weak
    and bony from unemployment and starvation,
And they grew nervous and sweaty, and opened and shut in anguish and doubt
    and hesitation and irresolution . . .

III

I am black and I have seen black hands, millions and millions of them—
Reaching hesitantly out of days of slow death for the goods they had made, but

Reprinted from: *New Masses*, No. 11 (June 26, 1934), p. 16.

the bosses warned that the goods were private and did not belong to them,
And the black hands struck desperately out in defence of life and there was blood, but the enraged bosses decreed that this too was wrong,
And the black hands felt the cold steel bars of the prison they had made, in despair tested their strength and found that they could neither bend nor break them,
And the black hands lifted palms in mute and futile supplication to the sodden faces of mobs wild in the revelries of sadism,
And the black hands strained and clawed and struggled in vain at the noose that tightened about the black throat,
And the black hands waved and beat fearfully at the tall flames that cooked and charred the black flesh . . .

## IV

I am black and I have seen black hands
Raised in fists of revolt, side by side with the white fists of white workers,
And some day—and it is only this which sustains me—
Some day there shall be millions and millions of them,
On some red day in a burst of fists on a new horizon!

### Rise and Live

Is this living?
Is this living here idle living?
Is this living here holding our empty hands,
Feeling with our senses the slow seep of time,
Rising, eating, talking, and sleeping,
And ever so often crawling to plead for a hand-out of crumbs . . .
Is this living?
Is this living here lost living?
Is this living here wondering why we have no future,
Enduring with our nerves the dread dross of our days,
Dreaming of a past irretrievably gone,
And feeling the dull breath of death in the wan flow of time . . .
Is this living?
And yet
They tell us we're human—
Tell us we're human beings—
They tell us that our lives in this world mean something!
Where are our days gone?
We see—
We breathe—

We feel on our faces the gold of the sun—
We feel on our bodies the sting of the wind—
We feel in our hearts the call of life—
Yet
Time covers us like cold damp sand!
Where are our days gone?
We're human!
Our lives mean something!
We want to taste again the fruits of our harvest!
We want back our lives—
Our hours—
Our days—
Our years—
We want to live again!
We're human!
We sit here idle
Feeding aliens in a world once our home . . .
Holding bare hands that once worked . . .
We sit here lost
Yet
Towering above our heads are the granaries we built!
Sinking beneath our feet are the vaults we dug!
Winding over the prairies are the rails we laid!
All overflowing with good and wealth,
All guarded by cold steel and burning gas,
All watched by the hard faces of authority . . .
Yes
We sit idle and lost.
Shivering in the dark shadows of our own success,
Drying under the weight of self-made irony!
Let's take back our own!
Let's take back our stolen lives—
Our stolen hours—
Our stolen days—
Our stolen years—
Let's feel in our flesh the rip of their steel!
Let's feel in our throats the burn of their gas!
Let's feel it all, and yet fight!
For we're human
And our lives in this world mean something!
Comrades, let's rise and slay this monstrous irony!
RISE AND LIVE!

### Obsession

Yet again I must speak of it
Yet again I must speak of it
For it has grown to an obsession
Become the pivot-point
Of my days and hours
Reswinging my center of gravity
And outlining for my life
One dark perspective . . .
This haunting American symbol
Of fire cooking human flesh
The dreadful flame that will not die
Has dwarfed and paled all other symbols
Has become the red splotch I see when my eyes are closed
The dragon of my dreams . . .

*II*

How long
How long
Shall I crouch huddled here in this lurid American night
Listening helplessly to the groan of my black brothers?
How long
How long
Shall their oppressed bodies press close to mine
And strainingly lift me on tip-toe
With muscles aching and fists clenched?
How long
How long
Shall my nails bite into the flesh of my palms?
How long
How long?

*III*

Because I am black
And because there is no other way out
Because I know I am black
And because I know there is no other way out
I accept it all
The stake
The torch
The noose
I accept it all
And make of the deaths of my brothers
And the knowledge of my surely promised own
The deep rock on which I stand to face the world!

Reprinted from: *Midland Left,* No. 2 (February, 1935), p. 14.

### I Am a Red Slogan

I AM A RED SLOGAN,
A flaming torch flung to lead the minds of men!
I flaunt my messages from a million banners:
WORKERS OF THE WORLD, UNITE!
I AM A RED SLOGAN,
The axe that whacks to the heart of knotty problems:
STOP MUNITION SHIPMENTS!
FIGHT FASCISM!
DEATH TO LYNCHERS!
I bloom in tired brains in sleep:
BREAD!
LAND!
FREEDOM!
I AM A RED SLOGAN,
Brawny knuckles thrust in the face of profiteers:
EXPROPRIATE THE EXPROPRIATERS!
I AM A RED SLOGAN,
Lingering as a duty after my command is shouted:
DEFEND THE U.S.S.R.!
I haunt the doors of your mind until I am taken in:
SELF-DETERMINATION FOR MINORITY PEOPLES!
I am the one red star in the workers' black sky:
TURN IMPERIALIST WAR INTO CIVIL WAR!
I AM A RED SLOGAN,
The crest of the wave that sweeps to victory:
*ALL POWER TO THE SOVIETS!*


### Ah Feels It in Mah Bones

Mister, things ain't never been all stirred up this way befo'!
It ain't never been that Ah couldn't place a stake.
Now everything's done changed, an' ain't nobody got no go,
An' all the folks talkin' 'bout something's goin' to break.
An' by Gawd Ah b'lieves it—
*Ah feels it in mah bones!*

Yes, sir! Ah sho thought for awhile things was goin' to pick up.
Ah was plannin' on winnin' rolls of yellow dough
An' long-lopin' mah old proud sweet stuff like a greyhound pup!
But shucks, seems like them days just ain't comin' no mo'!
The whole world just done changed—
*Ah feels it in mah bones!*

Look, here! It's done got so bad Ah can't even beg a dime,
An' may bread-basket's a-swearin' mah throat's been cut!
Ah's done got as naked as a jaybird in whistlin' time
Tryin' to make mah old rounds on a empty gut!
Ah'm's got to make a change—
*Ah feels it in mah bones!*

Naw, Sir! Ah ain't a-worryin' no mo' 'bout mah brownskin gal!
Done laid mah razor down an' told mah spotted boys good-bye!
(An' even mah good luck-piece don't seem to work so well.)
Ah'm's ready—mah sail's set for whatever wind's in the sky!
An' brother, there's something a-comin'—
*Ah feels it in mah bones!*


### Red Leaves of Red Books

Turn
Red leaves of red books
Turn
In white palms and black palms
Turn
Slowly in the mute hours of the night
Turn
In the fingers of women and the fingers of men
In the fingers of the old and the fingers of the young
Turn
Under the nervous flickerings of candles
Under yellow gas splutterings
Under dim incandescent globes
Turn
In the North and in the South
In the East and in the West
Turn
Ceaselessly and reveal your printed being
Turn
Until your crispness leaves you
Until you are dog-eared
Until the calloused hands that grip you
Are hardened to the steel of unretractable purpose!

### Spread Your Sunrise!

Good God Almighty
Open up your eyes
And look at what I see
Tearing through them Urals
And leaping over that Volga!
It's a bushy-haired giant-child,
Big-limbed and double-jointed,
Boisterous and bull-headed,
With great big muscles bursting through his clothes!
Over railroads and above stackpipes,
Past skyscrapers and power plants,
Across farms and through forests,
By mine tipples and water dams
He's plowing forward night and day
Leaving cities rocking and shaking as he goes!

Hoooly Chriiist!
What *is* that he's got in his hands?
By George, in one he's holding a bucketful of sunrise,
And in the other he's swishing a long tall broom,
And Jeesus, the fool's splashing crimson everywhere,
Just painting the whole world red!
Go on, Big Boy, go on!
March in your red brogans
And up-root the little fences between the nations!
Smear the capitols!
Coat the crosses on the steeples!
Dab every government building!
Say, when you come to Germany, finish the job old Goering started:
Make that Reichstag blaze, and no fooling!
Then, just for fun,
Fling a drop of red over in Rome on the Pope's nose,
And if he squawks, slip him the quiet ha-ha,
And keep moving!

Gallop on, Big Timer, gallop on!
If anybody ask you who your Ma and Pa were
Show your birth certificate signed by Lenin:
UUUU! SSSS! SSSS! RRRR!
And tell them you're a man-child of the Revolution:
Seed of fiery workers' loins,
Fruit of October's swollen womb!
Get along, Hot Shot, get along,
Gallop with a high hand and dash your brush of red!

Send out across the Atlantic
And as you skid toward the good old U.S.A.
Dip the bristles of your broom deep into the sunrise
And dress the Statue of Liberty in a flaming kimono!
Shucks, ain't nobody never seen the likes of you, Kid!
Shelve the Stock Exchange deeper into the red
And swab the dome in Washington!

Travel on, Man, travel on!
Slap-dash across the states in your Five-year boots!
I'll swing onto the cuff of your pants as you pass Chicago!
Tramp with your legs of steel,
Jar the millionaires in their summer homes
And make them feel who's on their trail!
Stride on, Big Shot, stride on,
Stride and spread your sunrise, red-wash the whole world!


### Between the World and Me

And one morning while in the woods I stumbled suddenly upon the thing,
Stumbled upon it in a grassy clearing guarded by scaly oaks and elms.
And the sooty details of the scene rose, thrusting themselves between the world
and me . . .

There was a design of white bones slumbering forgottenly upon a cushion of ashes.
There was a charred stump of a sapling pointing a blunt finger accusingly at the
sky.
There were torn tree limbs, tiny veins of burnt leaves, and a scorched coil of
greasy hemp;
A vacant shoe, an empty tie, a ripped shirt, a lonely hat, and a pair of trousers stiff
with black blood.
And upon the trampled grass were buttons, dead matches, butt-ends of cigars and
cigarettes, peanut shells, a drained gin-flask, and a whore's lipstick;
Scattered traces of tar, restless arrays of feathers, and the lingering smell of
gasoline.
And through the morning air the sun poured yellow surprise into the eye sockets
of a stony skull . . .
And while I stood my mind was frozen with a cold pity for the life that was gone.
The ground gripped my feet and my heart was circled by icy walls of fear—
The sun died in the sky; a night wind muttered in the grass and fumbled the
leaves in the trees; the woods poured forth the hungry yelping of hounds;
the darkness screamed with thirsty voices; and the witnesses rose and
lived:
The dry bones stirred, rattled, lifted, melting themselves into my bones.
The gray ashes formed flesh firm and black, entering into my flesh.

The gin-flask passed from mouth to mouth; cigars and cigarettes glowed, the
    whore smeared the lipstick red upon her lips,
And a thousand faces swirled around me, clamoring that my life be burned . . .

And then they had me, stripped me, battering my teeth into my throat till I
    swallowed my own blood.
My voice was drowned in the roar of their voices, and my black wet body slipped
    and rolled in their hands as they bound me to the sapling.
And my skin clung to the bubbling hot tar, falling from me in limp patches.
And the down and quills of the white feathers sank into my raw flesh, and I
    moaned in my agony.
Then my blood was cooled mercifully, cooled by a baptism of gasoline.
And in a blaze of red I leaped to the sky as pain rose like water, boiling my limbs.
Panting, begging I clutched child-like, clutched to the hot sides of death.
Now I am dry bones and my face a stony skull staring in yellow surprise at the
    sun . . .

### Transcontinental

(For Louis Aragon, in praise of *Red Front*)

Through trembling waves of roadside heat
We see the cool green of golf courses
Long red awnings catching sunshine
Slender rainbows curved above spirals of water
Swaying hammocks slung between trees—
Like in the movies . . .

*America who built this dream*

Above the ceaseless hiss of passing cars
We hear the tinkle of ice in tall glasses
Clacks of croquet balls scudding over cropped lawns
Silvery crescendos of laughter—
Like in the movies
On Saturday nights
When we used to get paychecks . . .

*America who owns this wonderland*

Lost
We hitch-hike down the hot highways
Looking for a ride home
Yanking tired thumbs at glazed faces
Behind the steering wheels of Packards Pierce Arrows

Lincolns La Salles Reos Chryslers—
Their lips are tight jaws set eyes straight ahead . . .

*America America America why turn your face away*

O for the minute
The joyous minute
The minute of the hour of that day
When the tumbling white ball of our anger
Rolling down the cold hill of our lives
Swelling like a moving mass of snow
Shall crash
Shall explode at the bottom of our patience Thundering
HALT
You shall not pass our begging thumbs
America is ours
This car is commandeered
America is ours
Take your ringed fingers from the steering wheel
Take your polished shoe off the gas
We'll drive and let you be the hitch-hiker
We'll show you how to pass 'em up
You say we're robbers
So what
We're bastards
So what
Sonofbitches
All right chop us into little pieces we don't care
Let the wind tousle your hair like ours have been tousled
Doesn't the sun's hot hate feel sweet on your back
Crook your thumbs and smudge the thin air
What kind of a growl does your gut make when meal-time comes
At night your hips can learn how soft the pavements are
Oh let's do it the good old American way
Sportsmanship Buddy Sportsmanship
But dear America's a free country
Did you say Negroes
Oh I don't mean NEEEGROOOES
After all
Isn't there a limit to everthing
You wouldn't want your *daughter*
And they say there's no GOD
And furthermore it's simply disgraceful how they're discriminating against the
      children of the rich in Soviet schools
PROLETARIAN CHILDREN
*Good Lord*

Why if we divided up everything today we'd be just where we are inside of a
    year
The strong and the weak The quick and the slow You understand
But Lady even quivering lips can say
PLEASE COMRADE MY FATHER WAS A CARPENTER I SWEAR SWEAR
    HE WAS
I WAS NEVER AGAINST THE COMMUNISTS REALLY
Fairplay Boys Fairplay
America America can every boy have the chance to rise from Wall Street to the
    Commintern
America America can every boy have the chance to rise from Riverside Drive to
    the General Secretaryship of the Communist Party
100% Justice
And Mister don't forget
Our hand shall be on the steering wheel
Our feet shall be on the gas
And you shall hear the grate of our gears
UNITEDFRONT—SSSTRIKE
The motor throbs with eager anger
UNITEDFRONT—SSSTRIKE
We're lurching toward the highway
UNITEDFRONT—SSSTRIKE
The pavement drops into the past The future smites our face
America is ours
10 15 20 30
America America
WOORKERSWOORKERS
Hop on the runningboard Pile in
We're leaving We're leaving
Leaving the tired the timid the soft
Leaving pimps idlers loungers
Leaving empty dinner-pails wage-cuts stretch-outs
Leaving the tight-lipped mother and the bare meal-can
Leaving the shamed girl and her bastard child
Leaving leaving the past leaving
The wind filled with leaflets leaflets of freedom
Millions and millions of leaflets fluttering
Like the wings of a million birds
AmericaAmericaAmerica

Scaling New England's stubborn hills Spanning the Hudson
Waving at Manhattan Waving at New Jersey
Throwing a Good Bye kiss to Way Down East
Through mine-pirred Pennsylvania Through Maryland Our Maryland
Careening over the miles Spinning the steering wheel
Taking the curves with determination

AmericaAmerica
SOFT SHOULDER AHEAD
AmericaAmerica
KEEP TO THE MIDDLE OF THE ROAD
AmericaAmerica
The telegraph poles are a solid wall
WASHINGTON—90 MILES
AmericaAmerica
The farms are a storm of green
Past rivers past towns
50 60 70 80
AmericaAmerica
CITY LIMITS
Vaulting Washington's Monument
Leaping desks of Senators Ending all bourgeois elections
Hurdling desks of Congressmen Fascist flesh sticking to our tires
Skidding into the White House Leaving a trail of carbon monoxide for the
    President
Roaring into the East Room Going straight through Lincoln's portrait Letting
    the light of history through
AmericaAmerica
Swinging Southward Plunging the radiator into the lynch-mob Giving no
    warning
Slowing Slowing for the sharecroppers
Come on You Negroes Come on
There's room
Not in the back but front seat
We're heading for the highway of Self-Determination
UNITEDFRONT—SSSTRIKE
Dim your lights you Trotskyites
UNITEDFRONT—SSSTRIKE
Lenin's line is our stream line
UNITEDFRONT—SSSTRIKE
Through October's windshield we see the road Looping over green hills Dipping
    toward to-morrow

AmericaAmericaAmerica
Look back See the tiny threads of our tires leaving hammer and sickle prints
    upon the pavement
See the tree-lined horizon turning slowly in our hearts
See the ripe fields Fields ripe as our love
See the eastern sky See the white clouds of our hope
See the blood-red afterglow in the west Our memory of October
See See See the pretty cottages the bungalows the sheltered homes
See the packing-box cities the jungles the huts
See See See the skyscrapers the clubs the pent-houses

See the bread-lines winding winding winding long as our road
AmericaAmericaAmerica

Tagging Kentucky Tagging Tennessee
Into Ohio Into the orchards of Michigan
Over the rising and falling dunes of Indiana
Across Illinois' glad fields of dancing corn
Slowing Comrades Slowing again
Slowing for the heart of proletarian America
CHICAGO—100 MILES
WOORKERSWOORKERS
Steel and rail and stock All you sons of Haymarket
Swing on We're going your way America is ours
UNITEDFRONT—SSSTRIKE
The pressure of our tires is blood pounding in our hearts
UNITEDFRONT—STRIKE
The steam of our courage blows from the radiator-cap
UNITEDFRONT—SSSTRIKE
The wind screams red songs in our ears
60 70 80 90
AmericaAmericaAmerica

Listen Listen to the moans of those whose lives were laughter
Listen to the howls of the dogs dispossessed
Listen to bureaucratic insects spattering against the windshield
Listen to curses rebounding from fear-proof glass
Listen to the gravel of hate tingling on our fenders
Listen to the raindrops mumbling of yesterday
Listen to the wind whistling of to-morrow
Listen to our tires humming humming humming hymns of victory
AmericaAmericaAmerica

Coasting Comrades Coasting
Coasting on momentum of Revolution
Look Look at that village Like a lonesome egg in the nest of the hills
Soon Soon you shall fly all over the hillsides Crowing the new dawn
Coasting Indulging in Lenin's dream


TUNE IN ON THE RADIO THE WORLD IS LAUGHING

*Red Baseball*
Great Day in the Morning

> *. . . the Leninites defeated the redbirds 3 to 0.*
> *Batteries for the Leninites: Kenji Sumarira and*

*Boris Petrovsky. For the Redbirds: Wing Sing and*
*Eddie O'Brien. Homeruns: Hugo Schmidt and Jack*
*Ogletree. Umpires: Pierre Carpentier and Oswald Wallings* . . .

The world is laughing The world is laughing
     . . . *Mike Gold's account of the Revolutin sells*
     *26 millions copies* . . .
     26 million copies . . .
The world is laughing The world is laughing
     . . .*beginning May 1st the work day is limited to*
     *five hours* . . .
The world is laughing The world is laughing
     . . . *last of the landlords liquidated*
     *in Texas* . . .
The world is laughing The world is laughing

Picking up speed to measure the Mississippi
AmericaAmericaAmerica
Plowing the richness of Iowa soil Into the Wheat Empire
Making Minnesota Taking the Dakotas Carrying Nebraska
On on toward the Badlands the Rockies the deserts the Golden Gate
Slowing once again Comrades Slowing to right a wrong
Say You Red Men You Forgotten Men
Come out from your tepees
Show us Pocahontas For we love her
Bring her from her hiding place Let the sun kiss her eyes
Drape her in a shawl of red wool Tuck her in beside us
Our arms shall thaw the long cold of her shoulders
The lights flash red Comrades let's go
UNITEDFRONT—SSSTRIKE
The future opens like an ever-widening V
UNITEDFRONT—SSSTRIKE
We're rolling over titles of red logic
UNITEDFRONT—SSSTRIKE
We're speeding on wheels of revolution
AmericaAmerica
Mountain peaks are falling toward us
AmericaAmerica
Uphill and the earth rises and looms
AmericaAmerica
Downhill and the earth tilts and sways
AmericaAmerica
80 90 100
AmericaAmerica
Every factory is a fortress

Cities breed soviets
AmericaAmerica
Plains sprout collective farms
Ten thousand Units are meeting
America America
Resolutions passed unanimously
The Red Army is on the march
AmericaAmerica
*Arise, ye prisoners* . . .
AmericaAmerica
Speed Faster
Speed AmericaAmerica
*Arise, ye wretched* . . .
AmericaAmerica
Speed Faster
Ever Faster America America
*For Justice* America America *Thunders*
AmericaAmericaAmerica


### Hearst Headline Blues

"Charge Reds Foment Revolution"
    "Lynch Negro Who Wouldn't Say 'Mister'"
"Mayor Proposes Tax Solution"
    "Weeps When He Learns He Married His Sister"

"U.S.S.R. Abolishes Ration"
    "Professor Simpson Lectures on Sperm"
"100 Educators Praise Nation"
    "Striking Miner Gets Twenty-Year Term"

"Student Rebels at Scolding; Stabs Teacher"
    "Nab Fifty in Red Light Raid"
"10,000 Hear Six Year Old Girl Preacher"
    "Broker Rapes and Murders Maid"

"Woman Dynamites Jail to Free Her Lover"
    "Starvation Claims Mother and Tot"
"Roosevelt Says the Worst Is Over"
    "Longshoremen Picket; Two Are Shot"

"Father Butchers Son With Axe"
    "Many Gold Voices to Be Heard on Air"
"Attorney Dodd Uncovers Facts"
    "The Right Reverend O'Connell Urges Prayer"

### Old Habit and New Love

Daybreak has its own desire, noon its peculiar longing, and dusk a tired demand—all for paths that lead to the rusty levers of smoky and familiar
landscape.

An itch eats at softening callouses, sweaty hands won't stay dry, and the body
limbs are eager, chafing to revitalize the sleeping speed of chilled
flywheels.

There is an ache for marriage, for the sight of halves grown whole, for cactus land
to blend with dingy dream, for the welding of iron and bleeding palms.

It is for fusion of number and nerve we strain, of cobweb and waterfall, of worker
and lonely machine, of old habit and new love.

Electric anger rises to smelt trolley-track to pliability of artist's brush, daring to
quicken the whirs of crankshafts till they drone, ring as meaningful as
music.

O Creators: Poets, Makers of Melody! Some first-shift dawn shall find us on equal
ground, holding in our hands the world's tools, drafting the hope-prints of
our vision on canvases of green earth!


### We of the Streets

Streets are full of the scent of us—odors of onions drifting from doorways,
effluvium of baby new-born downstairs, seeping smells of warm soap-
suds—the streets as lush with the ferment of our living.

Our sea is water swirling in gutters; our lightning is the blue flame of an acetylene
torch; billboards blossom with the colors of a billion flowers; we hear
thunder when the "L" roars; our strip of sky is a dirty shirt.

We have grown used to nervous landscapes, chimney-broken horizons, and the
sun dying between tenements; we have grown to love streets, the ways of
streets; our bodies are hard like worn pavement.

Our emblems are street emblems: stringy curtains blowing in windows; sticky-
fingered babies tumbling on door-steps; deep-cellared laughs meant for
everybody; slow groans heard in area-ways.

Our sunshine is a common hope; our common summer and common winter a
common joy and a common sorrow; our fraternity is shoulder-rubbing,
crude with unspoken love; our password the wry smile that speaks a common fate.

Our love is nurtured by the soft flares of gas-lights; our hate is an icy wind
screaming around corners.

And there is something in the streets that made us feel immortality when we
rushed along ten thousand strong, hearing our chant fill the world, wanting
to do what none of us would do alone, aching to shout the forbidden word,
knowing that we of the streets are deathless. . . .

### Red Clay Blues

I miss that red clay, Lawd, I
Need to feel it on my shoes.
Says miss that red clay, Lawd, I
Need to feel it on my shoes.
I want to see Georgia cause I
Got them red clay blues.

Pavement's hard on my feet, I'm
Tired o' this concrete street.
Pavement's hard on my feet, I'm
Tired o' this city street.
Goin' back to Georgia where
That red clay can't be beat.

I want to tramp in the red mud, Lawd, and
Feel the red clay round my toes.
I want to wade in that red mud,
Feel that red clay suckin' at my toes.
I want my little farm back and I
Don't care where that landlord goes.

I want to be in Georgia, when the
Big storm starts to blow.
Yes, I want to be in Georgia when that
Big storm starts to blow.
I want to see the landlords runnin' cause I
Wonder where they gonna go!

I got them red clay blues.

RICHARD WRIGHT AND LANGSTON HUGHES.


# Blues

### King Joe (Joe Louis Blues)

Black-eyed peas ask cornbread, "What makes you so strong?"
Black-eyes peas ask cornbread, "What makes you so strong?"
Cornbread say, "I come from where Joe Louis was born."

Joe don't talk much, but he talks all the time.
Joe don't talk much, but he talks all the time.
Now you can look at Joe but you sure don't read his mind.

Lord, I know a secret, swore I'd never tell,
Lord, I know a secret, swore I'd never tell.
I know what makes old Joe book and punch and roll like hell.

Reprinted from: *New Letters* 38, No. 2 (December, 1971), [pp. 42–45].

Rabbit say to bee, what make you sting so deep?
Rabbit say to bee, what make you sting so deep?
Bee say I sting like Joe and rock 'em all to sleep.

They say old Joe just lays down sleeps all day long,
They say old Joe just lays down sleeps all day long,
What old Joe does at night, Lord, sure ain't done him no wrong.

Been in Cleveland, St. Louis, and Chicago, too;
Been in Cleveland, St. Louis, and Chicago, too;
But the best is Harlem when a Joe Louis fight is through.


### Additional Lyrics

Old Joe wrestled Ford engines, Lord, it was a shame;
Say old Joe hugged Ford engines, Lord, it was a shame;
And he turned engine himself and went to the fighting game.

If you want to see something, just watch Old Joe roll with a blow,
If you want to see something, just watch Old Joe roll with a blow,
Lord, Lord, bet he didn't learn that trick at no boxing show.

Big Black bearcat couldn't turn nothing loose he caught;
Big Black bearcat couldn't turn nothing loose he caught;
Squeezed it 'til the count of nine, and just couldn't be bought.

Now molasses is black and they say buttermilk is white,
Now molasses is black and they say buttermilk is white,
If you eat a bellyful of both, it's like a Joe Louis fight.

Wonder what Joe Louis thinks when he's fighting a white man,
Say wonder what Joe thinks when he's fighting a white man?
Bet he thinks what I'm thinking, 'cause he wears a deadpan.

Lord, I hate to see old Joe Louis step down,
Lord, I hate to see old Joe Louis step down,
But I bet a million dollars no man will ever wear his crown.

Bullfrog told boll weevil: Joe's done quit the ring,
Bullfrog told boll weevil: Joe's done quit the ring,
Boll weevil say: He ain't gone and he's still the king.


### The FB Eye Blues

That old FB eye
Tied a bell to my bed stall
Said old FB eye
Tied a bell to my bed stall
Each time I love my baby, gover'ment knows it all.

Woke up this morning
FB eye under my bed
Said I woke up this morning
FB eye under my bed
Told me all I dreamed last night, every word I said.

Everywhere I look, Lord
I see FB eyes
Said every place I look, Lord
I find FB eyes
I'm getting sick and tired of govern'ment spies.

My mama told me
A rotten egg'll never fry
Said my mama told me
A rotten egg'll never fry
And everybody knows a cheating dog'll never thrive.

Got them blues, blues, blues
Them mean old FB eye blues
Said I got them blues, blues, blues
Them dirty FB eye blues
Somebody tell me something, some good news.

If he'd been a snake, Lord
He'd a jumped up and bit me
Said if he'd been a snake, Lord
He'd a jumped up and bit me
But old FB eye just hauled off and hit me.

Now kittens like milk
And rats love cheese
Said kittens like milk
And rats sure love their cheese
Wonder what FB eye loves, crawling on his knees?

Grasshopper likes to spit
In a bloodhound's eye
Said grasshopper likes to spit
In a bloodhound's eye
Lord, let that grasshopper meet the FB eye.

Breaks my heart in two, Lord
And I just can't forget
Said it breaks my heart, Lord
And I just can't forget
Old jealous FB eye ain't ended yet.

# Haiku

I am nobody
A red sinking autumn sun
Took my name away

Make up your mind snail!
Your are half inside your house
And halfway out!

In the falling snow
A laughing boy holds out his palms
Until they are white

Keep straight down this block
Then turn right where you will find
A peach tree blooming

With a twitching nose
A dog reads a telegram
On a wet tree trunk

The spring lingers on
In the scent of a damp log
Rotting in the sun

Whose town did you leave
O wild and drowning spring rain
And where do you go?

The crow flew so fast
That he left his lonely caw
Behind in the fields

Just enough of rain
To bring the smell of silk
From the umbrellas

Coming from the woods
A bull has a sprig of lilac
Dangling from a horn

Why is the hail wo wild
Bouncing so frighteningly
Only to lie so still

A balmy spring wind
Reminding me of something
I cannot recall

Reprinted from: *New Letters* 38, No. 2 (December, 1971), [pp. 100–101].

The dog's violent sneeze
Fails to rouse a single fly
On his mangy back

I would like a bell
Tolling this soft twilight
Over willow trees

The green cockleburs
Caught in the thick wooly hair
Of the black boy's head

Winter rain at night
Sweetening the taste of bread
And spicing the soup

An empty sickbed
An indented white pillow
In weak winter sun

For you, O gulls
I order slatey waters
And this leaden sky

An autumn sunset
A buzzard sails slowly past
Not flapping its wings

Merciful autumn
Tones down the shabby curtains
Of my rented room

From across the lake
Past the black winter trees
Faint sounds of a flute

Standing in the field
I hear the whispering of
Snowflake to snowflake

# An Interview with Simone de Beauvoir

The following interview with Simone de Beauvoir was conducted by Michel Fabre on June 24, 1970.

**Q.** What were the circumstances of your first meeting with Richard Wright?

**A.** I met him in Paris in 1946 before I went to the United States myself. I think we had lunch or dinner together, and he said: "You must come and see us when you are in New York." Of course, he had already met Sartre and Camus. He met Sartre in early 1946 when the latter was in New York with a group of - journalists. . . . The details of my stay in New York, of the visits I paid the Wrights, and our trips and going out together are documented very precisely in *America Day by Day*. We went to Harlem several times, to a dance, to several churches where spirituals were sung, to many parties and meetings where intellectuals were present. . . . When I came back, they were not long in coming to Paris too and settling there, and we had friendly relations for quite a long time.

**Q.** I suppose that you were interested in politics and racial problems before the war, before meeting Wright. Yet, was your first contact with him, or with his work, a meaningful event in your life?

**A.** I do not really remember whether Sartre had already made me deeply aware of racial problems. The fact is that I became extremely preoccupied with racial problems in the United States after the war only. Before the war I hardly knew the United States, they represented for me something extremely mythical. I was conversant with American literature: Faulkner, Dos Passos, Hemingway in particular. But I did not read any book by Wright before the war. Had they been translated then?

**Q.** No. But *L'Arbalète*, an underground magazine, published a translation of "Big Boy Leaves Home" in a number devoted to American literature during the German occupation.

**A.** Hadn't *Native Son* been published previously in English?

**Q.** Yes, in 1940.

**A.** 1940, that's it. Now, I remember. Sylvia Beach had told me: "You like violent books, well, here is a violent one, it will hit you hard." And I said: "Yes, I'll read it." I read it and I was very, very much impressed. So my first encounter with Wright's novels was some time in 1940, through Sylvia Beach. I was especially impressed by the beginning, when the adolescent says that he knows there are things he'll never be allowed to do, that he'll never fly a plane, for instance. It struck me as a new version of predestination. Later, we published a novella in *Les Temps Modernes*, "Fire and Cloud," the one in which blacks and whites hold a demonstration together. . . . But I must admit I became concerned with racial problems in the United States in a meaningful way only when I was there. The first thing a woman had said to me—she worked in the French Embassy in New York—was: "Above all, do not speak of the Negro problem; you are new in America, you are a French woman, you cannot understand." . . . And of course, I hastened to do the reverse.

**Q.** Did Wright play a certain part in *Les Temps Modernes?*

**A.** Not in its policy. We issued a special number on the United States, with articles and extracts by black writers, and Wright was instrumental in having pieces of Horace Cayton and . . . a Chicago anthropologist—St. Clair Drake—published in that issue. He told me to read *Black Metropolis,* if I remember correctly, long before it was translated. He would always indicate and suggest new titles. *Les Temps Modernes* published quite a lot of his own stuff: *Black Boy,* in installments, "The Man Who Lived Underground," his lecture on black American literature, I think, novellas. . . . Also there was some cooperation between him and Sartre in the field of politics. I'm alluding to the Rassemblement Politique Révolutionnaire: Wright was not exactly a member of R.D.R. because he could not, not being a Frenchman, but he was quite close to their aims. I remember a meeting we had organized, somewhere in the salons of a big hotel, with Daniel Guérin, with Sartre and Wright and a number of left-wing intellectuals. And I remember a discussion between Wright and Sartre when they disagreed: Wright wanted us to support his drive for equality between black and white soldiers in the American occupation forces, or was it NATO in 1950 already? And Sartre, purely out of principle, did not want to support him officially, because doing so amounted to recognizing the existence of NATO and he refused to do so. You see, when they ask me now to demonstrate against national service for women or against the reforms in national service the government is preparing, I refuse because my demonstration would mean that I recognize the validity of national service, and I do not. The discussion between Sartre and Wright had taken place on a friendly level and they had settled it amicably.

**Q.** They had about the same positions at the big R.D.R. meeting at the Salle Pleyel in 1949, hadn't they?

**A.** Yes, Sartre and Wright and a few others had issued a statement opposing the Atlantic Treaty and the Marshall Plan. Their opposition to the United States and their policy then was stronger than that of David Rousset and the American delegation—they were hardly socialists anyway. I also remember another meeting where Albert Camus was present. It must have been on quite a general theme, since he was there. Yes, it was l'Internationalisme de l'Esprit. Sartre gave a speech, then Camus, then Wright and I translated Wright's speech, which I had read previously, for the audience after he had given it. Wright was quite active on the political scene with us at that time. I saw him rarely at the end of his life, but we were especially close from 1947 to 1955. Of course, Sartre was very busy and I had more frequent relationships with the Wrights than he could. I would often visit them or come for dinner and meet writers. I met Truman Capote once and also Carson McCullers and her husband at their place on Rue Monsieur le Prince. But I have not kept precise memories of those occasions.

**Q.** But you have read most of his works?

**A.** Of course. I can read English pretty well and I can say I've read all his works in English. I liked his last one, *The Long Dream,* especially.

**Q.** Do you remember any striking details about his personality?

**A.** They are rather blurred. Well, here is one episode. This took place in New York when I visited them in 1947. While I was there he had the visit of a female friend who was rather plain and rough mannered, and she grabbed Julia who must have been six at the time—and pretended to be fighting with her. Well, Dick rushed and snatched the little one in his arms and shouted, "No violence, no violence," with a passion which quite astounded me. He was certainly disturbed by physical violence and wanted to protect Julia from even a show of it. Think of his own youth. . . . I also remember a time when we talked about Mexico at some length; he told me about the absence of a middle class and how it made contacts difficult for a visitor. He was concerned with the state of political affairs when he was there during the war.

**Q.** I was struck to find in your book, *Les Mandarins,* a kind of image I had already found in Wright's *What You Do Not Know Won't Hurt You"*: that of dogs howling soundlessly—because their vocal cords have been cut—used as a symbol of silent pain and oppression. Can one see more than a coincidence?

**A.** I do not think it was inspired by Wright's image. I have always found it horrible that some consciousness could exist within a being, a man, or an animal, who is incapable of communication, of expressing himself. I thought of people who have had strokes, like Valéry Larbaud, for instance. . . . Also, when I wrote that I was living in a tiny studio above a veterinary clinic, . . . I remember Wright's story now: he was working in a hospital, and they had thrown down tiers of cages and had to put the guinea pigs and rabbits and mice back into their cages without having the slightest idea of which was which. It was a fine, funny piece, with a good point against discrimination. Wright was a wonderful storyteller, you know. I recall a trip we made in a taxi from his place to the northern part of Harlem when I was visiting. During the whole ride he did not stop telling stories for one moment. When we arrived, the driver, who was black, said he wished all his customers were like him. He'd never get bored. When Dick was in a mood for telling stories, he could go on for hours, and everyone would laugh and laugh. He was different from many writers and intellectuals I met through him in New York. We once went to a meeting of a writers' guild, or association and all they could talk about was rights and percentages and such things. No real intellectual exchange. We also went to a dinner which was given by Dorothy Norman, where Mrs. Gandhi, Nehru's daughter, was present with Asians and black people. It was stimulating, but although Mrs. Norman is a sincere liberal, it was somewhat artificial. There was something deeper and simpler in Wright.

# A Letter From Dorothy Padmore

The following letter, written on March 13, 1963, was sent by the late Dorothy Padmore in answer to Michel Fabre's request for information concerning the relationship between Richard Wright and George Padmore for a biography of Wright Fabre was preparing. Mrs. Padmore was then in Accra, working as a special aide to Kwame Nkrumah, after her husband's untimely death in 1959.

After explaining how she first met Wright, she continues:

Very rarely Richard came to London, when he would always come to see us. And whenever my husband and he met, there would be long talks about the problems of fighting for freedom from colonial rule in Africa and the West Indies and the struggle for equality by the Negroes of the United States. Richard came to recognize George Padmore as the rallying point in London, the center of the British Empire, for all those who, in no matter how small a way, wanted to see an end of colonialist rule. How deeply Richard thought of George Padmore, you will have gathered from the introduction he wrote to my husband's book, *Pan-Africanism or Communism?*

There has been much criticism of Richard, very largely inspired by the U.S. State Department [and] from Negroes in America who equated his refusal to go back to America as a confession of his withdrawal from the fight for equality in that self-styled bastion of democracy. Nothing could have been farther from the truth.

Richard Wright was not a simple person, even though his manner was straightforward and he never let his initial success go to his head and change him from the very likeable southern-born Negro that he was. Fundamentally, Richard was a product of the race-ridden society into which he was born. But he was overladen with the acute perception of the artist-writer and the extra susceptibility of a highly intelligent colored man, understanding the political, social, and economic roots of that environment and trying to make his own adjustment to it, both as individual and writer.

That would have been difficult enough in itself, but Richard had been drawn early into the Communist Party, which he saw as a sympathetic fighting vehicle on which he could ride the cause of Negro emancipation. Unfortunately, it did not turn out that way, and he found himself being ridden as a hag along the tortuous maze of Communist Party subordination to Soviet interests and internal party intrigues. He made the sad discovery that Negroes were used by the Party to make it appear on the surface that the Communists support their cause, while behind the scenes the same old attitudes of colour line obtained.

What happened to Richard Wright had happened to George Padmore a lot earlier, in 1932, when he left the Communist Party as the Soviet Union prepared to enter the League of Nations, indicating thereby that it was subordinating the colonial struggle to its own national interests, though speaking in terms of internationalism. Padmore recovered to maintain an objective, though critical, attitude towards the Soviet Union. Wright, however, was for a while more subjective, though he later made a distinction between the behaviour of the American Communist Party and the policies of the Soviet Union. Nevertheless, he felt himself to be hounded by the Party, whom he felt never forgave him for refusing to surrender his independence of action in their service, a sin made doubly great by the fact that he had failed to know his place as a black man.

I had the impression that when Richard went to Paris originally, at the invitation of the French Government, he was captivated by French culture and the general atmosphere of freedom, with its apparent absence of colour discrimination. Cut off from his original environment and at a loose end politically, he was drawn into the vortex of French intellectualism and politics; and for some years I had the feeling that he was losing touch with his own background in seeking some esoteric anchor to which he could attach himself. He associated with Jean-Paul Sartre, without accepting his existentialism, and later worked with him in getting together a preliminary committee for the new political group that Sartre tried to get along when he had passed beyond existentialism towards a more empirical left ward attitude. Wright did not go along with that group, for what reasons his wife will be able to explain.

Richard, I think was puzzled by his reception in the Gold Coast when he went there in 1953. When I suggested that he should go and see an African colony poising itself for independence, I considered that it would provide him with an exceptional opportunity to see at first hand both colonial conditions and the organization of the fight for liberation. I had not yet myself visited the country, but my husband had. We both told Wright what preparations he should make, and my husband wrote to Dr. Nkrumah telling him that Richard was planning to come to the Gold Coast and was eager to see what was going on and would be glad to be facilitiated in the formal procedures and in being welcomed and shown around. Richard's own introduction to *Black Power* will apprise you of how things turned out.

Because I had not myself visited the Gold Coast at that time, I was unable to foresee the reception that might be given to an American Negro who came to Africa, not only enthusiastic to observe the environment and atmosphere at a time of liberatory struggle, but also partly in a mood of curiosity to know and understand the people from whom his ancestors had sprung.

Unfortunately, Africans have received the impression that both American Negroes and West Indians consider themselves a cut above the African, whom they regard, as a rule, as primitive, an attitude instilled into them by the pattern of education to which they are submitted. This puts the African on the defensive in his communication with these descendants of Africa from overseas societies. It was this reaction as well as the general secretiveness of the African in his relations with those outside his own society that coloured Wright's reception even from the higher coterie of the Convention People's Party. I think they in part resented his open expression of his view, attributed to his American background, and his curiosity and genuine desire for information in order to be able to appraise their environment and struggle. I believe they regarded it as prying for ulterior motives, which inspires so many of the foreign observers and commentators who interpret them in a distorted fashion.

It was a pity, because there is no doubt that the Africans' reaction to him colored to some extent Richard's view of them. Worst of all, it put him in his place as an outsider, so that he was unable to wrest their confidence and find his way about among them with ease. I myself visited the Gold Coast the following year at the invitation of Dr. Nkrumah and was his personal guest. Even so, I found difficulty in getting arrangements made for traveling over the country, though people were friendly enough when we met, and I was taken to their houses and entertained. I think that at the time they were too busy with the double task of pushing forward to independence and doing their job as administrators in the Government. Moreover, they did not control affairs as yet and were poor in means of transport and other things.

Richard, too, was anxious to understand why it was that Africans had sold other Africans into slavery, since this was something that concerned him closely. It was not a problem that involved me in the same way, and so perhaps I was not handicapped by what might, after all, have been a dormant need to apportion guilt. When *Black Power* finally appeared and Richard sent a copy to my husband and me, I found it absorbing. And since by that time I had made my own visit to the Gold Coast, I found in it an echo of many of my own thoughts and reactions. My husband shared this view to a large extent, and we both considered the book a pretty fair summing up of the society, with its aspirations and past and future perspectives. This was not how it was received, however, in the Gold Coast, where much of what it said was regarded as untimely observation and commentary. It was felt that part of the picture drawn fitted in too closely with the views of their critics that they were not yet ready for self-government.

On their side, the non-African critics of Wright considered that he was presumptuous in the terms of his open letter to Dr. Nkrumah that appeared at the end of the book. In the opinion of my husband and myself, this constituted the most constructive contribution and, to my mind, remains as valid today as it was at the time of writing. Had it then been accepted as the friendly guide it was intended to be, I think that a good many pitfalls might have been avoided, as it would have harnessed more positively at the proper time the fund of enthusiasm and inspiration that independence released.

Wright, I am sure, was disappointed in the book's reception in Africa, where opinion on it weighed against him for the future and precluded him from offering the contribution that he was so anxious to make to Africa's need of freedom and unification.

Seeking still to find a niche in which he could use his gifts and secure a larger measure of spiritual satisfaction, Richard seemed to have a period of flirtation with the leftish intellectuals of Great Britain. He seemed to have some leanings towards the labor socialism of Richard Crossman, for example, at the time when he was making his contribution to the symposium, "The God That Failed."

This period, however, seemed quickly to be left behind. Continued contact with George Padmore, whose absorption in Africa's problems could not but infect Wright, increased his interest in Africa, and he understood the reaction of that independence struggle upon the Negroes' fight for equality in America. He regarded with contempt the identification of Negroes with America's assumption of the leadership of the "free world" and considered that the rights they felt they were gaining were, in fact, entrenching segregation by other means. And even these he understood to be wrenched from a reluctant white ruling class that was forced to concede recognition to the rising tide of liberty in the coloured world as part of its cold war strategy.

Richard refused to fall victim to the angry rejection of him and his works from Negroes themselves, who criticised him for remaining abroad at a time when, so they averred, Afro-Americans were widening their freedom frontiers inside the U.S.A. These critics ignored the restrictions placed on freedom of thought and action in America under McCarthyism and beyond. He abhorred the very idea of having his ideas and work circumscribed by the current total subservience to America's hysterical anti-Communism, which he regarded as equally totalitarian as the ideology of the Soviet Union. It was impossible for him to live and work in such a milieu.

In fact, his spirit was oppressed by a growing inability to fit into the spreading illiberalism of France, but his efforts to obtain permission to live in England, even though supported by John Strachey and other prominent personalities, ended in his refusing to accede to certain inquisitions, and thus renouncing the idea. As a writer striving earnestly to uphold his creative integrity, he was discovering that independence of thought and expression was becoming a luxury in the present period of authoritarianism, one for which he must pay dearly in isolation and opprobrium, as well as in the increasing difficulty of finding a congenial atmosphere in which to reside and work. France's involvement in colonial wars, especially that against Algeria, was emphasising racialism in a country where it has not previously come much to the surface, despite indications of hidden undercurrents.

He was at first sympathetic to certain attempts to engage his support for antiracial protests, but I believe [he] withdrew when he found that it would involve him in factional and individual squabbles where use would be made of his name to damage his report and standing.

Our contact with Richard, that is, my husband's and mine, was, from the end of 1957, and even before, by correspondence only, for we then came to Ghana. When my husband planned to be in London for a medical check-up in September 1959, Richard made the opportunity to come to London, and they talked together. When my husband died a few days later, Richard returned for the funeral. George Padmore's death unnerved him considerably, as it did many others, and I think that, alone in Paris, he may have brooded intensely both upon the personal loss to him of one whom he regarded as a most valuable friend, even though so far away much of the time, as well as an irreparable loss for the cause of African independence and unity at a time when he could have done so much to assist that cause.

Richard was, I think, extremely unhappy during the last years of his life, though outwardly he may not have shown it. When I saw him during the two days I stayed in Paris in 1960, at the end of August or beginning of September . . . he was extremely tired, both physically, and I sensed, spiritually, too. He was working extremely hard on play, novel, articles, radio talks—all in the effort to keep the separate establishments in London and Paris, which were draining his resources. He also declared himself the victim of a plot, evidence of which he had gathered, and which implicated the French security, the American F.B.I. (perhaps C.I.A.) and ex-Trotskyists.

He was then under treatment by a Russian doctor living in Paris, whose name I forget, but whom I met on the second evening I spent with Richard, who took me first to the doctor's house, where he consulted him professionally, and then all three of us went to dinner at a restaurant run by an American Negro who served Southern American cooking. I remember not finding the doctor very sympathetic and thinking that Richard was taking far too many drugs; and when I saw his condition I could not help feeling that it bore many resemblances to that of my husabnd in the last weeks of his life. I was hesitant about criticizing both his doctor's personality and his treatment and feel that I made a great mistake in not doing so. But Richard seemed to have a relationship with him that struck me as rather peculiar. My own thoughts about the doctor, which I did not express to Richard, were that I found it difficult to understand how he had the means to follow the special medical research he was apparently interested in without taking many patients. It was difficult to reconcile the spacious accommodation he lived in on a fashionable boulevard with his Russian origin and a certain absence of necessity to work at his living. His father was residing with him, and there was no evidence of a woman in residence.

That the doctor had attached himself specially to Richard was evident from the manner in which he wrote about him. Among the last letters I had from him, he talked about the possibility of making a trip to Africa, for which this doctor friend would make the necessary flight arrangements through some contact he had with UMARCO, the French travel agency and transport house. As I understood it, the doctor would probably also defray some of the expenses, and Richard was most anxious to come along to West Africa to see the current situation for himself at first hand and to use his visit to present a truer picture to the world as a means of counteracting the false information that was being spread abroad about the independent African states generally and Ghana in particular. He asked if some itinerary could be arranged for him, so that he could meet the leading personalities and other sources of information. My reaction was that he would have difficulty in finding publication for such articles as he might prepare in view of the committedness of the Western press.

It is possible that this letter never reached Richard, as the next I heard was the news of his death, which shocked me terribly, and left me bowled over. It seemed so hard that my husband and Richard Wright should have gone within a little more than a year of each other. Even though I had not had as close contact with him as I would have liked, since we met only at long intervals, I regarded Richard as a friend and I think he had a fondness for me as a person quite irrespective of my engagement in my husband's work and ideas, though, naturally, this must have had a bearing.

Yours sincerely,<br>
Dorothy Padmore

# Index